The authors

John Silvester has been a crime reporter in Melbourne since 1978. He worked for *The Sunday Times* 'Insight' team in London in 1990, and has co-authored several crime books, including the best-seller *Underbelly*. He is currently senior crime writer for *The Age* and an expensive but strangely popular after-dinner speaker.

Andrew Rule has been a journalist since 1975 and has worked in newspapers, television and radio. He wrote *Cuckoo*, the true story of the notorious 'Mr Stinky' case, and has edited and published several other books, including the original *Underbelly*. He is a senior writer for *Good Weekend* magazine and charges much more reasonably for after-dinner speaking.

They won the prestigious Ned Kelly Award for True Crime writing for *Underbelly 3*.

GOTCHA

How Australia's baddest
crooks copped
their right whack

From the *Underbelly* archives

Published in Australia by
Floradale Productions Pty Ltd and Sly Ink Pty Ltd
August 2005
Reprinted Oct 2005, Feb 2006, Aug 2007, Sept 2008

Distributed wholesale by
Gary Allen Pty Ltd,
9 Cooper Street,
Smithfield, NSW
Telephone 02 9725 2933

Gotcha
How Australia's baddest crooks copped their right whack

Cover photograph: JAMES BRAUND

ISBN – 0 9752318 5 5

You got to know when to hold 'em,
know when to fold 'em
Know when to walk away, know when to run
You never count your money when
you're sittin' at the table
There'll be time enough for countin',
when the dealin's done

Now, every gambler knows,
the secret to survivin'
Is knowing what to throw away,
knowing what to keep
'Cause every hand's a winner
and every hand's a loser
And the best you can hope for
is to die in your sleep

– Kenny Rogers, *The Gambler*

1 *Cold-Blooded Murder* *1*

2 *One Hurdle Too Many* *21*

3 *Two-Time Loser* *35*

4 *A Dirty Business* *55*

5 *The Society Murders* *75*

6 *Butting Out* *97*

7 *The Face of Evil* *117*

8 *A Web of Deceit* *127*

9 *The Scent of a Killer* *137*

10 *Persistence Pays* *143*

11 *Outgunned* *183*

12 *The Seeds of Destruction* *193*

13 *The Nine Lives of Fatcat* *215*

14 *Dragnet* *227*

15 *Heat* *241*

16 *A Man's Best Friend* *257*

17 *Never to be Released* *277*

18 *Deep Undercover* *301*

19 *A Concrete Case* *317*

20 *Dead Man Talking* *329*

CHAPTER 1

COLD-BLOODED MURDER

'It is hard to think of a more callous, heartless, wicked person.'

AS a child, Colleen Moss loved to watch her mother in the warm country kitchen of their modest Bendigo family home.

Her once fun-loving father, Johnny, was gravely ill and the daily ritual of seeing her mother prepare evening meals as if nothing had changed was somehow soothing to the concerned and confused teenager.

Lorraine Moss was glad of the company. A good cook, she usually enjoyed answering questions from her curious children about recipes and ingredients.

But when Colleen watched her mother mix a white powder into a bowl of butter, her questions were met abruptly.

At first she said doctors had given her the powder to spread on John's toast.

But when the teenager asked further questions, her mother

suddenly snapped, Colleen was to recall. 'My mother became very angry and grabbed me by the scruff of the neck and then led me out of the kitchen, and then closed the door in my face.'

It was a strangely vehement reaction, out of all proportion to the apparently harmless question. Colleen never forgot it.

THEY were just kids when they married. It was the oldest story of all but, being young, they didn't realise it then. Boy meets girl. Girl gets pregnant. She was 17 and imagined she was in love; he was 21 and working at a local meat processing plant. From whirlwind romance to shotgun wedding took only a few months and then, suddenly, there they were: handcuffed together, for richer or poorer, in sickness and in health, until death do them part.

They had met at the Golden Square Fire Brigade country dance late in 1965. Johnny Moss was Lorraine Stone's first and only boyfriend and she was determined, back then, to make a go of their life together.

They were to have two girls and a boy in four years and settle into a house in Upper Road, California Gully, on the outskirts of Bendigo, a provincial city in the heart of the old goldfields in central Victoria.

They were both raised in the region, their horizons were limited and it seemed natural they would settle down there in the same way thousands of other couples had.

They had a decent-sized block of land behind the house and Johnny grew vegetables and fruit trees. He even dug a little dam to keep yabbies for fishing bait.

Money was tight but that wasn't unusual in that time and place. The young family looked forward to their regular fishing trips to the Murray River and seemed content enough.

Johnny liked to go to the Newmarket Hotel with his mates on

a Friday night, but mostly he enjoyed pottering around the house and garden.

He welcomed friends home for a beer and to watch the footy, particularly when Carlton was playing. Under the old VFL zoning system, promising Bendigo players ended up playing with Carlton, so there was always a lot of support for the Blues among the locals.

Lorraine was quiet and had fewer friends than the gregarious Johnny. She spent most of her time caring for her children.

Moss's work at Mayfair Hams and Bacon was hard and bloody but he didn't seem to mind. He eventually progressed to first man in the 'gut line', where his job was to open up freshly killed pigs and expose their internal organs for removal.

He was well-respected by bosses and fellow workers and was chosen by 50 staff to be their union representative.

Even after he lost his left eye in a car accident, he remained active and energetic. Honed by hard work and an outdoor lifestyle, he was hardly ever sick. 'I would think he was one of the fittest blokes at work,' his oldest friend, Cliff Johnson, was to say.

But, in November 1978, John Moss became ill, and began to suffer from unexplained night sweats, stomach cramps and diarrhoea.

At first, doctors diagnosed gastroenteritis. Later they would suspect leptospirosis – a disease suffered by vets, slaughtermen and people who regularly deal with domestic animals.

Those in contact with the urine or kidneys of infected animals are particularly susceptible. Moss, who made a living from handling freshly-killed pigs, was an obvious candidate.

He was to recover, but entered a cycle of ill-health that would include frustrating bouts of fatigue, dizziness, and numbness in his fingers and toes.

In September, 1982, he went to his local doctor after a vomiting attack. He told Doctor Jagat Singh he had developed a rash, a tender stomach and had been exhausted for 10 days.

Tests were inconclusive, but because the problems subsided no one could forecast it was the beginning of a slow, painful and mysterious decline leading to his death. Within weeks, Moss apparently began to recover and tried to wrest back control of his life.

It was a pattern that would continue for the next two years. He would appear to improve and then slide back, each relapse leaving him weaker and more disoriented.

Tracey Moss didn't know her father was seriously ill until the middle of 1983 when he came into the house after gardening and she noticed his back was covered with an angry rash and hundreds of blisters.

In February, 1983, Cliff Johnson was driving home from work with him when Moss said he was losing feeling in his hands. Then, at work soon afterwards, 'He turned white and started shivering,' Johnson was to say.

The once robust slaughterman began to take more and more sick leave. Sometimes he would have to leave in the middle of a shift and eventually he could not work at all. But Lorraine continued to take him to the pub on Friday, first with a cane and finally in a wheelchair, so he would not lose contact with his workmates.

'John became very frustrated with his illness and was very determined to get better,' Johnson said. He could not use his thumbs and had to use his fist to light a match.

In May, 1983, he went to the Bendigo Hospital complaining of numb hands, blurred vision and slurred speech. Doctors considered a stroke, encephalitis or heavy metal poisoning as possible causes.

He was admitted to hospital and again appeared to improve, although he could still only walk with the help of a frame.

Johnny Moss was not the only man at Mayfair to suffer from a mystery illness. A close friend of his, Dennis Thatcher, was one of the regular crew who would meet at the Newmarket Hotel. They worked on the same line at Mayfair – and had their lunch and 'smokos' together.

'Johnny would sometimes pass his lunch on to someone else because he felt too crook to eat,' Thatcher was to say. One day, Moss gave Thatcher a serve of home-made stew. Thatcher, a single man, took the meal home for dinner that night but after eating it he became ill and began to hallucinate.

'It was the worst I had ever felt in my life ... I couldn't eat anything or drink anything and I wonder how I survived,' he was to recall of his ordeal. Many of the symptoms were similar to those Moss had suffered in the early days of his illness.

'I started to put two and two together and after hearing a bit of talk about Johnny I thought that perhaps the meal I ate of Johnny's was laced with something.'

He was not the only one. Another worker took eight months to recover after eating one of Johnny's home-cooked lunches.

EVERYONE felt sorry for Lorraine Moss. Her once strong, fit husband was becoming an invalid and no one seemed able to help. Not only was he losing his strength but his mind as well.

He suffered from hallucinations, found it difficult to speak and his behaviour became increasingly bizarre. He would pluck at imaginary items on his blankets and lapsed in and out of consciousness.

His throat was stripped raw and he had difficulty eating. He lost weight and became a shadow of the tough worker he had once been. Doctors ordered tests in Bendigo, Ballarat and

Melbourne but no one could find why a seemingly healthy man was collapsing into delirium. What puzzled medical staff was that five times when he was admitted to hospital his condition improved, only to relapse on release.

During the battle, Lorraine Moss remained loyal and stoic. It seemed to friends, neighbours and relatives that she cared for him seven days a week, 24 hours a day.

When the weather was warm enough, she would take him into the garden he could no longer tend. He would reach out to try to touch the soil and foliage he loved.

When he grew so ill that he was admitted to the Austin Hospital in Melbourne, his wife stayed in the nurses' quarters to be close to him. She refused help from the District Nurse, saying it was her duty to care for her husband.

When he was well enough to be at home she would feed him, even though he had lost his appetite. Home-cooked meals when he felt up to it, tinned fruit when he wasn't. She would race off to buy Chinese food when he asked, only to find he had lost the urge when she returned.

Even Johnny's mother said Lorraine was devoted to the point of obsession to her ill husband. 'Lorraine insisted on doing everything for John. She would not allow anyone else to help John in any way,' Marjory Moss was to say.

Victims usually recover from leptospirosis within weeks but in some cases it can cause damage to the kidneys, liver and heart. Only rarely is it fatal.

But Moss continued to fade. His one good eye rolled in his head, his tongue lolled from his mouth. His feet and hands were swollen and numb. He could not walk and hardly ate. It was painfully clear he was dying.

In August, 1983, doctors took nail and hair samples to test for lead arsenic poisoning. In an act, described by a Supreme Court judge nine years later as 'gross carelessness', the results were mislaid and didn't get to the doctors at the Austin Hospital until January 12, 1984.

It was too late … Johnny Moss died the next day. He was 38.

When the doctors told her he was dead, Lorraine Moss at first refused to believe it. Then she collapsed. Hospital staff, although conditioned to the irrationality of grief, were still puzzled by her reaction.

She asked one of them a strange question: 'Am I going to jail?'

WHEN doctors found the cause of death they notified police and it was handed to the homicide squad.

Four days after John Moss died, police searched the house and found nothing but, two days later, they came back and searched again. This time they discovered a small brown Tupperware container hidden on rafters in the garage. It contained an off-white powder, later found to be arsenic.

A fortnight later, on February 3, 1984, Detective Sergeant John Hill spoke to the new widow and asked her if any arsenic was kept on the premises.

She was adamant: 'There's never been any of that around here.'

But her 17-year-old daughter, Tracey, said, 'Yes we did, remember, we bought it for Dad once, years ago.'

Police were later to establish that the Mosses bought a tin of Lanes brand arsenate from a local nursery in 1978 – around the time Johnny Moss first reported feeling ill.

The powder – used to spray apple trees for codling moth – was withdrawn from sale in the early 1980s.

Lorraine asked Hill: 'Does this mean we are in trouble? I don't want to be blamed for something I didn't do.'

Police sent samples from Moss's body to the Atomic Energy

Commission in NSW to be tested by analytical chemists. Commission experts using neutron activation analysis showed Moss's hair had 80 times the normal level of arsenic. Tests on hair and nails showed Moss had been methodically poisoned and had developed a tolerance to arsenic. Finally, he was fed four massive doses over the last eight weeks of his life.

Months later, Detective Senior Sergeant Jack Jacobs and Senior Detective Brendan Murphy took Lorraine to the Bendigo police station for questioning. She had now changed from victim to suspect.

She told the detectives she had devoted herself to her husband – 'helping him swim, exercise, lifting him, carting him around everywhere. I loved him, I had him 18 years, no 20 years … I did not hurt him. The children loved him, we loved him and our whole life was fishing, gardening and loving him. He loved me. I loved him and he loved the kids.

'I bathed him, washed him, powdered him, put cream here, powder there, and I watched him go down to nothing. Why would I do all that, then hurt him?'

Murphy said, 'It seems someone wanted to hurt John.'

She said: 'Johnny didn't have any enemies; everybody loved Johnny.'

The detective said, 'Someone was killing him in a slow, painful way and we've already explained that the chances of it being a stranger are remote.'

She responded, 'Yes, but I didn't hurt him. I saw him trickle away to nothing. I looked after him. I did everything I could. I asked professors, the doctors, what was wrong with him. They'd say, "We'll do this test, we'll operate this day or that day." We had plans for the future.'

Which was half true, anyway. It turned out that Lorraine had plans for the future. But they hadn't involved her husband.

The detectives asked her if she had been faithful. The widow said, 'I'd never been unfaithful to him and he'd never been unfaithful to me … Johnny was my man.'

But some were not so sure. Sisters-in-law Brenda and Dorothy Murley joined a Thursday morning tenpin bowling team at Bendigo and one of their team-mates was Lorraine Moss.

In the late 1970s, the team finally won a premiership but Lorraine missed the celebration because she was in hospital for an ear operation.

The Murleys decided to take Moss her trophy and flowers. They soon wished they hadn't. They walked in to her room to see their team-mate cuddling a man with his head resting on her stomach. It was not her husband.

'I wished the floor had opened up and swallowed me up because I was so embarrassed,' Brenda Murley would recall more than 20 years later.

It was around the time Johnny Moss started to get sick. A defence lawyer would call that coincidence. But police don't believe in coincidence.

IT didn't take long for the rumours to start. Lorraine Moss killed her husband to run off with another bloke.

The Mosses had always struggled financially; with three kids there was never anything left over for luxuries. During her married life, Lorraine rarely used make-up and wore practical, hard-wearing clothing.

But, according to daughter Colleen, 'Our whole family life fell apart after Dad died. Mum changed. She started wearing a lot of make-up and provocative clothing.'

Bobby Whyte worked at Mayfair with Johnny and had started doing odd jobs around the Moss home when his work-mate became an invalid – but it was no act of charity. Johnny sometimes expressed mild annoyance that Bobby was always around his home but the gravely-ill man didn't have the strength for a confrontation. Lorraine apparently didn't feel the tension, saying Whyte was 'a tower of strength' during her husband's long illness.

A few months after Moss died, Bobby Whyte moved in. 'It wasn't long at all before my mother and Bobby were sleeping in the same bed,' Colleen said.

Lorraine once raised the issue of the rumours with her daughter, Tracey. 'What would you do if I told you I killed your father?' she asked.

Tracey responded, 'I would kill you.'

Lorraine then said, 'Well, I didn't anyway.'

Lorraine Moss worked part-time with the local council providing home-cleaning help for people suffering physical disabilities. One of her clients was Aileen Crack.

Months before Johnny died Lorraine asked Aileen if she could borrow an old medical book kept at the house. She said Tracey needed to study first aid because she hoped to join the police force.

The book was on poisoning and insect bites. It was never returned and Tracey would later tell police she had not seen the book.

Daughter Colleen would also recall her mother's sudden interest in research.

She remembers going with her mother to the temporary library at Bendigo, puzzled why her mother was in such a 'frenzy'. They checked reference cards together and gathered a series of text books before using her daughter's library card to borrow the heavy reading material.

They all covered one topic … poisons.

Police forensic experts took samples from tiny food and fat

residue trapped in cracks near the kitchen sink. They were found to contain a one to one lead and arsenic mixture similar to that found in the Tupperware container in the garage and sold at the local nursery years earlier.

It was enough for police to charge her with murder. But, in August, 1986, coroner Hugh Adams found that while Johnny Moss had been 'maliciously and unlawfully' poisoned by someone there was insufficient evidence to establish who was responsible.

Adams was not one to be swayed by a circumstantial case, and correctly decided that there was not enough evidence to implicate Lorraine Moss in her husband's death. (Adams was to be dogged by cases that became controversial – the year before, in 1985, he had conducted the first inquest into the death of Bonnie Doon farmer's wife Jennifer Tanner. The open finding he made on that occasion was subsequently quashed after a new investigation was launched in 1996.)

The charges against Lorraine Moss were then dropped. She said after the inquest, 'I am not guilty. I've never done anything to hurt anybody.'

If she had been tried and acquitted in front of a jury she would have been in the clear but, as there had been no trial, the case remained open.

In Bendigo, the rumours persisted. One woman would jokingly tell her family if they didn't behave she would 'do a Lorraine Moss' and poison them. But what she would tell police much later was no joke.

Nancy Henderson was only 18 when she married and moved into a house in Upper Road, opposite the Mosses. Almost every day she would put her infant son in a pusher and walk over to visit Lorraine, an older mother she saw as a role model.

'I used to go across to Lorraine's for a cuppa and a chat every day after a while. I had a great respect for Lorraine as I thought she knew everything.'

Eventually, Nancy began to confide to Lorraine that she was trapped in a violent marriage. She said her then husband drank and beat her. Lorraine first advised her friend to avoid any confrontations and to 'keep your mouth shut'.

But, as the beatings increased in severity and regularity, Lorraine's attitude hardened. She said, 'You shouldn't let him get away with it. You know what you should do – put some Ratsak in his tea each night, that'll get rid of him for you.'

The two women became soul sisters. Lorraine showed her how to avoid violence by side-stepping possible arguments and how to save a little money by inflating the grocery bill to keep the change.

The older woman said she was also unhappy in her marriage. 'I used to ask her why she didn't leave him. She said that she wasn't giving up her house and stuff for anybody,' Nancy Henderson (now Arthur) said.

'A few weeks later, after I had received another hiding from John, Lorraine said, "I've told you what to do: a bit of Ratsak each night will do it".'

According to Nancy, her friend offered the same advice at least six times. 'Just a bit at a time. It'll eventually do him in, but they'd never know how it got there. There's plenty at my place if you want some.'

LORRAINE refused to discuss the controversial death of her first husband and married Bobby Whyte soon after the charges were dropped.

But, according to her daughter Colleen, she marked off every year after Johnny died. She was convinced that after 15 years no one could be charged with murder. Lorraine may have taught herself about poisons but she didn't know much about criminal law. She was wrong.

Colleen said her mother asked: 'Can they arrest me for it after 15 years? Can they do anything about it after 15 years?'

Colleen continued: 'As the 15th anniversary of my father dying got closer and closer, my mother kept asking me these questions more often. I also recall her telling me one time: "It's been 14 years Col, only one more to go". It was as if she thought that once the 15-year barrier was up she could not be charged.'

But it was after 16 years, in early April, 2000, that Lorraine rang Colleen and asked her to visit the following day. When Colleen arrived, her mother was alone. As they sat together on a couch Lorraine finally said, 'I think I killed your dad, Col.'

Lorraine's story was that John Moss brought a tin of sausage 'thickener' home from Mayfair and kept it under the sink. She said Moss was disorganised and kept tins of poisons near the thickener and she had accidentally mixed them together.

Colleen couldn't believe what she heard. She knew her father was careful with poisons and kept them locked away. Lorraine had earlier told police Moss kept all chemicals securely locked in the shed. 'Johnny was very careful, terribly protective of me and the kids.'

Colleen Moss didn't buy the thickener story for a moment. Why had no one else in the family become ill when they all ate the same home-cooked food?

She reminded Lorraine about the incident where she put the powder in her father's butter. 'My mother then snapped and said, "Is there anything else that you remember that I should know?"'

But, after years of denials, Lorraine was on the verge of a nervous breakdown. Next day she took an overdose of pills and Colleen rushed back to the house.

This time, Lorraine didn't try to explain the death as an accident. She claimed John smoked and drank away his pay. 'She then went on to say that she killed my father for the $11,000 superannuation money,' Colleen told police.

'Mum got out of bed and just kept saying, "I did it, I did it".'

She then rang her sister, Robin Ivins, in Mackay in northern Queensland and said, 'I've got something important to tell you … I killed him … Colleen's here and Colleen knows.'

Robin Ivins said later: 'John's death has been like a cloud hanging over the family for all these years.'

Lorraine's younger brother, Tony Stone, and his wife, Rhonda, moved in next door to Lorraine in Myers Flat. Bobby Whyte yelled from their yard that he needed help as Lorraine had taken an overdose of pills. Rhonda asked Lorraine what had happened. She replied, 'I killed John'.

She was starting to unravel, telling people that police were following and persecuting her. Rhonda thought she was so confused 'I don't think Lorraine knew whether she did or didn't kill John.'

Colleen's partner, pilot Alfred Assouad, was also at the house. He sat on a step outside the open bedroom door and heard Lorraine confess 'she had killed him for the $11,000 superannuation money and that everything that had been said in court about how she killed Johnny was right.'

A few days later she again took pills and was taken to hospital. One nurse heard her say to Bobby Whyte. 'I killed someone and I need to tell you … I need to talk to the police. I need to tell them.'

When Tracey Moss heard of her mother's confession, she rang the man that she knew had not forgotten the case – former homicide detective Jack Jacobs.

Jacobs had retired from the force but kept in touch with some of the relatives of murder victims, including Tracey. Women tended to like and trust the veteran investigator, who was more polite and attentive than some of his gruffer colleagues and skilled in the art of gentle probing. Jacobs knew which buttons to push, and when. After talking to Tracey he pushed the ones on his telephone – contacting the homicide squad and urged the case be re-opened. It was handed to Senior Detective Kira Olney, of the cold case crew.

Olney asked Colleen whether she would secretly record her mother.

On December 20, 2000, Colleen went to meet her mother at the Malmsbury Botanical Gardens, an attractive country park beside the Calder Highway between Melbourne and Bendigo. In her handbag she carried a tiny tape recorder that police had given her.

As Lorraine arrived, Colleen said, 'She's here, guys. Wish me luck.'

Colleen tried to trap her mother into admissions but Lorraine had by now reverted to her standard denials.

'I don't want to talk about the past, all right?' she said.

Colleen: 'Well, I want to.'

Lorraine: 'Well, I don't want to … If this comes back again ... I don't want to know about the past. The past is the past. I only just want to look after me and Pa (Bobby Whyte). I never killed him. I didn't.'

Colleen: 'You did.'

Lorraine: 'I didn't.'

Colleen: 'You did, mum.'

Lorraine: 'I didn't.'

Colleen: 'I need to know why you made that choice. Did you make it because you were trapped? Did they have a single parents' pension back then or what?'

Lorraine: 'No, there was nothing back then. There was nothing.'

Colleen: 'Tell me.'

Lorraine: 'I'm going home now.'

Colleen: 'Oh, fine. See ya. Have a good life. I hope it's fun.'

Colleen Moss then spoke into the recorder: 'Well, you know I really thought there, for a minute, that she'd tell me. Oh, she's cunning isn't she? What mother would do that? What person could do that? God, I hope you've got enough to get her, Kira. A person like that doesn't deserve to be roaming around. She needs to go through some personal hell of her own.'

On January 17, 2001 – 17 years to the day after her house was first searched for poisons, and 15 years after she was first charged with murder – Lorraine Whyte was arrested again.

This time she appeared to be beyond defending herself. 'Just lock me up,' she said. They did. On May 3, 2002, in the Bendigo Supreme Court, Justice Bill Gillard sentenced Lorraine Whyte. He didn't try to conceal his disgust.

'In the year 1982, the deceased was suffering from regular patterns of illness. He complained to his workmates and suffered bouts of illness whilst at work. Arsenic is odourless, tasteless and does not dissolve in fluids,' he said.

'It is apparent from the evidence that you were poisoning your husband over an extensive period of time. You placed arsenic in his lunches on occasions. Sometimes he would complain to his workmates about the taste of his lunches and often would be very critical and throw the lunch away.

'Two of his workmates, bachelors who were only too happy to have a home-cooked meal, ate his lunches and suffered extreme illness lasting for weeks. Their symptoms were similar to the symptoms suffered by your late husband and with hindsight, they were clearly symptoms of arsenic poisoning.

'I am satisfied beyond reasonable doubt that by 1982, you were systematically and regularly poisoning your husband with arsenic. Consistent with the views of the experts, he was building up some resistance, which explains his ability to keep going.

'The same could not be said of his workmates who, having been poisoned, were violently ill for weeks, and in the case of one person, took eight months to recover.

'Some time during the year 1983, you took your daughter, Colleen, then aged 14 years, to the Bendigo Library to acquire books on poisons.

'You told Colleen that you were anxious to find out what was wrong with her father and to see whether you could do something that the doctors could not do, namely, find a cure.

'In my view, the real reason was because you wanted to know more about poisons and their effects. What amount of arsenic is required to gradually kill a person, or kill a person with one dose, is something the average person would have no knowledge of.

'Instead of seeking to help your husband, what you were seeking was information as to what quantity was needed to kill him. Your wickedness knew no bounds.

'He again relapsed and on 20 June 1983, he was admitted to the Austin Hospital. He was suffering from anaemia. It was thought that he may have had glandular fever. He had problems with his peripheral nerves. He was developing problems with sensation in his fingers and feet. His bone marrow was not working properly. The doctors could not find any infection. They could not find any evidence of malignancy or tumour. He had episodes of confusion and delusions. These features were consistent with arsenic poisoning.

'His illness and symptoms continued in 1983 and he gradually got worse. He would go to work, suffer a relapse, rest, return to work, and then again suffer an illness. This went on for some five to six months.

'By May 1983, he was so ill he could not work. He ceased work and never returned. His work record to that date was good, save for the mystery illness which he suffered in September, 1982. He was highly thought of at the works. He had been elected a union representative. This demonstrated the respect that was held of him by his 50 workmates.

'By May, 1983, he was so ill that life became a living hell, getting worse each day. In that month, he was admitted to Bendigo Hospital for two weeks. He was speaking strangely, slurring words, and his right eye was rolling in his head. His tongue was hanging out and he was blue in the face. That is a description that you gave to the police, as to how he was in May, 1983. You said he was so bad, he was too weak to hold a knife.

'The doctors were mystified, but you knew; you were torturing him to death. He had all the symptoms of arsenic poisoning. That was not appreciated by the medical profession.

'Despite the excruciating effect the poison was having on his body, you continued to administer it. He improved a little while he was in hospital in May, but on his discharge, he became worse. You were continuing your nefarious practices.

'The hospital investigated, looking for causes, but could not find one. It was all very confusing to the medical profession. Whilst there, there was some improvement and his rash disappeared. He was discharged 11 days later.

'It was not surprising that he was showing some improvement because his body was not being bombarded with arsenic. But he was back again in hospital on July 7, 1983, and he stayed there for six weeks. More intensive investigations were carried out but without determining the cause.

'In July, he described increased numbness to knees, difficulty walking and holding things. There was numbness in his hands. It was thought that there may be some problem with his nerves. By July 20, 1983, he could only walk with a frame. He had decreased power in his hands and feet and had foot drop. He was dragging his toes. He was in a very disabled state. By August, he required a wheelchair. He was discharged home on August 17.

'It was at this stage that somebody in the medical profession or involved in the administration at the Austin Hospital, badly let him down. A test was taken during August 1983 which showed significant levels of arsenic and lead in his body. However, the test results never caught up with his file until January 1984, by which time it was too late. This gross carelessness played into your hands; you were able to continue your callous, heartless activities, unchecked and undetected.

'You were caring for him on a full-time basis. You were nursing him, but you were not nursing him to health, you were nursing him to certain death. You were making sure that he died.

'It is hard to think of a more callous, heartless, wicked person. Your husband was suffering excruciating pain, he was getting weaker and weaker, nobody knew why, yet you continued to feed him large doses of arsenic.

'As I have said, the effect upon your children must have been devastating, yet you persevered. You had no compassion, you were heartless. You were hell-bent on finally killing him. You gave him a number of massive doses of arsenic in the last months of his life.

'You did succeed in killing him. He died on January 13, 1984. On his last admission to the Austin Hospital, he was still vomiting, had stomach pains, was confused, disoriented, hallucinating, could not walk and was suffering from skin problems. It was at that time that the August test results of the year before caught up with his file, and there was a realisation that he was suffering from chronic arsenic poisoning. Your conduct over a period of about 15 months, ensured the progressive destruction of the father of your children in the most excruciating, distressing circumstances. As I have said, your wickedness knew no bounds.'

Justice Gillard sentenced her to a minimum of 18 years jail. She will not be released until she is 70. The judge ordered police to confiscate and destroy the Tupperware container and a red spoon used to poison Johnny Moss.

Senior Detective Kira Olney said, 'Lorraine liked to portray herself as a simple woman but she was cunning and cold.'

Jack Jacobs investigated more than 100 murders in his record sixteen and a half years in the homicide squad but he found the Moss case 'the most intriguing' of all.

'Most murders involving spouses are heat of the moment crimes but this was just so cold-blooded. Lorraine killed him by degrees over years. It was a case of cold-blooded torture.'

He said he couldn't find a solid motive. As is so often the case in murders, when judged on facts alone it didn't make a lot of sense because the risk far outweighed the apparent reward. But who knows what secret motives move people to desperate acts? Perhaps Lorraine Moss yearned for a man who was skilled in the act of love. Jacobs puts it another way: 'I think she just wanted a change of lifestyle.'

He remembered another thing about the black widow of Bendigo: she was always polite and hospitable when the homicide squad went to interview her.

'She always offered us a cup of tea. I always made sure I never took it.' When it came to wily women, Jack knew when to say no.

CHAPTER 2

ONE HURDLE
TOO MANY

*'They want you to be the one that cracks and gives
everybody up. We're stronger than that.'*

ANDREW Fraser was a lawyer always on the lookout for his
next case. That's why some of Australia's most notorious
criminals always carried his business card and why he always
carried a mobile telephone.

Some criminal lawyers, like police, are always on duty.

But when Fraser walked into one of his many favourite bars
in late spring in 1998, he was looking for a drink, not a client.

The Dogs Bar in St Kilda's trendy Acland Street was part of
Fraser's hectic beat.

He mixed easily with the eclectic crowd, made up of the
fashionable, the questionable and the unmentionable.

Fraser saw a friend drinking with a tall, middle-aged man
who spoke with a strong German accent.

He walked over and was introduced to Werner Paul Roberts.

a man who was looking for a lawyer to help him settle a Workcover case.

Fraser was a specialist in criminal law but business had slowed and his expensive lifestyle hadn't. He would take the case.

But it didn't take long for the two men to realise they had more in common than a Workcover settlement. For years, Fraser had loved to use cocaine, while Werner was in the business of selling it. Snap.

Werner didn't need long to work out he had found both a lawyer and a customer in the appropriately named Dogs Bar.

He could see what many, including police, judges and fellow lawyers couldn't. Fraser was a hopeless coke-head and slavishly devoted to the Colombian white powder.

The drug dealer would later tell detectives there were 'certain signs' that convinced him from the first meeting that the high-flying lawyer was a high-flying user. 'He sniffed and he was hyperactive ... He was pretty keen on it, from what I gathered.'

Fraser, had been using cocaine 'off and on' for more than a decade. Despite having seen hundreds of clients whose lives had been ruined through drugs, he had the arrogance to believe he would be different; that he could control it. He was wrong.

The former star schoolboy athlete was a full-blown addict and, by September 1999, with Roberts as his dealer, he was consuming at least four grams of cocaine, valued at $1000, every day.

Battling bankruptcy and a shrinking law practice, Fraser became a drug-trafficker to fund his own insatiable appetite for cocaine. He would later admit to 3AW talkback radio host Neil Mitchell that 'in the last year I would have spent over a hundred grand' on the drug.

Fraser spoke to Mitchell after he was charged, but even then his answers seemed insincere. He was trying to build a defence for the indefensible.

Just two years after the chance meeting at the Dogs Bar, Fraser was forced to stand in the dock of the County Court as he was sentenced to prison for helping Roberts import up to $2.7million worth of cocaine from Africa.

One of Australia's best-known lawyers, whose client list included business tycoon Alan Bond, footballer Jimmy Krakouer and killer Dennis Allan, had become a professional wreck whose 30-year career had fallen, by his own admission, 'down the shit-chute'.

His barrister, Con Heliotis QC, argued in court that Fraser was a victim and that it was foolishness, not greed, which turned him into a criminal who pleaded guilty to trafficking cocaine, possession of ecstasy, and being knowingly concerned in the importation of cocaine.

Many witnesses were called to give character evidence on his behalf: the Fraser they knew was a caring and compassionate man, a 'completely idiosyncratic Australian character', a loyal friend and an adoring father.

He was of the 'work hard, play hard' school. Long, boozy lunches, meetings with notorious criminals and living on the edge were part of the lifestyle he loved. But he wanted more.

Fraser was first introduced to cocaine at a party around 1987. Some years later, suffering burnout because of his constant working hours, he found out his neighbour was a dealer, and soon graduated from 'the occasional line' to frequent use.

But with Roberts able to supply his demands, Fraser's cocaine use became chronic and uncontrolled. He claimed he was never high when representing clients, but police listening devices recorded a man seemingly obsessed with cocaine.

'He was clearly out of control and many of his associates had no choice but to distance themselves from him,' Heliotis said during Fraser's plea hearing.

But not all his colleagues turned away.

Police recorded some legal identities speaking to Fraser in cryptic terms. One asked for a 'book', with Fraser later asking if he liked the volume and then saying it was 'suitably inscribed'.

Detectives suspect Fraser was selling small amounts of cocaine to fellow lawyers and associates, including well-known former psychologist Tim Watson-Munro. Contrary to rumours that swept Victoria's court system, no judges were ever implicated.

Heliotis told Judge Leo Hart that Fraser's addiction highlighted his characteristics of being driven and narcissistic, suffering mood swings, and wrestling with 'a constant conflict between his ego and his insecurity'. It sounded like a fair summary.

His constant exposure to the hard edge of the criminal underworld, a family history of substance abuse, and a desire to be accepted left him flawed and vulnerable, the court heard.

'He was a person who had to succeed, who had to be liked by his peers, or, at least, if not liked, admired,' Heliotis said.

Fraser was a juggler who lost his nerve. 'I think he thought as if he needed the drug to keep him at the top of the profession, which was where he aspired to be,' said one character witness, David Brown, a Melbourne senior counsel who had known Fraser for many years.

'He developed the personality of someone who thought he was bullet-proof, who thought he was beyond others. His greatest friend became cocaine.'

August 16, 1999, was the beginning of the end for the man who believed he was indestructible. At around 5pm, Fraser arrived at his Lonsdale Street law office. Werner Roberts, no longer a client but a close associate, was waiting for him in the reception lobby.

The drug dealer was due to leave Australia on a business trip. He was to meet an associate in Benin, West Africa, to buy 5.5 kilograms of high-grade cocaine.

The plan was simple. Roberts would travel with his former girlfriend, Carol Brand, on a seemingly innocent holiday, first to Europe and then on to Africa. The cocaine, 65 per cent pure, would be specially sealed inside eight decorative wall plaques, and smuggled into the country inside the pair's hand luggage.

Brand was the innocent abroad. She believed the expenses-paid trip was a peace offering from Roberts after their less-than-amicable split a few years earlier. She thought that they might rekindle their romance.

But the aspiring actress knew nothing of the cold-blooded Roberts' plan to use her as the cover for the importation. She would be the unwitting 'mule' who would carry the drug-filled plaques through airports and who would, if necessary, take the fall for the real villains.

Customs officers are trained to pick drug smugglers through nervous body language that betrays guilt.

The best 'mules' are the ones with nothing to fear because they don't know what they are carrying. But this mule would buck the system and was to give telling evidence against her former lover. She told the court how she had caught up with Roberts in early 1999, three years after their split.

Believing they could become friends, she occasionally met him for coffee and conversation. One day, he gave her the holiday offer. 'He explained to me that he would like me to accompany him on a trip overseas, since it was something that we never managed to do while we were together.'

The day before the trip Fraser and Roberts discussed the plan, in between glasses of wine and lines of cocaine, cut and divided on the marble slate table of the lawyer's seemingly private conference room.

But the office was bugged as part of a covert police investigation into local drug trafficking, in which Fraser was the main suspect.

It had not begun that way. In February 1999, police started an investigation designed to trap members of the notorious Moran family who were considered the major drug traffickers in Melbourne's north-west.

The drug squad had gathered intelligence that the suspect family had become heavily involved in dealing in amphetamines, cocaine and ecstasy. But it would not be the drug squad that would eventually cripple the Moran family. They would be destroyed in a vicious underworld war as the senior members of the family were hunted down one by one by a rival drug syndicate. First it was Mark Moran, shot dead outside his $1.3million Aberfeldie home on June 15, 2000; then his half brother Jason was shot dead with friend Pasquale Barbaro in front of a group of children while watching junior football in Essendon North on June 21, 2003. Finally, the head of the family, Lewis Moran was murdered inside the Brunswick Club on March 31, 2004.

But before the underworld war police had sufficient information in 1999 to justify installing court-authorised telephone taps and while Lewis Moran was too cunning to implicate himself, detectives found repeated references to Fraser's involvement with cocaine.

Within three months, investigators shifted their attention to the well-known lawyer. Fraser believed he could keep his habit a secret, yet it was already the subject of conversation among many criminals. One said the lawyer had turned up at his home to discuss his upcoming case, and ended up sharing a line of cocaine with his client.

Knowing that he had many contacts, and enemies, inside the force, Fraser was referred to in *Operation Regent* only as 'Target A' – both after his first name and as a bid to keep the investigation confidential.

Investigators felt that if it became known in police circles that he was a target, it would spread through, and beyond, the department within days.

Fraser had a reputation as a street-smart and cunning lawyer. He often used underworld slang picked up from his many high-profile, low-life clients. He prided himself on his knowledge of investigative techniques and made a handsome living advising suspects on the best way to counter police tactics.

Yet when it came to drug dealing, Andrew Fraser was incredibly dumb. His was a high-profile case but, ultimately, he was an easy pinch for the drug squad. Like an animal raised in captivity, the private school-educated Fraser was not equipped for life in the wild. He realised too late that his wings and claws were clipped.

In a Prahran restaurant-bar, Fraser slipped into the men's toilet to do a deal. He had become so nonchalant that when he heard a mobile telephone ring in a cubicle, he yelled out to the occupant, 'Don't you hate it when that happens?'

The man from behind the locked door just laughed. He was a drug squad detective there to observe the deal.

Police listening devices installed in his office recorded the damning meeting with Roberts.

The conversation was pivotal in building the case against the man one detective admitted in evidence was not exactly 'liked' by 'certain people' in the force. It also showed how he was prepared to risk the freedom of an innocent woman to feed his obsession with cocaine.

In a drug-fuelled, rambling conversation filled with obscenities, gossip and schoolboy stories, surveillance detectives heard Fraser counselling his ex-client on ways to avoid suspicion during the trip.

He advised Roberts that it might be risky having both his and Brand's name on the same itinerary if she was eventually to take the fall, and tried to discourage him from giving her $8000 for accompanying him overseas. Fraser believed it would arouse suspicion and instead suggested that $2500 would be enough of a gesture to entrap the innocent woman in drug trafficking. The once rich and generous lawyer had turned cheap and nasty.

'Look, I understand, mate. I've done this. I've given pertinent advice before in these situations … ' he was recorded as saying.

He also made sure Roberts had his correct contact details, and that he, in turn, had a copy of his itinerary. He also advised him to be careful coming back through customs when he returned with the drugs, but stopped short of agreeing to meet him when he arrived because it would look too much a like a 'conspiracy'.

Instead, he told him to call from a pay phone to let him know that he had returned safely. And, according to the prosecution, he agreed to be the 'legal backstop' if things didn't go according to plan.

Roberts left Melbourne the following day, leaving his wife, Andrea Mohr, and long-time friend, Carl Heinze Urbanec, to supply Fraser with his much-needed cocaine.

Mohr was a younger woman, about fifteen years Roberts' junior, and prone to fits of jealously. She was a devoted wife – and a chronic heroin addict.

Urbanec was Mohr's former boyfriend and had become one

of the couple's oldest friends. He was also a drug user. They were a cosmopolitan modern family unit.

The drug deal seemed to go according to plan. On September 8, 1999, a man named Cornelius arrived at the Hotel DuPont in Cotonou, Benin, to meet Roberts and Brand.

There, he delivered eight wall plaques, about thirteen centimetres long by eighteen centimetres wide, with tribal faces carved on them. The cocaine was sealed in the hollow interior of each item.

Shortly after returning to Sydney, Roberts called Mohr to let her know he had arrived. At about 8pm, he notified Fraser, with the cliché coded message 'The eagle has landed', which some critics consider was alone worth an extra three months' jail.

According to Brand's evidence, she and Roberts checked into the El Toro Motel, in the Sydney suburb of Liverpool, at about 11pm. They had decided on staying overnight before driving back to Melbourne in a rental car, a vehicle Australian Federal Police had secretly bugged in order to track the pair's movements.

Brand said they ordered breakfast, arranged a wake-up call and went to sleep. But about 4am, an agitated Roberts woke her up, wanting to leave immediately.

'I was woken abruptly and quite rudely by Werner. I remember asking why,' Brand told the jury. 'We had agreed to a 7am wake-up call. He had agreed to breakfast. I remember asking what the hurry was and why he was being so rude and he didn't elaborate.'

It was early September 11, 1999, when the couple headed south for Melbourne. It was a long, tense trip and it didn't get any better. Soon after they got to Melbourne, police raided Roberts' Elwood apartment and arrested him and Mohr. The eight plaques were seized from the boot of his rented car.

The drug dealer was taken into custody and, following their emergency plans, he requested Fraser as his solicitor. Detectives told him he would need a different lawyer because his first choice had just been arrested during raids at his beachside home and city office.

The group was charged and remanded but unlike his co-offenders, who have spent more than two years in jail since, Fraser was granted bail and continued working as a solicitor until September 4, 2000, when he voluntarily gave up his practising certificate and pleaded guilty to the charges against him.

Many detectives were furious that Fraser was allowed to continue to appear in criminal courts while facing serious charges. Police who are charged with criminal offences are immediately suspended from duty.

Mohr also pleaded guilty, but Roberts and Urbanec fought the case over a four-week trial.

On the surface, it appeared to be a straightforward case. Crown prosecutor Richard Maidment told the court that Roberts, both a drug dealer and drug user, was the principal importer of the cocaine.

Meanwhile, Fraser, Mohr and Urbanec formed the 'support crew' to the scheme, were ready and willing to receive the cocaine, and provided advice, encouragement and logistical support to aid its importation.

But on the second day of the trial, Roberts' barrister, George Traczyk, presented the jury with a 90-minute line of defence that alleged that police had hated Fraser for years and wanted to set him up. Traczyk suggested his client was being used to get the despised criminal lawyer.

He claimed Fraser was disliked by police for his role in defending Anthony Farrell, one of the men accused, and later acquitted, of the 1988 Walsh Street police murders of Steven Tynan and Damian Eyre.

Many police felt Fraser had crossed the line when he represented Farrell and was no longer just a lawyer doing his job.

On September 3, 1988, Fraser was taped in the Melbourne watch-house urging his client to stay strong.

The notorious section of transcript seems rather damning, given that Fraser's first sworn duty was to the court.

Fraser: 'We're going to blow these c.... out of the water on this … so you just keep your trap shut, mate, this is the rest of your life here … We've put the word out that you've said nothing … They've fucking nailed you because they reckon you're the weak link in the chain. They're putting enormous pressure on you in what they are doing. They want you to be the one that cracks and gives everybody up. We're stronger than that.'

More than thirteen years after the conversation was recorded Traczyk asked one drug squad detective, Senior Constable Paul Firth, if police still felt a sense of anger or betrayal towards Fraser after the Walsh Street acquittals.

'It would be fair to say that certain people didn't like him as a person,' the witness replied.

It took two days for the jury to dismiss Roberts' version of events and find him guilty of the importation. Urbanec, who had argued that his involvement was limited to sending $900 to Roberts after he had lost his luggage and plane tickets (and not, as the Crown suggested, to help facilitate the deal), was found guilty of being knowingly concerned with the importation.

Roberts returned to the County Court three weeks after his trial for his pre-sentencing plea. The division between him and his former solicitor could not have been more apparent.

They sat at opposite ends of the criminal dock and, on the second day of the hearing, a security guard sat between the pair.

Heliotis, a softly-spoken, yet robust and convincing barrister, urged Judge Hart to impose a 'short, sharp' minimum sentence of about six to twelve months against Fraser.

He told the court that his client would 'do it hard' in jail, partly because he was an outspoken person, partly because he might have disgruntled ex-clients in the prison system and mostly because he had given evidence to police against his co-offenders, agreeing to testify against them on behalf of the Crown in expectation of a lesser sentence.

However the prosecution submitted that a six to twelve-month minimum term would be an inappropriate punishment, given Fraser's role in the importation.

The prosecution argued that the disgraced lawyer might not have been an essential part of the plan, but he actively encouraged the deal in the expectation that he would benefit from it.

It was clear that the seriousness of the offence, particularly because Fraser knew that an innocent person could take the fall for a crime she did not commit, was aggravated by the fact that he was a solicitor at the time.

Outside the court, a group of lawyers and detectives ran an informal sweep on Fraser's likely sentence: a minimum of about four years was the most popular guess.

Fraser lost his job, his reputation and his dignity. The family home, his car and even the wine collection he had started when he was eighteen all went. But there are no excuses. As an officer of the court he knew very well the consequences of drug trafficking.

Days before his sentencing, Fraser was still telling friends he was hoping for a suspended jail term, showing that the once street-smart lawyer had lost touch with courtroom reality.

Judge Leo Hart was waiting to bring the high flier back to earth. On December 3, 2001, Hart sentenced him to a minimum of five years. 'You had bound yourself by oath to uphold the law and to conduct yourself honestly. To behave in the illegal, dishonourable and disgraceful way that you did ... involves a degree of public scandal, which reflects on the profession as a whole,' the judge said.

Such conduct warranted a sentence that would act as a deterrent to others, including lawyers who might be tempted to commit such crimes, he said.

'A legal practitioner must not succumb to such temptations,' he said. 'A legal practitioner must not cross that line.'

Judge Hart said Fraser was 'a hardened user' of cocaine, and rejected submissions by his defence counsel that he was so 'off his face' at the time of his conversation with Roberts that his judgment was severely impaired.

While he accepted that Fraser had freely given time to pro bono and community work, Judge Hart questioned his previous good reputation. 'For the last twelve to thirteen years you have not had a good character at all,' he said. 'On your own admission, you have been breaking the law with increasing frequency by possessing and using cocaine.'

Werner Roberts, 54, was found guilty by a jury of the importation and was sentenced to thirteen years, with a minimum of ten; Andrea Mohr, 38, was sentenced to eight years with a minimum of five; and Carl Urbanec, 46, was sentenced to nine years with a minimum of six.

*The listening devices hidden in Fraser's office also picked up an interesting piece of intelligence. One of the biggest underworld murders in Melbourne was the killing of Alphonse Gangitano, who was shot dead in his Templestowe home in January 1998.

Police believed that the dead man's former close friend, Jason Moran, was the gunman who carried out the hit. When Moran was to be interviewed over the crime his long-time lawyer, Andrew Fraser, was there to protect his client's rights and accompanied him to the homicide squad office.

But in what he thought was the privacy of his own office Fraser had a chat with a friend on August 11, 1999, about many things and in that conversation described his valued client Jason Moran as 'crazy'. The friend asked the lawyer who killed Gangitano. He said just one word: 'Jason'.

CHAPTER 3

TWO-TIME LOSER

'Well, I want to stop him breathing.'

IT was just after midnight in a seedy, dead-end lane in St Kilda. A man, his body trussed with black tape and with a hood over his head, was wedged into the back of a white van. The portly, middle-aged man who had ordered the abduction approached quietly. He was smiling, eyes sparkling with anticipation.

Philip Peters had planned this moment for months. The crooked lawyer who specialised in laundering cash had branched out. He was in the big-time now. He was about to turn killer.

Peters had planned it carefully. He was going to drug and abduct the man he believed responsible for losing him $200,000, then kill him. It was payback time.

Peters, known in the underworld as 'Mr Laundry', was going to take his victim to a remote farmhouse in St Arnaud in central Victoria, where he would be dismembered and buried in pieces by a butcher recruited for the job. 'Where do we kill him?' asked the former butcher.

'Put a bag over his head,' said Peters.

'I've already done that, I've got him trussed up, hands and …' said the accomplice.

'Can he breathe? … Well, I want to stop him breathing … Put a plastic bag over his head,' ordered Peters.

But, apparently just in the nick of time, police arrived after a concerned neighbour yelled out. Frantically, they worked on the victim with mouth-to-mouth and heart massage, but the body remained deathly still. There was no flicker of life. Which was hardly surprising.

The police's apparently desperate actions were the final movements in an elaborate, three-month masquerade designed to snare Peters, the ambitious lawyer turned gangster, who had been determined to become a millionaire in six months – and was prepared to kill to get there.

As Peters was secretly taped in the back of a police car working out his alibi, police crowded around the lifeless body. It was lifeless because it was not the victim Peters had ordered killed. It was the dummy from Channel Seven's television series, *Full Frontal*.

The producers had agreed to lend the police the dummy as part of *Operation Soli*, a sting to catch Peters, who had been taped for months planning the abduction, torture and murder of his enemy. He had provided the drugs to dope his victim and found a stooge to do the actual killing – or so he thought.

In 1997, Peters, a former lawyer for the Crown Solicitor's Office and State Treasury, was jailed for attempted abduction, perjury and cultivating marijuana.

He was released just 22 days after being sentenced because of a deal where his original, more serious charges, including conspiracy to murder, were dropped in exchange for his guilty plea. It seemed a tiny sentence for an ongoing conspiracy where a man could have died, but the deal was cut outside the court. The pressure is on to save money by avoiding long trials. A deal is a deal and Peters, having worked for the Crown and the other side, knew the unspoken rule that much of modern law enforcement is budget driven. Justice is not only blind, but broke as well. The fact that Peters was released so early was, perhaps, to have tragic consequences much later.

According to police, Peters was a brilliant thinker but, gripped by greed and vindictiveness, he planned to torture a man he believed had contributed to his financial ruin.

The man Peters hated was another manipulative figure in Melbourne's underworld, Peter Kypri, a man with a love of money and a reputation as a double-crosser.

Peters knew from personal experience that in his circles the loss of money could prove fatal. At one point there was a $30,000 contract taken out on his life by an amphetamines dealer over a 'misunderstanding' involving between $450,000 and $600,000.

Police believe the drug dealer organised four men to beat an elderly member of Peters' family as a warning. Peters took the hint and changed his appearance, dyeing his hair and eyebrows, and he began to carry a gun.

Peters had taken possession of huge amounts of dirty money from the drug dealer and promised to launder it through a Melbourne computer firm and a property development in the Whitsunday Islands. The money went missing - and Peters would have too, but for a bizarre legal twist. The drug dealer took his case to the Solicitors' Guarantee Fund and was repaid around $500,000 in compensation and legal costs, even though it was known the money was drug profits.

A former client of Peters said he was 'known as Mr Laundry because he can launder millions for you'.

Peters, who was educated at Trinity Grammar and Melbourne University, spent ten years working for government departments before he started private practice in Essendon.

He soon earned the reputation in the underworld as a 'no-questions asked' type who cleaned dirty money. He engineered property developments using a string of shelf companies and false names. He used his secretary's name without her knowledge in one development. She began to understand she was in over her head when she started receiving anonymous funeral wreaths as none-too-subtle threats.

A New Zealand family asked Peters to wind up the affairs of a relative, Michael Joseph Smith, who had died in Melbourne. Smith, an oil rig worker, died in January 1989, aged 33. His brother, sister and their spouses flew from New Zealand to tidy up his affairs and arrange the funeral. They needed a solicitor and, as they didn't have a car, they picked the closest lawyer to the motel they were staying in at Essendon. It was Peters. The family asked him to complete all legal details. He agreed to do so for a substantial fee, but later decided that wasn't enough.

Peters assumed the dead man's identity, taking out a licence, opening bank accounts, registering his car and working as a financier under Smith's name. In fact, Peters became Michael Smith in all his business dealings after his legal practising certificate was cancelled in 1989.

The Law Institute of Victoria moved on Peters late that year. It found money missing from his trust account. In each discrepancy the money had been redirected to companies controlled by two drug dealers.

One witness described being in the office when a drug dealer arrived with money he wanted laundered. The man said the dealer produced $50,000 in cash from a paper bag to set up a bogus mortgage on a historic property in Essendon. The cash had previously been hidden from police in the ceiling of a house in Moonee Ponds.

Peter Kelly, a St Kilda solicitor, said Peters worked for him in the early 1990s using the name Michael Smith. He was supposed to help organise commercial and home loans. 'He said he had a legal degree from New Zealand, but had never practised. What I remember most about him was his eyes, which looked straight through you. It was like he was from another planet.' Peters did not conclude any loans, Kelly said. 'I think, looking back, he was trying to set me up as another front for him.'

In 1994 Peters manipulated a client to perform minor criminal acts for him. In the end he asked the man, John, to help him kill someone he believed was responsible for a loss of $200,000 in an insurance fraud gone wrong.

The proposed victim – Peter Kypri – allegedly 'stole' computer equipment from Peters' company so the loss could be claimed, but the brilliant lawyer had made an unbelievable blunder. The insurance cover on the business had lapsed and the burglar, given the green light, would not return the gear or cough up the money he'd made.

Peters' planned revenge was to organise a drug deal and then rip off Kypri for the money. He planned to take the man to a pit under a farmhouse in St Arnaud and torture him until the victim provided the cash. To do this, he wanted John, a butcher, to help abduct Kypri and ultimately to chop up his body so it would never be found.

John had been running two businesses when he was introduced to Peters, but both had failed after he was effectively manipulated into signing over his interests to Peters.

John said Peters used his legal experience to plan crimes. 'He said he read files to see how criminals had worked. He read legal transcripts and his notes to see where they went wrong.'

Once Peters had effectively taken over John's firms, the once successful businessman was at the mercy of the master manipulator.

John became involved with Peters at the lower end of crime. 'We had no money and were in debt. We had to go with them. I was going to lose my house. They had me.' He grew marijuana seedlings to be planted at the bent lawyer's Sunbury property. It was not a great success. 'The sheep ate the plants. They ended up stoned,' John said.

Each crime was the same. Peters did the planning and John did the dirty work. Peters was almost never there when there were any risks to take.

He planned several major frauds, but when the plans turned to a murder plot, John went to the police with three boxes of documents to prove his claims. Police turned John into an undercover agent in early 1994. More than 4000 pages of conversations between the two men were taped, including plans to drug and kill the proposed victim. John had no doubt Peters wanted his enemy dead. 'He was going to kill him for sure.'

The policeman in charge of *Operation Soli*, acting Detective Sergeant Jeremy Oliver, said Peters always used middlemen as fall guys to try to protect himself from prosecution. 'He always wanted someone else to do the dirty work.' There was no doubting Peters' intelligence. 'He would just make up a story as he went along which would sound quite credible. He was able to think on his feet,' Oliver was to recall.

Another policeman who had dealt with Peters made a blunter assessment. 'His looks were deceiving. He looked like a fat idiot, but he had an incredibly quick mind.'

At one point Peters developed a plan to rip-off the Solicitors' Guarantee Fund. He set up a false investment portfolio under the fictitious name of Giovanni Sanetti. The file said that Sanetti invested $60,000, which would eventually mature to $100,000. Police said that in 1993 Peters approached John and asked him to pretend to be 'Sanetti'. The plan was to apply to the Guarantee Fund for the investment money that had allegedly been lost or stolen by Peters.

According to police tapes, Peters also planned an insurance fraud by buying a fish and chip shop in Gordon, near Ballarat, and burning it down three months later.

Peters' plans to be a crime boss folded when he was arrested in the culmination of the sting. Mr Laundry forgot his golden rule: don't get your hands dirty and always use a patsy. As agreed with police, John rang Peters to say he had drugged the target, who was in the freezer in the back of his St Kilda shop. Peters wanted John to put Kypri's body in the van and drive to the St Arnaud farm. Peters, naturally, would be in another car, away from any potential problems.

As part of the police plan, John persuaded Peters to come to the shop. When he arrived he was told Kypri was still alive. It was then that Peters showed himself to be a would-be killer.

Even when police arrived he remained cool, discussing possible legal defences with his partner, still unaware that the victim was a television dummy. As police 'worked' to save the alleged victim, Peters was plotting a plan that would put him in the clear, but leave his mate John out in the cold.

PETERS: 'Just don't worry about him, John.'

JOHN: 'So, who … who … drugged him, what … what if they ask me questions like that? Hey?'

PETERS: 'Well, we're gonna have to say you did, John.'

Peters was originally charged with thirteen major criminal

charges including incitement and conspiracy to murder. The charges were later amended after he agreed to plead guilty to incitement to kidnap, cultivate marijuana and perjury.

County Court Judge Byrne sentenced him to three years and six months' jail with a minimum of five months. When pre-trial detention was taken into account he was freed 22 days after he was sentenced. John was handed a two-year suspended sentence for his activities with Peters and on his release worked eighteen hours a day in two jobs to recover financially. 'I always knew he would get away with it. It's a joke what he got.'

FOLLOWING is an edited transcript from 4000 pages of secretly-taped conversations between John and Peters the corrupt lawyer in which they discuss the plot to abduct and torture Kypri before butchering him to dispose of the body.

Tullamarine, February 11, 1994:

JOHN : '… You and Phillip were gonna take him up to St Arnaud and stick him in a fucking pit and things like that, now I've been trembling, you know for a fucking week.'

PETERS: 'Well, that's what I was gonna do. I really was. Because the bastard had pinched $200,000 worth of stock.'

JOHN: 'Yeah, and what would have happened if he got out of the pit?'

PETERS: 'Well, he wasn't gonna get out. He wasn't gonna get out, ever. We were gonna get the stock and then he was gonna vanish. He was gonna vanish, John, believe me.'

JOHN: 'All I could think was my wife, my kids, you know, things like that – nothing else.'

PETERS: 'No, I would never, ever have let it get to a situation where there could be any risk at all. He was going to vanish totally.'

JOHN: 'As in totally dead, dead.'

PETERS: 'Dead, dead. Well, he … he has pinched so much from so many people that the world … you would get a medal. Apart from the stuff he pinched from Phillip, he pinched a car from me and sold it and then told the coppers that I told him to do it.'

PETERS: 'Yeah, well, Danny has I believe … no, not has … had put a contract out on him.'

JOHN: 'That'd explain the way sort of you know he rang, yeah.'

PETERS: 'Yeah, yeah. No, that's why he's got seven around with him … I made some inquiries and Danny had apparently put a contract out on him two years ago.'

JOHN: 'Yeah.'

PETERS: 'The bloke took Danny's money then told K … '

JOHN: 'Like I said to you believe … with the pit, it's the wife and kids, I'm not worried about anything else.'

PETERS: 'No, well look, don't worry about that, there is no way on earth I would let that sort of thing happen. No, he was never gonna get out of the pit. I was gonna get as much as we could, because he owes me … he took $200,000 worth of stock … the business went down.'

PETERS: 'When you're talking on the telephone be very cautious because I just don't trust telephones.'

Tullamarine, February 16, 1994:

JOHN: 'Well if there's money to be made, I'll … I'll go along with the original idea, mate.'

PETERS: 'Right. Well, if he turns up with the cash.'

JOHN : 'Yeah.'

PETERS: 'Then as long as we can get him away, where we can see what the hell is going on.'

JOHN: 'Yeah.'

PETERS: 'You know, if he brings the cash up the bush or

whatever, then we can do it … providing things go right we can, but, you know, we're … step number one is protection.'

JOHN : 'Yeah.'

PETERS: 'Step number two is the money. You know, money's no use at all, if you're not protected. It's something to think about.'

JOHN: 'I think he's … he's greedy enough to fall for it … If he smelt the dollar, yeah.'

PETERS: 'He is, but the one thing you've got to be careful of … is that you're not followed. You know, you're going to need back roads and all sorts of things.'

A St Kilda pizza parlour, February 17, 1994:

PETERS: 'This is getting beyond me, but I … I want to get this bastard … . . . . . Yeah, well he's a lying, thieving, nasty little bastard.'

JOHN: 'Yeah.'

PETERS: Once that's happened, you're free, and then we can hit him with impunity.'

Tullamarine, February 24, 1994:

Peters talks of buying a fish and chip shop and then burning it down for the insurance.

PETERS: 'What's gonna happen, gonna buy this fish and chip shop and go into … three months or whatever and then there's gonna be a fire in the place and that's gonna be … Fish and chip shops go all the time.'

JOHN: 'What exactly is going to happen to him eventually? Is he … ?'

PETERS: 'He's going to vanish. You don't need to know about that … I want to get some money out of him first.'

February 28, 1994:

JOHN : 'I mean, are we really going to kill him? What are we going to do?'

PETERS: 'Well, look, that's up to them. I don't give a stuff.'

JOHN: 'Yeah.'

PETERS: 'All I want is … is my money back and Phillip's money back.'

JOHN: 'Yeah.'

PETERS: 'I don't give a stuff what they do with him. But obviously, if he vanishes, it's going to be better for you.'

(They talk of the marijuana John grew for Peters, later eaten by sheep.)

JOHN: 'The sheep ate them, Philip. Go outside and see if there's any stoned sheep running around the paddock.'

PETERS: 'There's dead sheep all over the place, they probably suicided.'

(They discuss getting drugs to knock out Kypri.)

JOHN: 'And make sure you bring it down to the shop and I've got it there.'

PETERS: 'Yeah, yeah.'

JOHN: 'I'm not running around for three days like we did with the bloody sample.'

PETERS: 'No. It's got to be there first.'

(He returns to the subject of the fish and chip shop).

'But basically what it is, we run the fish shop for three months or something and then the fat boils over … you've seen it happen.'

At a St Kilda pizza parlour, March 2, 1994:

JOHN: 'And with Kypri, what's going to be the outcome with him, mate?'

PETERS: 'Well.'

JOHN: 'Is he still goin' up to St Arnaud, or what?'

PETERS: 'Yeah, providing we can get him up to a big enough deal.'

JOHN: 'All right.'

PETERS: 'I'm not interested in knocking him off … over four, five grand or ten grand, but if we can get up … get him up to fifty or a hundred grand, yes, it's worth it, to get my money back.

JOHN: 'All right.'

PETERS: 'Bloody rotten little shit, he is. He … look, John, you've got no idea of what a bloody, lying, devious, dishonest, nasty little shit he is.'

JOHN: 'He … he looks like that, that's why he … he … just like a little ferret.'

PETERS: 'What I'm trying to do is build the bank … the bank roll … for other operations. I've got to find a million dollars within the next six months.'

JOHN: 'That's … that's a small order.'

PETERS: 'Well, I'm gonna do it, John.'

Tullamarine, March 23, 1994:

JOHN: 'Is there really a pit, up at St Arnaud, or what?'

PETERS: 'Yeah, there's a cellar in the house.'

JOHN: 'Right.'

PETERS: 'Brick, you know, with a very narrow staircase, so, you know.'

JOHN: 'I just hope he doesn't get out of there mate.'

PETERS: 'Well, that's why I'm thinking we might need a third person, we might need a third person, we might need someone to go and sit up there.'

JOHN: 'And how long do you think you're going to need to set up somebody to sit up with him?'

PETERS: 'I would think only a day or two, he's going to give us the information. If he doesn't then, he vanishes, which he's gonna do anyway.'

McDonald's car park, Tullamarine, April 1994:

PETERS: 'Well, I think he's got to vanish anyway.'

JOHN: 'Yeah.'

PETERS: 'The minute we do that, for your, our, for your sake, he's got to vanish.'

JOHN: 'Yeah.'

PETERS: 'But what I was … what I had originally intended to do, was either get the two hundred, or get some satisfaction.'

(The two men talk about how that will be able to get Kypri to St Arnaud.)

PETERS: 'It'll be something like an old-fashioned Mickey Finn.'

JOHN : 'We, the other thing, if he was … who is gonna kill (Kypri), up at St Arnaud, then?'

PETERS: 'If necessary, I will, but I … I think we've now got to the stage, where … you know, it's got to be you and me and no-one else, John.'

JOHN: 'All right.'

PETERS: 'I don't need, I don't want a third person involved, either.'

JOHN: 'Fine with me, mate.'

PETERS: 'That way, if something goes wrong, we know there's only two people to blame.'

PETERS: 'You'd take him out and bury him.'

Tullamarine. McDonald's car park, April 14, 1994:

(The two men discuss how they will drug the target.)

PETERS: 'But it's basically knock-out drops.'

JOHN: 'Yeah. Where do you get 'em?'

PETERS: 'They used to be all over the place. I'm finding it very difficult … I've got a half a dozen people looking for them.'

JOHN: 'It must be the signs of the times, mate.'

JOHN: 'But can you use anything else?'

PETERS: 'Look, I'm sure you can, but I don't know … you know, I've got no idea what three or four moggies tastes like.'

JOHN: 'What are moggies?'

PETERS: 'Mogadons.'

JOHN: 'Oh.'

PETERS: 'Sleeping pills ... but you know, presumably, that'd be the same ... I've got a couple of blokes having a hunt around for me, so we'll see what they come up with. There was a woman, Poison Ivy, convicted a couple of years ago, and if I could find a copy of the court transcript, I'd know how to make the stuff, even, because she was using it, but it ... it's around.'

(The two men discuss disguising the taste of the Mogadons.)

PETERS: 'What does (Kypri) drink?'

JOHN: 'Coffee.'

PETERS: 'They tell me it (the drug) is fairly bitter, so it'll have to be coffee with sugar, or something ... anyway, you can do some tests on it, John, try it on the girls.'

(By April 19, as they are getting close to abducting Kypri, Peters also considers killing a woman.

PETERS: 'You said you wanted to kill her ... There is no way on earth I'm going to do business with her, but have a think about it ... what we should be able to do, is set her up in the same way we've set up (the target) and do the same thing. I'm getting enough ... and don't call them 'Mickeys' (knockout tablets) on the phone ... you never know who's listening.'

PETERS: 'But if we set her up in the same way, we can achieve the same result, and pick up a substantial quantity of material.'

(Peters said he would like to experiment with the drugs to get the dose accurate.) 'The bloody things have turned out expensive. It's costing a hundred bucks for the what, three doses I'm getting. I'm picking them up tonight.'

JOHN: 'All right and (the murder is) gonna be done this week?'

PETERS: 'Mm, I think you should give this stuff a test. If it doesn't work, then we review everything.'

On April 20 Peters hands the drugs to John.

JOHN: 'So, how do … how many of these do we have … do … do I use?'

PETERS: 'I would put … I'd give him four, two and two.'

JOHN: 'Well, after he's asleep, what'll I do with him?'

PETERS: 'You're going to have to secure him reasonably … very, very well.'

JOHN: 'What, so he's gonna be slapped about?'

PETERS: 'Mm, as long as he's properly secured … that's gonna be the … real trick … A tape around the mouth, cuffs on the hands and ankles, and you haven't got a problem … Make sure you've got some heavy, sticky bandage, or whatever, we may need to wrap that round his mouth.'

JOHN: 'Right. They're not gonna find him, up at St Arnaud, then?'

PETERS: 'No.'

JOHN: 'They're not gonna find the body, are they?'

PETERS: 'Nuh, nuh, they're not going to find anything.'

April 21, 1994:

(John rings Peters and tells him he has drugged the victim. Peters drives to a shop in St Kilda where, he believes, the unconscious Kypri is trussed in a van outside. But it is the dummy in the van, and police hidden nearby.)

JOHN: 'Well, the moggies you gave me, mate, worked beautifully.'

PETERS: 'Good.'

JOHN: 'Where do we kill him.'

PETERS: 'Put a bag over his head.'

JOHN: 'I've already done that, I've got him trussed up, hands and feet.'

PETERS: 'Yeah, but.'

JOHN: 'I'll show you.'

PETERS: 'Can he breathe?'

JOHN: 'Yeah, come on, I'll show you.'

PETERS: 'Well, I want to stop him breathing.'

JOHN: 'Well, come and have a look.'

PETERS: 'Put a plastic bag over his head.'

UNIDENTIFIED SPEAKER: 'Hey, what are you doing there? Hey, what are you doing there? Police, call the police.'

POLICE OFFICER: 'Police, don't do anything, get on the ground.'

POLICE OFFICER: 'Get on the ground, go on. Get on the ground.'

POLICE OFFICER: 'Put your hands behind your back. Hands behind your back.'

The police then pretend to find the 'victim' in the car.

John and Peters are put in a police car. Peters sets out to concoct a legal defence, unaware he is being taped.

POLICE OFFICER: 'Who's gettin' the ambulance?'

POLICE OFFICER: 'They didn't … they didn't call an ambulance.'

POLICE OFFICER: 'Well, arrange an ambulance now.'

JOHN: 'What do we do now, Phil?'

PETERS: 'No conspiracy to murder.'

JOHN: 'You're fucking kidding me.'

PETERS: 'Well, all we were trying to do, is get some money out of this bloke that owes me and Phillip some money.'

JOHN: 'What do I tell 'em?'

PETERS: 'Just that.'

JOHN: 'So what did we do to him?'

PETERS: 'Nothing.'

JOHN: 'How did he get in the back of the van?'

PETERS: 'Just don't worry about him, John.'

JOHN: 'So, who … who … drugged him, what … what if they ask me questions like that? Hey?'

PETERS: 'Well, we're gonna have to say you did, John.'

JOHN: 'With what. What did I use?'

PETERS: 'Just a couple of Mogadons.'

JOHN : 'And where'd I get 'em? Who am I … you gave me the shits, mate.'

PETERS: 'Yeah.'

JOHN: 'Come on, what do I say, Phil.'

PETERS: 'I gave you a couple of moggies, that's all.'

JOHN: 'If they ask me, how many'd you give me, how many?'

PETERS: 'Two. Two.'

JOHN: 'If they ask me when you gave them to me, what, what do I say?'

PETERS: 'A couple of days ago.'

JOHN: 'All right. How much shit are we in?'

PETERS: 'Oh, a bit.'

Philip Peters was released from prison in April 1997, but returned to jail in early 1998 to serve a further three months for fraud. If he hated Kypri before *Operation Soli* his vindictiveness must have grown while inside. After all, the man he believed had stolen $200,000 from him and ruined his life was on the outside, still doing deals and doublecrossing anyone he dealt with.

Peters was a man who had showed he was prepared to organise a hit on Kypri. He was also a man who believed he could learn from his mistakes. So the million-dollar question (literally) is, did Peters decide to have another go at the Kypri family as a payback?

The mysterious Peter Kypri lived with his family and

conducted his equally mysterious business from a neat but nondescript house in Muriel Street, Niddrie.

It was the same street where young mother, Jane Thurgood-Dove, was shot dead in the driveway of her home in front of her three children on November 6, 1997, just a few months after Peters was released from prison.

For years there were theories and whispers. For years detectives believed there was strong circumstantial evidence that the most likely suspect was a serving policeman who had been obsessed with the married woman.

But, in 2003, after lobbying by Jane's parents, John and Helen Magill, the state government announced an unprecedented $1million reward fund for specific murders, one of which was the Thurgood-Dove case.

The hook was baited and it didn't take long. A phone call was made to police, confirming what some had suspected from the day of the murder … it was a case of mistaken identity and the real target of the paid killers had been Peter Kypri's wife, Carmel.

Police had known within days of the murder of the wrong victim theory and that the Kypri family was the real target, but this time the caller put a name to the face of the potbellied gunman who chased the innocent woman around her car before repeatedly shooting her.

Jane Thurgood-Dove's house in Muriel Street, Niddrie, was three houses from a corner. The Kypris lived on the same side of the same street, also three houses from the nearest corner.

In 1997 Carmel Kypri and Jane Thurgood-Dove had similar hairstyles. There were only three young mothers living in the street but the third's appearance was markedly different from the other two. And, of course, the third woman did not live three houses from a corner as Thurgood-Dove and Carmel Kypri did.

John, the man who went undercover to help police trap

Peters, said in 1997 he believed Carmel Kypri must have been the target of the killer who shot Jane Thurgood-Dove.

'They had the same facial features and same hairstyle. Carmel's hair was more fawn than blonde, but they were very similar. And when I saw her (Jane) on Australia's Most Wanted the hairs on the back of my neck stood up.'

There was another similarity. Both women drove four-wheel drives and often used them to pick up their children from school.

Oddly, in the months before the murder, neighbours noticed that the cautious Kypris became even more security conscious.

A friend who visited Kypri's home in Muriel Street said if Peter Kypri saw a strange car in the street, he would give a distinctive whistle as a signal for his wife and two children to lock themselves indoors. Kypri always backed his cars into the driveway as if he needed to be ready to leave in a hurry and insisted visitors not block his escape route by parking in front of his car. When the authors knocked on the Kypris' door and spoke to Carmel Kypri, then telephoned her husband where he was working in a nearby suburb, he made threats and raced home within a few minutes.

After Peters was released, the Kypris tightened security even more. The two children stopped playing in the street, were rarely seen outside and were driven to the nearby secondary school. After school they often went to the homes of other relatives. The Kypris had their reasons for being careful. They knew they had enemies. Carmel Kypri admitted just three weeks after her neighbour's murder that she may well have been the stupid gunman's intended target.

'If it wasn't meant for her (Jane) it makes you wonder. It has made us wary. My husband says to watch out when we come into the drive, to look around the place,' she hesitantly told the authors from behind a heavy screen security door.

'I keep the door locked. Maybe it was for us. Who knows? But you can't let it stop your life. The kids still go to school.'

It showed Peters was not worried about killing women and in 1994 had contemplated drugging, abducting and killing a female rival.

The Kypris were not liked in Muriel Street and residents tended to leave them alone. But they did notice their shady neighbours' behaviour. In the weeks before the murder Carmel Kypri stopped driving her four-wheel drive and began using a relative's sedan.

That left only one young mother living in the street still driving a 'Toorak tractor' – Jane Thurgood-Dove.

The 2003 tip-off finally let police identify the potbellied killer who killed the wrong woman. He was a former Rebels Motorcycle Club member, Steven John Mordy.

Mordy rarely left his home in the eighteen months after the murder because his description matched that of the gunman. After the new information was passed to police a witness identified him as the killer from a series of photos.

He was a violent man who had already been accused of being a killer. He had been acquitted of a NSW murder in August 1996.

But the breakthrough came too late for the law to take its usual course, though some might see a poetic justice in what happened to Mordy. He died of a drug overdose and related health problems in September 2001.

And the man who was said to have arranged the stolen getaway car, Jamie Reynolds, died in a boating accident off the seaside holiday town of Ocean Grove in April 2004. Few people mourned either cowardly killer.

But Peters was alive. He remains a prime suspect in the murder of Jane Thurgood-Dove. A woman he had never met, gunned down by mistake.

CHAPTER 4

A DIRTY BUSINESS

*'I was left with the impression he wanted
me to knock (kill) somebody.'*

MURDER cases are usually prised open rather than cracked. They are solved by degrees rather than with a blinding breakthrough.

But in the case of the cold-blooded abduction and murder of a harmless Melbourne solicitor, two seemingly unconnected acts a world apart combined to expose the carefully planned killing.

The first was the decision of German engineers to incorporate a foot pedal in the handbrake design on late-model Mercedes Benz motorcars. The second was the decision of two young police in Altona to follow a set of retreating tail-lights during a boring nightshift in May 2000.

It was that combination of idle curiosity and eccentric German engineering that punched a hole in what could have been a perfect professional hit. The case shows that not only gangsters – but also the law-abiding – can be the targets of paid hit men. It also proves that you don't have to have a body to prove a murder. It began when an insignificant conveyancing clerk, appropriately named Julian Clarke, pulled off a massive fraud on a trust account in the suburban law firm where he worked. When Clarke realised he was about to be exposed, he needed a patsy to blame. He decided his boss, Keith Allan, fitted the bill perfectly.

Clarke's plan was fiendishly simple. He reasoned that if Allan disappeared, the authorities would blame the solicitor for the thefts. That is why he calmly planned his boss's murder and effectively put the contract out for tender.

As it turned out, he was only one set of traffic lights away from the perfect crime …

THREE hours into a nightshift, police can go into cruise mode. So when a car went past them on an almost-deserted road in Altona in Melbourne's western suburbs just after 2am on a deadly dull Monday, Senior Constables Travis McCarthy and Michael Strongman were entitled to keep going.

But, for no good reason, they turned their vehicle and followed in the direction of the rapidly-disappearing tail-lights.

And for no good reason the two policemen continued to search for the tail-lights until they found two cars parked in a dead-end street.

They were not to know that those tail-lights were from a recently-purchased old model Jaguar and they were not to know the driver had bought the car with $12,000 in $100 notes he had been paid as an advance for taking the contract to kill a likeable lawyer.

It would take another 21 months to lay charges and four years to gain convictions, but the crime was exposed the moment the two young police pulled up in Ayr Street, Altona, to make a routine check.

There they found two cars, the old white Jaguar with NSW plates and a late model blue Mercedes with the Victorian registration, KWA 111.

The Mercedes was registered to Keith William Allan. When police looked in the back seat they saw a shovel and a hoe with soil still on the blades.

KEITH William Allan was a walking contradiction – a man who loved a bet but who hated taking risks. At 53 years of age he remained devoted to his elderly mother, choosing to live next door to her in the quiet Northcote street where he had grown up.

Born on November 19, 1946, Keith was the younger of two brothers. He went to Northcote High then to Melbourne University, where he completed a law degree. Hardworking rather than naturally gifted, he struggled in one subject – trust management. Ironically, it was his trust – personal as well as financial – that would destroy him.

But after graduation he bought a solicitor's practice in Military Road, Avondale Heights, and built a solid business under the banner of Keith W. Allan and Associates. He was successful enough to open a second practice in Springvale in 1992.

When his parents finally sold the family home in Beavers Road, Northcote, they simply moved across the road and seven houses down the street. Keith and his schoolmaster elder brother, Lyle, bought the house next door to their parents and moved in.

Keith worked up to twelve hours a day and then would most often go straight home to eat and watch a little television before bed. He had a close platonic relationship with a childhood friend, Cheryl Sutherland. Almost every Saturday they would go to the harness racing together.

'Keith and I were very similar in that neither of us drank alcohol or smoked,' Cheryl was to say about her lifelong friend. 'We are not party people and were more than happy to sit in front of the television ... Keith is a very likeable character and is easygoing. Every person I know, particularly my family, all love him. He is generous to a fault,' she would later tell police.

Allan was a creature of habit and liked order in his life. Each Wednesday and Friday he would visit Cheryl after work before going home at a respectable hour. Saturday was trots night and on Sunday he would have dinner at a Preston hotel with Cheryl and friends. He would invariably order the roast of the day.

While Keith Allan loved harness racing he was not a big punter, betting no more than $50 each weekend.

In 1984 he was the secretary of the Harness Racing Owners Association and for many years he enjoyed the social and official sides of the industry.

A former Footscray league footballer, Jack Collins, met the amiable solicitor at the trots and they became friends. 'I would describe Keith Allan as being an honest, hardworking, mild-mannered man who never looked for any trouble and wouldn't hurt a fly. He was not an aggressive person but a shy individual with not a lot of self-confidence,' was the way Collins described him later.

Collins and other friends say that Allan's life was simple and that he had no secrets. His life revolved around his practice, his family and his interest in harness racing.

He was honest, decent and hardworking but even those closest to him admitted he was not great with numbers. 'Keith was a poor financial manager,' his brother Lyle says, without reproach. In the early 1990s, Lyle had to bail him out of a financial disaster involving a failed stud farm. By 1995 the solicitor who couldn't add up realised he needed help and he employed a conveyancing clerk.

But Allan sometimes had another flaw besides weak arithmetic: on this occasion he was a fatally poor judge of character.

JULIAN Michael Clarke was born on June 13, 1956, in Marrickville, the working-class inner western suburb of Sydney that was also to produce a future world boxing champion, Jeff Fenech. Clarke was one of five children. Soon after he was born, the family moved to Belmont, near Geelong.

Like Keith Allan, Clarke grew up to live a seemingly respectable life, at eighteen joining the public service, where he worked for ten years before becoming a law clerk.

Clarke married but it lasted only eighteen months. It was not surprising the marriage failed, as he was gay.

In February 1995, he joined Allan's firm as a law clerk but his influence soon grew with the older but more naïve confirmed bachelor. He showed interest in the financial side of the business – Allan's obvious weakness. The solicitor was happy to leave the books to the clerk and in 1996 he made Clarke a co-signatory to the firm's trust account – a move that breached trust account guidelines.

In effect, Clarke became the business manager, leaving Allan free to work with clients and complete his official duties in the harness racing industry.

But while Allan was a weekend punter, Clarke was a problem

gambler. The insignificant clerk with the beer income and champagne tastes soon became a regular at Crown Casino's Mahogany Room.

What Allan didn't know was that his trusted clerk was stealing hundred of thousands of dollars to feed his own gambling addiction and that of his friends.

While Clarke was paid just $150 a day for his work in Allan's firm he was living the life of a millionaire. Perhaps it was because Clarke liked to back long shots that he couldn't see the one sure thing: that his ferocious raids on the trust accounts could not remain undiscovered for long.

Records show that between November 9, 1998, and September 14 the following year, $4.3million was deposited and withdrawn from the trust account.

Much later it was found that Clarke was responsible for 58 thefts totalling $929,478. He was found to have improperly used that account for $2,795,000. By then, of course, it would be the least of his legal problems. Meanwhile, it was inevitable the thefts would be discovered. The surprise was that it took so long.

In August 1999 the Law Institute received the first complaint involving a possible theft of a $75,000 cheque from the trust account. Two months later Marie Ryan, an accountant working for the institute, visited Keith Allan's office for a chat – the first of many, as it turned out.

Immediately, the accountant was told that the account's key paperwork was missing.

Oddly, Clarke was to give two explanations: the first was that he had taken records home in a cardboard box, left them in the car and they were stolen.

The second was that he left them on the nature strip and forgot them. He claimed that by the time he remembered where he had left the records, the garbage man had collected them. Despite his apparent confusion, Clarke remained unfazed and, at least initially, seemed helpful. He offered to reconstruct the ledger using bank records to the satisfaction of the inquisitive Ms Ryan.

But there were always delays. Clarke was ill or he was too busy. Allan was always apologetic – saying he 'felt sick about the situation' – while Clarke put up a bold front, rudely saying the institute should spend more time investigating crooked lawyers and 'stop hassling me'.

By May 2000 even the patient Ms Ryan was tired of excuses.

FRIDAY May 26, should have been a great day for the painfully shy solicitor. He had won a raffle and the prize was to have a harness race named after him. He took his friend Cheryl, her brother Norman and Norman's wife to Bendigo to the harness races and they stayed overnight.

But before he left his office he told his staff, in the absence of his shifty conveyancing clerk, that he was going to telephone Ms Ryan on Monday to ask her to come out to the practice.

It may have been an attempt at face-saving. Although Allan was financially inept he knew the trust account was hopelessly compromised. He also knew that Ms Ryan had given him a deadline for the reconstructed accounts – June 5 – just over a week away. He knew his business was on the verge of collapse.

On May 27, on the way home from Bendigo, he confided to Cheryl that he had a big week coming up. He told her he was determined to sort out his financial problems and intended to try to recover money owed to him.

On Sunday May 28, Allan went to his office with his brother Lyle, who later described a painful scene as his brother confessed his problems. 'He told me that he was in fairly serious financial trouble. He asked me if I was able to access any funds urgently. He told me that he needed $100,000 very quickly. He told me that a lot of people owed him money and that he may have been able to raise some of this money from the debts he was owed.

'I was angry with him because I had helped him once before,' Lyle said. 'He also said he thought that Julian would soon be leaving the firm.'

A drowning man will clutch a snake to try to save his life and Allan was sinking fast. So when Clarke rang him on that Sunday and said he may have found an investor who could provide cash to float the sinking trust account, Allan wanted to believe him. He clutched for the snake, too desperate to heed the danger.

During the day Clarke made several attempts to speak to Allan. On their way to their regular Sunday dinner at Cramers Hotel, Allan told Cheryl that Clarke had asked to meet him at the Avondale Heights office at 7pm but the solicitor had said he was busy. They had then arranged to meet at 9.30pm. According to Ms Sutherland, Allan said, 'Julian wants to meet me with a man'.

She joked that he should be careful and he responded with a light-hearted comment. 'Keith joked that he was worth more alive than dead.'

He was wrong.

Backed into a corner, the solicitor who liked to avoid confrontations knew he would have to act. But Clarke had read the play more than a month earlier and had already stolen a further $70,000 from the trust account in four instalments to pay for Allan's murder.

Now Clarke wanted value for his boss's money.

HOW do you find a killer? For Julian Clarke it was as simple as attending a social function in a suburban home in Muriel Street, Niddrie, near Essendon in Melbourne's north-west.

Birds of a feather flock together. Somehow Clarke the greedy, crooked law clerk had become a friend of a mysterious minor Melbourne underworld figure called Peter Kypri. They had one thing in common: lack of scruples. Clarke soon concluded that members of the Kypri clan were available to perform duties not discussed in polite social circles.

Over the years Kypri had developed a wide group of friends and just as many enemies.

In 1994, a crooked lawyer called Philip Peters tried to hire professional killers to abduct and murder Kypri over an alleged $200,000 debt. Peter's plan was to lure Kypri into a $200,000 marijuana deal, drug him with a sedative, and take him to a farmhouse at St Arnaud in central Victoria, where he would be tortured in a hidden cellar, then killed.

But police used a man that Kypri trusted to play the role of the hit man in order to trap Peters in a sting operation, code-named *Soli* (see *Two-Time Loser*). Police believe that Kypri and later his wife Carmel were murder targets.

DESPITE the fact that Peter Kypri and his wife had both almost become victims of paid hits, it did not stop a member of his family accepting a job as a contract killer. It was Kypri's cousin, Costas 'Con' Athanasi who would eventually organise the murder of Keith Allan.

In early 1999 Julian Clarke met Athanasi at Kypri's Niddrie home. Later that year Athanasi's de facto wife, Vicki Lester, needed a lawyer to represent her over a routine .05 drink-driving charge. Clarke recommended his boss.

Allan would also represent Peter Kypri in a 1999 court case

where the underworld figure was found guilty of assault. If Kypri were grateful he had a strange way of showing it.

Vicki Lester had endured a fractured ten-year relationship with Athanasi after meeting him in a nightclub where she worked. He was always jealous, but not jealous enough to work at their relationship because his first love was always gambling.

'Con has been a gambler for the entire time I have known him,' Lester was to say.

'He gambles on horses, cards, sport or the pokies, in fact he would gamble on anything. I believe that he is addicted to gambling … No amount of money for Con is enough, he has to double it and quite often he would lose.'

Life with Athanasi was often grim but rarely boring.

Born in Cyprus, the second youngest of four, he migrated to Australia with his family when he was six.

The family moved to St Albans, then to Loxton North in South Australia to farm a fruit block.

They moved back to St Albans when Con was twelve, and ran a greengrocer's shop. He went to a local high school and also worked in the family shop.

He enjoyed indoor soccer and developed a strong friendship with team-mate Sudo Cavkic. They were mates for about three years but lost contact.

In 1996 Athanasi and Lester went to Cyprus to help establish a family bar. If it was supposed to be a new start it turned out to be the same old story. One day Athanasi told Lester he would be returning to Australia – in twenty minutes. He had been caught drug trafficking and had to get out of the country before his passport was flagged at the airport.

He returned to Australia and continued drug trafficking, but not successfully. Lester later told police that she was once taken hostage in Melbourne when three men came looking for Athanasi.

Faced with the choice of chivalry or self-protection, he chose the latter. He jumped through a plate glass window to escape and later needed surgery. After recovering from his injuries he returned to the nightclub beat for pleasure and profit, selling drugs and socialising. He ran into his old mate Cavkic at the High Society nightclub in Doncaster. Sudo Cavkic was born in Bosnia on January 1, 1968, and migrated to Australia with his family at the age of two. Brought up in Melbourne, he later moved to Western Australia with his de facto wife and child but returned alone in 1998 and tried to find work as a plasterer.

After their chance meeting at the nightclub, the old soccer buddies agreed to stay in touch. They met from time to time at the Crown Casino.

Kypros Kypri is another in the Kypri family who gives the impression of being unfazed by his brother Peter's shady connections.

Kypros met Julian Clarke at Peter's home and knew the overweight clerk as 'Slim'. He also knew Keith Allan and called the bespectacled solicitor 'Mr Magoo'.

Kypros was running a coffee shop in Queensland when he received a phone call from 'Slim' in March or April in 2000. 'Julian wanted me to do something for a fair bit of money. I asked what was it, and he said it required a gun. He said it would pay about $100,000. I was not interested and he wanted to know if I knew anybody that could do it. I was left with the impression he wanted me to knock (kill) somebody.'

Around that time Kypros's cousin Con Athanasi came to visit in Southport, where he made and took a series of calls to and from Clarke.

Another curious figure in the Kypri social set was a coffee

shop owner, Salih Hudaverdi. He was a friend of Peter Kypri and they had mutual interests – not always lawful.

'I started to associate with him as Peter was always looking for little scams to make money and I was interested in making money.'

About three weeks before Allan disappeared Hudaverdi and Kypri met for coffee in Lygon Street, Carlton. Hulaverdi said Kypri had a telephone conversation with Clarke. 'When Peter got off the phone he asked me if I wanted to do a job.

'I asked him what sort of job and he said, "Do you want to make some money, around 50 grand?" I said yes. Peter then explained that the job was to "take out a solicitor." Straight away I said no and he didn't talk about it any more.'

Typically, Kypri tried his traditional doublecross and, following Allan's murder, he went to the homicide squad and offered information on Clarke.

In return he wanted to be paid as an informer and have pending charges against him dropped.

Police said they wouldn't deal and the would-be middleman disappeared. But he managed to sit just under the surface of the investigation and was never charged in relation to Allan's murder.

Privately, he told police Clarke had offered him the contract at least ten times but each time he had refused.

ON the Sunday night, after dropping Cheryl Sutherland home and stopping at a supermarket to buy some lollies, Allan drove to his practice for his 9.30pm meeting with Clarke.

As usual, the conniving conveyancing clerk was one step ahead. He had arrived early and used the office computer to lay a paper trail calculated to make him look like a concerned whistleblower.

At 9.27pm he finished a note on the computer that read:

'Keith, It is with great reluctance that I write this letter.

I cannot however go on with the charade that you have demanded of me.

Keith, I like you very much and there is nothing that I would not do to save your practice and the jobs of (the staff). I feel that this has not been better illustrated than my complicity in covering your tracks and the sham in trying to delay the investigation by the Law Institute these past eight months.

It cannot go on any longer.

Unless you have adequate funds in trust to trade and by that I mean to cover all trust balances by 9.30am Monday 29 May 2000 I will have no alternative but to report the matter to the Law Institute unless you have already done so.

Please do not do anything rash.

Lastly Keith you have indicated to all and sundry your preparedness to take your own life. Put this thought out of reach Keith.'

When Allan arrived at the office Clarke was able to persuade him to travel to meet a man who supposedly might be able to help them.

They drove separately to a Mobil service station in Milleara Road, East Keilor. Police were able to get the security tape from the service station that showed the two men there at 9.53pm. It was the last voluntary act Allan would make in his life.

Almost certainly, Cavkic was waiting in the car park and Allan was abducted at gunpoint.

Clarke then drove to his home in Port Melbourne, arriving around 10.30pm secure in the knowledge he would never see his boss again.

The men who know what happened after they left the service

station aren't talking but it is possible to trace the movements of the suspects through their mobile phone chatter.

That morning Clarke received a call from Athanasi's mobile phone. Police suspect the paid killer was scouting for and possibly digging a grave in the Mt Macedon area. Less than twenty minutes after the abduction Cavkic rang Athanasi from the Broadmeadows area. About 40 minutes later he rang again from Mt Macedon.

There were a series of phone calls between Cavkic and Athanasi in the Mt Macedon, Mt Blackwood and Taylors Lakes areas in the next few hours. One theory was the men were talking until they found the pre-arranged burial site.

Allan's phone was used to ring Athanasi at 12.45am. Police believe Cavkic made the call and the lawyer was already dead.

Certainly the plan was to abduct Allan, kill him and bury the body in the hills, but police have been told that not all went as arranged.

They were told the men could not find the gravesite and that Allan was hurriedly buried near the Melton tip.

About a week later Clarke asked a friend if he could borrow his van. Police say the van may have been used to move the body from the temporary grave and dump it elsewhere. Detectives did find a freshly dug hole near the tip that could have been used to conceal a body, but no strong forensic evidence.

But what is beyond dispute is the killers needed to dispose of Allan's Mercedes to lead police to the false conclusion that the solicitor had either disappeared or committed suicide to avoid exposure by the Law Institute.

The plan was simple. They would torch his car. Indeed, they had already bought a container of petrol, which they had wedged tightly in the front seat.

But there was a technical problem. After returning from Mt Macedon in the dead lawyer's car Cavkic had for the first time engaged the handbrake. And he couldn't release it.

Athanasi had driven off first, to meet Cavkic at a prearranged spot to burn the car but Cavkic had not moved.

Twice Cavkic rang his partner, at 1.54 and again at 2.18am. It was then that Athanasi agreed to return to help get the Mercedes moving. Just two minutes later the two senior constables on night patrol saw the tail-lights of his white Jaguar and decided to follow.

Much later, when the Mercedes was seized, tow truck driver William Brincat would tell police the handbrake was applied by a foot pedal but released by a small lever in the dash.

'Generally speaking if you applied the handbrake without being familiar with how to release it, you would have difficulty locating the lever … this would have been even more difficult if you were trying to locate this release lever in the dark,' he said.

He took it to the police station and found the wheels were locked up and he had to spray his tray with water to slide the Mercedes into the police compound.

But there was something else. The interior light globes in the car had been removed by someone who wanted to be sure that whatever was to happen in the car could be carried out in darkness.

WHEN Senior Constables Strongman and McCarthy spoke to the two drivers it became immediately obvious that their routine car check was anything but routine.

Cavkic gave a false name and an obviously false story as to why he was driving the Mercedes. He claimed that he had met Keith Allan in a pub and had borrowed the car for the chance to drive a luxury vehicle.

Police could see a spade and a hoe in the back seat of the Mercedes. They also found a silver petrol tin wedged in the front seat. If this was not enough to make them suspicious there was something else to raise concerns about the man who gave the false name. He was wearing a shoulder holster.

Back at the Williamstown station he was found to be carrying a 1950 7.62 x 25 millimetre Russian-made self-loading service pistol. The serial number had been erased. It had an eight-shot magazine but was loaded with only five live rounds.

Police rang Keith Allan's mother, Mavis. Her reaction and that of Keith's brother, Lyle, was enough to tell them the missing man would not have lent his car to a virtual stranger, was a teetotaller who would not have met the men in a pub and would not be out in the early hours.

It was enough for police to conclude that the two men they had found in a dead-end street needed to answer some serious questions.

It was time to call the homicide squad.

DETECTIVE Senior Sergeant Lucio Rovis is one of Australia's longest serving homicide investigators, experienced enough to know that a man found in someone else's car in the middle of the night is not necessarily a murderer.

He knows that a few stern words, followed by a few snappy answers, often result in nothing worse than a case of a broken night's sleep rather than a homicide investigation. But this time the answers were so vague and the circumstances so bizarre the matter had to be pursued.

Cavkic told Rovis: 'Look, I can clear this up with a couple of phone calls. I told the other cops this already. I can't believe this shit.'

Rovis responded: 'We want to clear this matter up as well. I don't know if we should even be involved. All we want to know is where the owner of the Mercedes is. We're not interested in the firearm or why you had the car.'

Cavkic persisted with trying to lie his way out of trouble. It left Rovis unimpressed. 'Sudo, some of what you're telling us seems a bit far-fetched. There are two possible scenarios that I can think of. One is that Keith has been killed and somehow you have his car and two, that Keith is alive and for some reason has not come forward. If he's alive and well and you know where he is, tell us now before this whole thing gets out of hand.'

But while Cavkic would never tell the truth he unwittingly did provide the answers. Police were able to find tiny traces of blood on Cavkic's trousers, sock and shoe. They took a sample from a hairbrush in Allan's room and it proved to be a perfect match.

Finally the case was handed to the missing person cold case unit of the homicide squad in January 2002. Proving a murder without witnesses is difficult. Proving it without a body is more so.

Senior Detective David Rae said rumours that Allan led a secret life and was a heavy gambler and womaniser were exactly that: only rumours. 'We examined his background deeply. He was just a decent man who was the victim of cold-blooded murder.'

Even though they knew they were suspects, Cavkic, Clarke and Athanasi remained confident they had got away with murder.

Certainly Athanasi remained an active drug dealer and was later arrested and convicted for trafficking amphetamines. While he refused to talk to police frankly, he certainly was a chatterbox to others. Police found that between February 18 and March 21 2002, there were 11,442 calls made to and from his mobile phone.

BERNIE Smith is an experienced used car dealer and knows it pays to keep potential customers happy. But on March 30, 2000, he had second thoughts about giving a loud and obnoxious browser called Con Athanasi a test drive of an old Jaguar in his Flemington lot.

The car was parked about ten deep and it would require moving a large number of vehicles. 'Con then pulled out a wad of cash from his pocket and showed it to me.'

'Con said, "Do you want to sell the fucking car or what?"'

'Con gave me the wad of cash, which was approximately $12,000 in $100 bills.'

He took the car for a test drive, rang on his mobile and said he liked the car and would return the next day to complete paperwork. But he didn't come back. Two weeks later he returned saying he had changed his mind and wanted to swap the car.

The Jag was now in poor condition and full of rubbish. But Smith agreed and he swapped the Jag for a Mercedes and a BMW. Several months later he again returned with the two cars and swapped them for a 1985 Jaguar.

Almost two months later Athanasi approached him and asked if the used car warranty had expired. When informed that it had, 'Con smiled and said "Well you're going to go fishing like the other bloke".'

On February 18, 2002 Cavkic was charged with the murder. On October 31 Clarke was charged and a day later Athanasi was also charged.

The defence was as simple as the prosecution was complex.

Lawyers for all three men simply said the prosecution had not established that Allan was dead.

The jury disagreed and found all three guilty.

On May 10, 2004, nearly four years after Allan's murder, Justice Philip Cummins sentenced Clarke to a minimum of 25 years, Athanasi to 24 years and Cavkic to 23 years. He said, 'The prosecution case was that you, Mr Clarke, were the architect and intended beneficiary of the murder; you, Mr Athanasi, were the arranger and you, Mr Cavkic, the killer.' He said of Clarke, 'In order to enable yourself to blame Mr Allan for your own conduct, you had him killed. You even paid for the killing with money you stole from his trust account.

'You, Mr Athanasi, were paid $70,000 by Mr Clarke to arrange the murder of Mr Allan. This was done by the payment to you of four trust account cheques between 12 April 2000 and 19 May 2000 arranged by Mr Clarke. The cloak for these cheques was the pretence that they were repayments to you of a loan. All false.

'It is not known, Mr Cavkic, what was your reward for doing the killing. Probably you were paid an amount of cash by Mr Athanasi.'

'Mrs Allan, the mother of the deceased, was grievously afflicted by his disappearance. First the shock of his disappearance, then the cruel uncertainty of what had happened to him, and the even crueller oscillation between hope and despair, all took their toll on her health and her emotions. She died on 3 February 2002, never knowing what had happened to her loving younger son, and never having been able to lay his body to rest.

'Mr Lyle Allan, the elder brother of the deceased, too has been grievously afflicted by the loss of his brother. I have given attention to his victim impact statement filed with the

Court and which is a moving and impressive document. Mr Lyle Allan has been afflicted by the loss of his brother, by the cruel, longitudinal uncertainty of his brother's fate, and by being denied his fraternal right of placing his brother's body in its final resting place and at peace.'

Senior Detective Rae said, 'It is a tragedy how one event can take a life and change so many others. Keith's brother, Lyle believes his mother (Mavis) died of a broken heart.'

He said it was a complex investigation, 'But without the keen observation of the senior constables (Travis McCarthy and Michael Strongman) I don't think we would have got anywhere.'

CHAPTER 5

THE SOCIETY MURDERS

He sold his self-respect for access to the family trust accounts.

MATTHEW Wales might have been dim, but he was determined. The youngest of five, he carefully selected a date to kill his wealthy mother and stepfather – but had to abort the plan just before the deadline.

His infant son, Domenik, became ill just hours before Matthew was to poison his mother, Margaret Wales-King, and her husband, Matthew's stepfather Paul King, at a family dinner. But Matthew had been planning the murders for months so, while the cancellation was technically a matter of life and death, in practical terms it would only delay the inevitable.

Although he would tell police much later he had dreamed of killing his mother since he was a child, it was in early 2002 that his fantasy began to turn into sick reality.

Matthew's anger was honed by his reliance on his mother's

wealth, which gave her control of his life. He needed her cash but there were always apron strings attached. It was a recipe for resentment, but no-one realised just how much so until it was too late. With an IQ of just 83, Matthew was on the thick side but he was convinced he knew one thing: if his millionaire mother was dead, along with her invalid husband, he could have the money without having to please her to get it.

Or so he thought.

For as long as he could remember, his mother's very existence was a constant reminder of his own inadequacies. His brother and sisters had attained financial independence and no longer needed to rely on their mother's inherited wealth, which had come from the road-building empire her father had established between the wars.

But Matthew was seen as the runt of the litter. Incapable of making his own way in business, too weak to stand up to the family matriarch, and too pathetically greedy to refuse her money, he sold his self-respect for access to the family trust accounts.

As murders go, police see the Wales-King case as a classic domestic motivated by a deadly blend of resentment and greed. To them, it was an open and shut case. At least, it would be once the bodies were found.

But Matthew Wales' family maintains there is more to the killing than has been exposed in court. After failing to persuade the media of this, they employed a prominent public relations firm to help promote their assertion that Matthew was a pawn in the hands of his manipulative and cunning wife, Maritza.

According to some people close to the family, they see Maritza as a hot-blooded Chilean bombshell who helped turn the malleable Matthew into a cold-blooded killer. In an orchestrated publicity campaign, family members made it clear they were convinced she was a key player in the murder plot. Yet police say there is no evidence to support their theory and believe she may simply have been caught up in the web of greed, malevolence and violence.

Both husband and wife have denied the claims, with Matthew telling police, 'Maritza had nothing to do with this at all'. But she did originally give her husband a false alibi and was charged with attempting to pervert the course of justice. The family still maintains she is guilty of much more.

They believe that while Maritza didn't physically kill her in-laws, she was deeply involved. They publicly suggested that the young mother callously stood by while the couple lay dying after being bludgeoned in the front yard of Matthew's rented Glen Iris town house.

They say the autopsies show that Margaret and Paul Wales-King were still alive after the initial attack and that if Maritza had called an ambulance they might have survived.

'She could have saved them,' one said. 'If she gets away with a suspended sentence or a rap across the knuckles, then certainly we will be very unhappy.'

For more than a year the real-life soap opera surrounding the Wales-King murders fascinated Australia. The rich family, the intrigue and their internal squabbles made headline news. The *Herald Sun* published more than 70 articles on what it dubbed 'Society Murders', including twelve on page one. *The Age* published more than 50 reports, including six on the front page.

For days, reporters and television crews stood outside Matthew's home yelling questions and waiting for his inevitable arrest. Police who were quietly trying to build their case found many of their moves telegraphed in media reports.

A former homicide squad detective rang a crime reporter to ask for the inside story. He said he wouldn't pester the detectives on the case, but wanted to know the unpublished details for his wife. He said he had investigated dozens of murders without his wife showing a great deal of interest but she was riveted by the Wales-King case.

Even the Prime Minister, Mr Howard, while waiting to go on air at a Melbourne radio station, asked the host what the 'real' story was behind the double murder. So who is the family whose secrets were exposed through this public tragedy?

MARGARET Wales-King was born on June 16, 1933, the eldest of two daughters of Doreen May and Robert John Lord, a man who made a fortune through road construction.

She went to boarding school and the exclusive Loreto Mandeville Hall in Toorak. She later went to business school and, while always an astute manager of money, her loves were the arts, paintings, decorating and antiques.

On June 17, 1957 – one day after turning 24 – she married Brian John Wales and a year later had their first child.

They lived in Camberwell and, like many affluent families, spent summer holidays at Sorrento and winter breaks at the snow.

They had five children – Sally, Damian, Emma, Prue and Matthew, who was born on February 18, 1968. That year the couple met Paul King while on holiday at Brampton Island. Brian Wales was a commercial pilot who was often away from home. Paul and Margaret were to become friends, then lovers. It was to prove a fatal attraction, if Matthew Wales' claimed motives are to be believed.

In 1975, Brian and Margaret Wales separated. A year later, they divorced. Soon after the separation, King moved in with Margaret. This created a split in the family, a rift that never completely healed.

Paul Aloisius King was five years older than Margaret and lived in Sydney until the 1960s, when he moved to Melbourne to take up a position as advertising manager for a wool company. He did not marry and lived alone in a small flat in Prahran. He retired in 1976 and, according to friends, was besotted with Margaret.

The four elder Wales children blamed him for their parents' break-up. They dismissed him behind his back with the nicknames of 'The Butler' and 'The Shadow' because he was so subservient to Margaret.

But King did become a father figure to Matthew, who was just seven when his parents split. While four of the Wales children would spend holidays with their father, Matthew stayed home with his mother and stepfather.

This drove a wedge between Matthew and his brother and sisters. Put simply, they felt he was a spoiled brat. 'Mum adored Matthew to the stage where we used to call him "Golden Boy" – he could do no wrong in Mum's eyes,' sister Emma was to say. 'Matthew was the baby of the family and I feel he was Mum's absolute masterpiece because he was so beautiful and she was so very into aesthetics.'

But 'golden boy' would prove to be fool's gold. He struggled at school, lied at home and grew into an uncontrollable teenager, prone to violent outbursts.

His brother and sisters felt he was allowed to get away with fewer family duties and could always rely on his mother to support him, even when he was clearly wrong.

Tellingly, Emma recalls that he was cruel to animals. 'I used to tell Mum, but Matthew would lie and get out of it.' Crime profilers maintain that a consistent trait in cold-blooded killers is a tendency to torture animals when they are children.

His mother (and her money) was always there to bail him out.

But Matthew was far from grateful. He knew he was different. Like a cuckoo chick in the nest, he just didn't fit in. His brother, Damian, was to say, 'Matthew was a prick of a kid. We were never close'.

Homicide detectives trying to establish Matthew's motives for murder decided he 'felt he had been alienated from his family by the deceased Wales-King and harboured this anger for years. He has also felt that his mother constantly used money as a bargaining tool to enable her to exercise her will over him and the rest of the family, which also upset him and affected him deeply.'

He left Caulfield Grammar for the John Morrey School of Hairdressing where he completed his apprenticeship. In 1997 he opened a franchised hairdressing salon in the Knox shopping centre, called Hair House Warehouse.

He had a small but loyal client list. One was an attractive girl from Boronia – Maritza Pizzaro.

The youngest of three children, Maritza had migrated to Australia from Chile at thirteen with her parents, Mario and Honoria Pizzaro, in 1976 to settle in Melbourne's outer east.

She went to Aquinas College in Ringwood where she completed Year Ten and then worked at *The Age* office taking classified advertisements. Her relationship with Matthew was her first serious one.

According to Emma Wales, Matthew often confided in her about his love life: 'He was a real kiss-and-tell merchant'.

She said Maritza asked Matthew to go to her house to do her hair. 'When Matthew arrived at her door, apparently Maritza was wearing a see-through negligee and a g-string and apparently the hairdo went out the window, as did all caution … from that moment on he was besotted with her.'

They married in 1999 and had their only child, Domenik, the

following year. Emma told police she saw her sister-in-law as a gold-digger. 'She seemed like a vulgar little guttersnipe really … Maritza aspired to being rich, rich, rich, that's all she wanted to be. I've never met anyone as blatant a liar as Maritza.'

Marriage did not mature Matthew. If anything, it made him worse. He walked out on the hairdressing business after an argument over rent and did not even bother to collect his equipment.

While Matthew clearly loved Maritza as deeply as his shallow intellect allowed, other members of his family felt he had simply added another dominant woman to his life.

Even when the couple moved in together, they were not truly independent. Their house in Horace Street, Malvern, had been bought by Margaret Wales-King ten years earlier on the condition that her wayward son pay off a $50,000 mortgage.

When the property was sold in 2001, Matthew demanded his share of the profits. His mother tried to keep $70,000 in trust for him but, after a dispute lasting months, finally agreed to hand over all the money. Some family members questioned the wisdom of selling his only solid asset. Having sold their house, the couple and Domenik moved into a rented four-bedroom townhouse in busy Burke Road, Glen Iris.

Matthew used the money from the sale to help set up his wife in what they hoped would be a trendy women's fashion shop in High Street, Armadale. They called it Maritza Imports.

Emma would later tell police that her sister-in-law lacked the business and sales experience to succeed. She claimed Maritza's brother once said his sister's only retailing experience was to 'wiggle her arse in a men's shoe shop'.

In December 2001 the simmering tensions between members of the family threatened to break out into open warfare. As always, it was about money, power and control. The children wanted to free themselves from their mother's financial interests. Margaret and her sister, Sydney socialite Di Yeldham, controlled a trust that owned a Gold Coast unit bequeathed to them by their father. But the real owners were their children. When Mrs Yeldham decided to sell, Margaret wanted her share invested back into her trust, but she needed her children's agreement.

According to police, 'Much to the deceased Wales-King's irritation, all the children wanted to be involved in the negotiations and were initially hesitant to sign their consent'.

Mrs Yeldham said, 'Marg was concerned about winding up her trust because she didn't want the children to have control of the money'.

Margaret's son-in-law, Angus Reed, told police she was motivated by power: 'I would say Margaret tried to manipulate her children through the use of money'.

The dispute went on for two months. The only person whose opinion didn't matter was Matthew – his mother gave him the documents and demanded his signature. Margaret either believed that after all she had done for him she could rely on his loyalty – or she thought he was too stupid to understand the document.

He signed but clearly believed it was the final proof that his mother would always treat him like a child.

Matthew didn't speak to his mother for a month and when he finally did it was almost certain he had already decided their relationship was over.

In late March 2002, he went to his in-laws' home in Kew and stole some blood pressure pills, prescribed for Maritza's mother Honoria, from the kitchen cabinet. Matthew was preparing to poison his mother.

He invited Margaret and Paul for dinner that week but the

arrangement had to be cancelled when Domenik became ill. But time was on his side. The dinner date was reset for Thursday, April 4.

FOR years Paul King had devoted himself to his strong-willed wife. He had few friends of his own and was happy to be the submissive partner in their relationship.

'The boys called him "The Butler" because he doted on Mum and did whatever she wanted … Mum directed him in what she wanted him to do, which he was fine with. It worked well for both of them,' daughter Sally was to say.

Or, as Prudence said: 'Paul was like a slave and he did everything for her'. In early 2000, Paul King suffered a stroke while at their property at Red Hill. At one stage he was so ill Margaret began making funeral arrangements. He survived with diminished speech capacity but, after a series of setbacks, ultimately needed 24-hour care.

Margaret Wales-King had to rein in her lifestyle to care for her incapacitated husband. 'Mum found this complete turnaround of roles difficult to deal with,' Sally said.

Her social life began to shrink as she nursed Paul. She took bridge lessons as an escape from her duties. The idea of an evening meal at the home of her problem child must have seemed a welcome, if brief, respite.

Maritza saw her mother-in-law on the Tuesday. 'She was very busy; she said we should catch up. She told me she was taking Paul to a centre on Wednesday, which is like a nursing home, to see whether he likes it or not.'

Margaret and Paul spent the Thursday afternoon entertaining friends, Janette and Fred Roach. They had two glasses of wine each and just after 6pm Margaret told her friends, 'I'm sorry, I'm going to have to kick you out now because I'm expected at my daughter's (in-law) home for dinner'. She was always punctual. The invitation was for between 6.30pm and 7pm. She rang and said she would arrive at 6.50pm.

Margaret drove their silver Mercedes sedan into the driveway of the double-storey town house, which was enclosed by a large concrete rendered fence. No-one could see in off the busy road so no-one would have seen Matthew carefully hiding a piece of pine timber in the garden hedge before the arrival of his guests.

As the househusband, it was his job to prepare dinner. While Maritza played with their son, Matthew prepared the first course of homemade vegetable soup.

In the kitchen he crushed his mother-in-law's blood pressure tablets and the prescription painkiller, Panadeine Forte, and mixed it into Paul and Margaret's soup bowls. He then served vegetable risotto accompanied by a Chilean red and an Australian white wine.

He would later tell police he picked the drug cocktail because the blood pressure medication would make them drowsy and the panadeine forte would numb the pain when he beat them to death. And people said he was heartless.

On April 9, Maritza made a statement to police. In it she said she didn't know how her in-laws came to disappear in suspicious circumstances five days earlier.

She lied.

But about a month later, on May 10, she made a conditional confession. She did not speak to police but made a 'can say' statement to her lawyers on the condition it could not be used against her.

In the statement she gave her version of what happened that night. 'I only had a small glass of white wine that evening and I can recall Paul and Margaret drinking red wine.'

'During the course of the dinner I noticed Paul and Margaret appeared to be drowsy and Margaret appeared to be slurring her words. I simply thought this was due to the alcohol that was consumed.'

She did the dishes and made them camomile tea and honey while the three others went into the lounge room. 'At this stage Margaret appeared less affected by alcohol.'

She said she went upstairs to change and feed Domenik. She was gone 30 minutes.

When she came downstairs she found the house deserted and the lights off. She thought her guests had gone home without saying goodbye because they did not want to disturb Domenik.

'I noticed that the front door was open and I looked outside and found Paul and Margaret lying on the ground.'

Police were later to establish that at some time after 9pm the drugged couple tried to go home. They were drowsy and unsteady on their feet. As they walked across the courtyard Matthew picked up the piece of wood and hit his mother over the back of the neck 'with great force'. She fell face first to the ground breaking her nose in the fall. He then struck the frail and helpless Paul King across the left arm and then the forehead. He also fell face first.

'My head was going bananas and I just kept on hitting. I just kept on hitting,' Matthew later confessed to police.

He checked for signs of life by listening for breathing and searching for a pulse. He found neither.

Matthew also expected to be arrested within minutes. After he attacked the couple he looked up and saw a girl in the bedroom of a flat opposite on the phone and looking directly at him. He thought she was calling the police. Police were able to establish that she was on the phone at 9.08pm talking to friend but had seen nothing.

In her confession Maritza, then 38, recalled: 'I said, "What happened?" and Matthew told me to "get inside". He was crying and shaking and said, "I hit her".

'I ran upstairs crying and was violently ill. I did not know what to do. Later, upstairs, I looked out the window and saw Matthew drag Margaret and Paul over to the fence. This was by the wall on the grass. I then saw him put two doona covers over them.

'Matthew then came upstairs looking white and pale and said to me, "Do you hate me for what I have done?" I said, "I don't know". I felt sick. I said, "What are you going to do?" and he said, "I'll cover them and fix it". I can't remember exactly when but I asked him what he did and he said he'd hit his mother over the back of the head with piece of wood.'

She asked why he did it and he replied, 'I had to do it. It's a relief'. Matthew put on a pair of latex gloves from the kitchen and drove his mother's car to the corner of Page and Armstrong Streets, Middle Park. He then walked to Beaconsfield Parade where he hailed a taxi and went home. Almost as an afterthought he dumped the gloves down a drain near his house.

They were never recovered.

He went upstairs and tried to sleep but returned several times to check on the bodies, eventually covering them with his son's deflated wading pool.

He also ripped a sheet in half and used it to cover their faces in what crime profilers say was a classic attempt to depersonalise his victims.

As he had so many times in his protected and self-obsessed life, Matthew made plans without thinking through the consequences. Usually, he could rely on his mother to work out a way to rescue him from himself but she was lying dead in the garden.

This time he was on his own and out of his depth.

As a criminal, Matthew made a good hairdresser. He left a trail a trainee policeman could follow without breaking into a sweat. The next day he withdrew $200 from an automatic teller machine, hired a trailer and bought a heavy shackle from a local service station.

He then bought cord, chain and three concrete bricks. His first rather unoriginal plan was to dump the bodies in the Yarra. He returned home and slipped the bodies into two doona covers, then chained and weighed them down. He put them in the trailer and again covered them with the deflated pool.

Maritza would later confess, 'Matthew told me he was going to get a trailer. I went to work. Matthew told me later that he'd put Margaret and Paul in the garage. I didn't look in the garage and I didn't know what to do.'

On the Saturday, two days after the murders, he decided it was time to move. First he rang his mother's home to leave a message on her answering machine. He reasoned that once she was discovered missing the message from a concerned son could conceal his involvement.

He then left with the bodies. 'About 11.30am he went out with the car and the trailer. I knew that Matthew was going to dispose of Margaret and Paul. He told me it was best if he didn't tell me where. I can't recall when but within a few days he told me that he had buried Margaret and Paul at Marysville. I have never been there and didn't know where it was,' Maritza said.

He drove along the Woods Point-Warburton Road looking for a track where he could dig a grave, undisturbed. But he couldn't even get that right. Two men, Jamie Tonkin and Craig Lamont, were returning from a camping trip when they spotted a red Nissan Patrol about to turn up a track off the main road. The bodies were later found only 50 metres from the intersection.

Matthew didn't usually take to hard work but this time he

made an effort, digging a grave over a metre deep. He put his mother in first and Paul on top. He later told police that he put his stepfather on top because Margaret had dominated him for years. Again, placing her face down to hide her face was a way of depersonalising her in death.

He made some ham-fisted attempts to make it look as if robbers had killed the couple by stripping them of jewellery, money and a mobile phone. But he left his mother with her $90,000 diamond ring – not for any sentimental reasons but because he panicked.

He returned home and ordered topsoil for his garden, believing the new earth would conceal any forensic evidence left on the grass in the garden.

On the Sunday his sister Sally rang and left a message on the answering machine saying she was concerned because she hadn't heard from Margaret. Matthew did not return the call.

The following day the soil arrived and he dug up the murder scene, spreading the new soil over the area. Then, worried that animals would disturb the grave site he returned to Marysville with six large river rocks and the remaining soil.

He knew that Sally was going to her mother's home that day and the couple would be reported missing within hours. He went to the house for a family meeting. The police were already there.

According to Emma, Matthew was as bad an actor as he was a killer. 'He burst into the front room, his head looked like it was going to explode and I could see the veins in his neck and his body was puffed up like a blowfish. He looked very emotional and asked, "What's going on?" acting as though he was surprised to see the police and acting as though he feared the worst. He then walked himself into the corner of the room and let out a distraught cry and moan … His face was distorted,

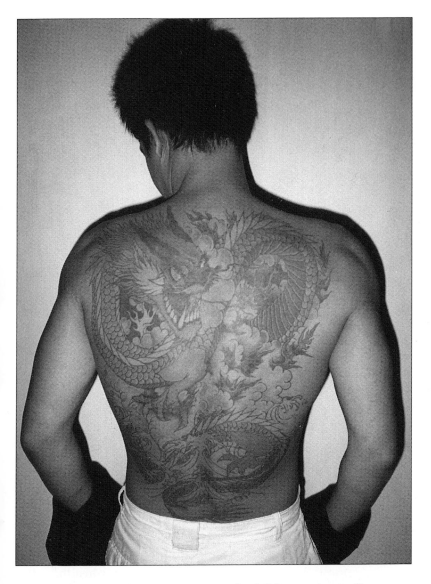

Rat-a-tat-tat … this man never stood trial for an Australian contract killing because he had a date with a machine gun execution squad in an Asian jail.

Smoking is bad for your health ... the Marlboro hat that police used to track the killers and the vases used to import heroin.

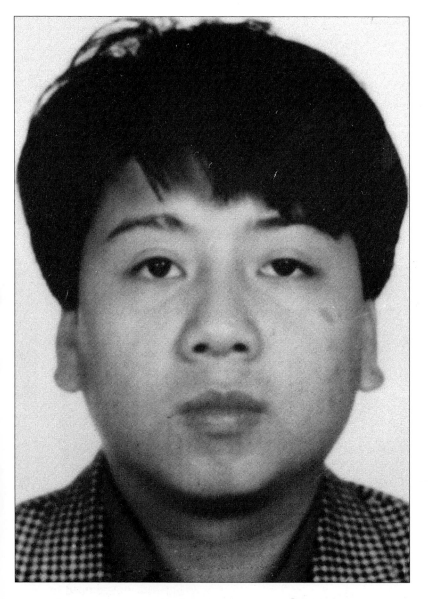

The victim … murdered in Melbourne by American killers on the orders of a Hong Kong crime boss.

Steve Tragardh with The Executioner.

Lunch in a Vietnamese prison … pond fish and dog. Yum!

Prison snaps … Australian detectives with Vietnamese prison authorities. Don't skip lunch.

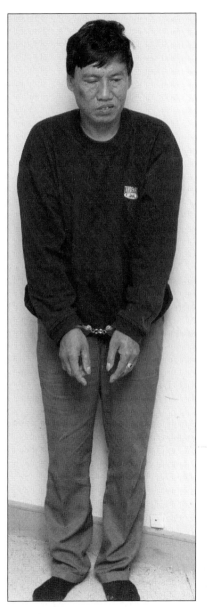

Brother Phuc's 'black pawns' … arrested while

trying to collect money for *The Brotherhood*.

Brother Phuc about to get his last airline meal before landing in an Australian jail.

Not so yummy ... the list of phone numbers rescued from a black pawn's mouth as he tried to swallow the evidence.

Suburban solicitor Keith Allan … a victim of hitmen.

**Keith Allan as a child with
his brother Lyle (right).**

Real-life melodrama … Keith Allan (front) at a theatre restaurant with office staff, actors and friends. At the back is Julian Clarke, who robbed the trust fund and ordered Allan's murder.

Service is our business … Telstra disguises used by would-be amphetamine thieves George Lipp (top), Paul Elliott (centre) and Brian Zerna. Their point of entry (below).

Magnetic drill ready to go (top) in the safe door and semi-automatic pistol ammunition clips.

**'Til death do us part … the late John Moss with
his killer bride Lorraine.**

Lorraine Moss with her daughters and (below) the kitchen crime scene.

Andrew Fraser … a high-flying lawyer who hit a hurdle.

he seemed overwhelmed by the whole situation, which I thought was an absolute over-reaction as no-one had mentioned anything about what had happened to them. The police had not even had a chance to introduce themselves to Matthew. 'For all he knew, Mum and Paul could have been away for the weekend. Sally and I were not crying – we didn't look distraught and we didn't alarm him in any way.

'This made me believe that his reaction was fake.'

EVEN before the bodies were discovered, police were treating the case as a double homicide and Matthew as the main suspect. As always with a suspicious disappearance, detectives begin at the last known sighting.

They immediately felt that something was rotten and it wasn't the leftover risotto.

On April 9, Matthew made a statement to police saying he hosted a pleasant dinner party for his mother and stepfather and they had then headed home. He could shed no light on their disappearance.

On the same day, Maritza was interviewed and backed up her husband's story. She said that at the dinner Margaret mentioned she had sufficient American Express points to fly around the world. 'She said she needed a holiday because she had been looking after Paul for two years.'

Maritza said the couple would not disappear without contacting the family. 'If she goes somewhere she would always ring. She was always busy, we practically had to make an appointment to see her.'

Maritza said she referred to Margaret as 'Mum' and they would often just have a coffee and a chat. But in her first interview she did betray underlying tensions. 'The family has always had its ups and downs but everyone got along fine.

Mum was sometimes a bit standoffish. She was a bit snobby.'
By April 10, the homicide squad was in control of the investigation. Later that day the couple's Mercedes was found abandoned in Middle Park. Forensic tests found traces of blood in the driver's foot-well area that proved to be a positive match to the victims.

Matthew may have been wearing gloves when he dumped the car but he still left traces of scientific evidence. But it was not sophisticated forensic tests that would expose Matthew Wales as a liar and a killer – it was a detective's nose for simple clues. On April 11, police went to his home and one immediately noticed a strong smell of cleaning fluid coming from the garage and a pile of fresh mulch on the front garden beds.

Five days earlier Matthew had bought the fluid to clean blood spots from the concrete floor of the garage. Typically, he didn't quite finish the job.

When police checked the floor they were able to find a small amount of blood, which proved to be a positive match to Paul King. They also found four blood spots inside the house.

Officially, the case was still a 'suspicious disappearance' but police knew it was murder.

What they needed were the bodies.

On April 29, two Parks Victoria rangers noticed a mound they first thought to be a lyrebird's display area in the forest east of Marysville. But it seemed too big and the wrong shape so they returned for a second look and discovered a male body. When police examined the grave they soon found the second body.

On April 30, police seized a doona cover, 'D' shackles, green twine and a mattock from Matthew's house.

Detectives established that Matthew had bought a child's pool on January 11 from Toys R Us, identical to the one found at the grave site. The pool was missing from his Glen Iris home.

They found he hired a trailer and bought chains and digging equipment. He bought the concrete cleaner on April 6 – two days after the murder. While police were trying to build a case against Matthew, the media was camped outside the house, making the homicide investigation increasingly difficult. It was Melbourne's worst kept secret that Matthew Wales was to be arrested.

On May 9, a forensic examination of the river rocks found at the gravesite showed traces of three layers of paint identical to the layers from the trailer hired by Matthew Wales. The following day Maritza Wales made her 'can say' statement to police via her lawyers – telling them her husband was the killer. It was the final piece of evidence they needed.

Matthew was arrested the next day and made a full taped confession.

He maintained he did not kill his mother for his share of $6million – the value of the family estate. 'Everybody will probably think this is about money, OK? And it is about money. Not in the use of me getting money.

'It's the way she used her power for money – she used it against us all the time. I just feel like every time she wanted me to do something she used it.'

But if it was about money, then Matthew was again the loser.

He and his brother, Damian, were joint executors of the will. Each of the five children and Paul King were to receive equal shares and all would have been millionaires.

But Margaret Wales-King put a strange condition in her will: her children could collect their share of the estate only after the age of 40. Matthew, the youngest, was 34. As the convicted killer, he loses all claims on the estate.

As always, he missed out. Effectively, he shot himself in the foot when he hit them over the head.

Under the terms of the will, the share assigned for Paul King will be divided among Margaret's eleven grandchildren.

This means that Matthew's son, Domenik Wales, is entitled to around $110,000. But some members of the family were determined that the money should not be controlled by the woman they fear may have got away with murder, Maritza.

On the day, they were to be sentenced the court was packed with family members watching the guilty couple and the media watching the family. Many members of the Wales family felt angry and betrayed by the coverage of the double murder.

They felt their loss had been turned into sport and that they had been portrayed as rich and uncaring. They were victims of a terrible crime but their private relationships had become fodder for gossip. They felt that, in death, Margaret was unfairly vilified as a manipulative and grasping matriarch, rather than a woman who tried her best to care for an invalid husband and a deeply flawed son.

Several members of the family stared aggressively at Matthew, but he did not look back, not because he wanted to avoid them, but because he remained oblivious to their glares. He appeared unconcerned about his fate as he was sentenced and seemed worried only about Maritza's future.

On April 11, 2003 – one year and one week after the murders – Justice John Coldrey delivered sentence in the Victorian Supreme Court after the pair had pleaded guilty.

'Matthew Wales, you told the police of great animosity and hurt between your mother and yourself and of anger that had been building up in you for years. You stated that your motive was not to be found in any desire to obtain your mother's money, but in the reaction against her using that money to manipulate you. You asserted that not only had your mother used the power of her money against you but also against your sisters. Indeed, your sister Prudence Reed, speaking to you prior to the funerals, had the impression that you believed that the family had been done a favour by your mother's death.

'That impression was shared by your father, Mr Brian Wales. When he spoke to you at Port Phillip Prison on May 29, 2002, it appeared to him that you thought of yourself as a hero and as having done the family a favour in killing Margaret and Paul, no-one else in the family having the guts to do so. That was certainly not the view of your siblings.

'Family members also make it clear that their upbringing, in which you, Matthew Wales, participated, was a privileged one involving access to several farms, a beach house, a unit at the snow and the benefit of a number of overseas trips. Moreover, all the children, including you, benefited from your mother's assistance in obtaining a primary residential property. At the end of the day it should not be forgotten that it was up to Mrs Wales-King to determine how she used her own money and how prudent her approach should be in retaining or distributing it. Ultimately, it was being preserved for the benefit of her children, all of whom, at this time, were adults.

'On their various accounts (those of his brother and sisters), you were adored by your mother, who showered you with gifts, love and support. She was proud of you and your brother Damian as fathers; she was an advocate for you, always trying to be positive and to build you up.

'It was also your view that your wife Maritza who, I accept, you idolised, and her family, were looked down upon by your family.

'According to Maritza's record of interview, you were reluctant to introduce her to your family, labelling them as "a bunch of snobs". It was put that when eventually driving to meet them in Boronia, your mother queried where the suburb was, how she could leave a Mercedes parked there, and asked your view whether it would be stolen. Your sister, Sally Honan, speaks of you passing on Maritza's views that your mother felt her family were just "wogs". Your own view of your wife was that she was intelligent, stylish and elegant, and accomplished in retail business. Indeed you believed your mother to be jealous of Maritza's business achievements.

'These murders were premeditated. The victims were elderly and vulnerable. After the killings you made a persistent and systematic effort to avoid detection. Moreover your lies and dissembling conduct, which continued until the time of your arrest, has caused your relatives, particularly your sisters and brother, an added level of distress and anguish.

'Maritza Wales, the Crown does not allege that you had any role in the planned killing of Mrs Wales-King and Paul King and I am quite satisfied that you did not. Apart from the factors to which I have already referred, it is inconceivable that you would have been a party to the killing of your parents-in-law in the front yard of your family home and without any plan for the disposal of their bodies. As I have already endeavoured to make quite clear, I am quite satisfied that your husband acted alone in perpetrating these crimes.

'It follows that you were confronted with a totally unexpected and horrific situation. In the accounts of both you and your husband, your reaction to the revelation of these crimes has been detailed. It involved shock; distress, (which manifested itself in vomiting); anger; a withdrawal from physical contact with your husband; an endeavour to distance yourself from these events and the frequent urging of him to go to the police. Your husband's procrastination about contacting the authorities, phrased in terms of wanting to spend more time with you and Domenik, had the effect of you living a lie in the days and weeks that followed the killings. Eventually, faced with his continuing failure to contact the authorities, you took matters into your own hands and, through your solicitor, informed the police of what had occurred.

'In the course of your interview, you were asked, in effect, why you had not earlier told the police what had happened. You responded, "Because I was thinking of Domenik. I was thinking of Matt. I was thinking of everything except for the right thing".

'I have no doubt that as a wife and mother you were faced with a conflict between doing the right thing and loyalty to your family manifested in the fear of losing a husband with whom you were deeply in love and the loss to Domenik of his father. No-one would wish to be confronted with such a dilemma.

'I accept that you have already suffered greatly through the publicity generated by this case. In itself this constitutes a measure of punishment.

'Further, one of the consequences of your decision to contact the police has been the effective destruction of the marriage which was the cornerstone of your life.

'Whilst the serious nature of your offence and the need for general deterrence dictates that a prison sentence be imposed, the requirements of justice may best be achieved in the circumstances of your case by wholly suspending that prison term. The length of the sentence will be two years suspended for the whole of that period.

'Mrs Wales, I am giving you the opportunity of a future in which you are free to bring up your son.

'Matthew Wales, in your case I have concluded that the appropriate sentences are as follows: on Count One, the murder of Margaret Wales-King, you are sentenced to be imprisoned for twenty years. On Count Two, the murder of Paul King, you are also sentenced to be imprisoned for twenty years. I order that ten years of Count Two be served cumulatively with Count One, resulting in a total effective sentence of 30 years. I fix a minimum of 24 years before you become eligible for parole.'

Members of the family shook their heads in disbelief when they realised Maritza would not be jailed. She left the court with her head bowed. Matthew was escorted to a prison van. He did not look back.

Outside the court the family released a statement calling for an inquest into the deaths. 'Tragically, the confession of our brother today stands as the so-called factual account of the details and reasons behind these brutal crimes. To us, his account was self-serving and based on selfish opportunity and selfish greed. We believe we have a right to the full facts. We believe the public has a right to know.'

Damian Wales had the last word. 'We are just at the mercy of what two people have said, two people who are proven liars, and who are obviously criminals.'

CHAPTER 6

BUTTING OUT

The prisoner indicated he was concerned
the chunky metal cuffs could scratch his
gold watch. It was a Gucci ...

AT 12.46am on April 20, 1996, a United States citizen about to
head overseas walked into the North America Shop, a duty-free
store at the Tom Bradley Terminal inside the frantically busy
Los Angeles Airport.

He picked up four cartons of Marlboro cigarettes and took
$65 from his pocket to pay. He was lucky. Not only were the
cigarettes much less than the retail price, but he was presented
with two black baseball caps emblazoned with a red M on the
front.

It was part of a special promotion. From June 1, 1995 until
June 30 the following year 150,000 of the caps were produced
for duty-free outlets in the United States and on its borders with
Canada and Mexico.

When the traveller bought the cigarettes he had to produce his boarding pass as confirmation. It showed he was heading to Hong Kong on Cathay Pacific flight 881 from Los Angeles. His allocated seat was 55B.

The man, Nguyen Hoa Ngoc, was not alone. In 55A, the seat next to him, was Bui Quang Thuan, 23, who was to continue on to Australia on family business. Bui's elder brother, another United States citizen, had already flown to Australia from Hong Kong a week earlier.

The brothers were on the way to Melbourne to kidnap and kill a man they had never met. It was nothing personal, just business.

The elder brother, Bui Tai Huu, 27, was not worried if the kidnap plot turned sour. He was a cold-blooded international hit man with prior convictions in the United States for manslaughter, drive-by shootings, and other violent crimes in San Francisco. His bosses knew he could be trusted to follow orders without question. In an organisation that required specialists he had developed his own niche. He was the executioner.

The executioner had already visited Australia twice on business earlier in 1996. Both times he was involved in moving hundreds of thousands of dollars of drug money to Hong Kong.

He had a passport made out in a false name and in January had flown to Melbourne from Hong Kong, then travelled to Sydney, where he stayed for a week at the luxury Furama Hotel in Darling Harbour. At the busy ground floor reception desk, he filled in his registration giving his address as Eastondale Avenue, Long Beach.

A few days later he was to meet his syndicate boss, Truong Hong Phuc, who had flown in from Hong Kong. Together they were able to collect $365,000 cash in just three weeks. A further $214,000 was also transferred to Hong Kong and US accounts controlled by the group – known as *The Brotherhood*.

Police were to find that Truong went to a house in Sydney with a suitcase containing $250,000 in cash. A few days earlier he arrived with a plastic Grace Brothers bag. It contained $50,000.

TRADITIONAL Australian gangsters tend to be territorial. They may dominate a street, a suburb or even part of a city, but they rarely go beyond the borders where they were brought up. Some have become huge shoplifters in Europe or bar owners and drug dealers in Asia, but few have had the organisational skills or the contacts to control international syndicates.

But there are networks in Australia that are part of crime conglomerates with branches around the world. Organisations that can develop business strategies in London to target heroin addicts in Bourke Street or Kings Cross. Men who can decide from an office in Hong Kong to kidnap a man in suburban Melbourne because a woman who made a fortune in Russia resisted instructions to launder the organisation's massive drug funds.

By contrast, policing is hampered by being geographically based. Local police worry about crime trends in their suburbs, while senior police remain concerned about state-wide problems. There are ten main law enforcement bodies in Australia, each with its own problems and priorities. Police officers have power only in their own jurisdiction – outside their own area they are just tourists.

But an examination of *The Brotherhood* exposes classic organised crime aided by modern technology and also shows the problem that traditional policing has in combating international crime syndicates that ignore national boundaries.

The modern crime cartel sees opportunities, not boundaries; and markets, not borders.

The size of *The Brotherhood* will never be known, nor whether Truong, 41, was its undisputed international leader. But what can be established is that virtually anywhere in the world where there was a Vietnamese community Truong, or 'Brother Phuc', as he was known, had real power. People did what he asked – almost without exception. And he rarely needed to ask twice.

When he was in Australia, he ran up a phone bill of $6000 in just four weeks. He made calls to Hong Kong, the United States, Iceland, Russia, England and Canada.

Bui, the executioner with a huge tattoo of a dragon on his back, made calls to Britain, Hong Kong, Macau, Hawaii and Vietnam during the same period. For police, Brother Phuc was difficult to track. He would 'ask' Vietnamese people he knew to transfer money to accounts in Hong Kong – nearly always around $9000, just under the amount checked by law enforcement authorities. They would be paid $1000 for their trouble.

He would give them money to buy mobile phones to be registered under their names. He would then take them so he could pass messages throughout the world without police knowing he was behind the calls.

Brother Phuc ran his network from his small house in London although the drug syndicate operated out of an office in Hong Kong. His syndicate was alleged to be behind the massive importation of heroin into Australia, including a shipment worth $25million smuggled in to Sydney in specially-designed metre-high pottery vases and a $4million shipment inside Buddha statues and children's clothing.

Truong was small, polite and, in his own way, quite charming. He could afford to be pleasant. Most people are when they get their own way.

On March 9, 1996, Truong turned up at a twenty-first

birthday party in the Sydney suburb of Belmore. He was introduced to a couple he had never met and was told they were going to Vietnam the next day. He peeled off $10,000 in $50 notes from a wad held together by rubber bands. He asked the couple to take the money to his mother who was on holiday in Vietnam from England. They agreed without hesitation.

'Brother Phuc' then peeled off a $100 note and gave it to the couple's baby boy.

THE small and elegant Ha Que Thi Mai is an international success story. A woman who runs and owns her own businesses around the world, she had made it big from her base in Russia, where she was living with a former Soviet intelligence officer. In 1993 her son, Le Anh Tuan, migrated from Russia to Australia. It seemed a good idea at the time, but it was to lead to the young man's violent death – and, indirectly, to the end of his mother's relationship with her Russian lover. When the Russian was brought to Melbourne from Moscow for the committal hearing he was clearly mentally distressed. From the witness box of the Magistrate's Court he gave the startling evidence that he was a Russian Tsar with the real name of 'Prince Bigdash'. He said he spoke seven languages, had studied law and medicine and if anyone commented on the weather it was a KGB code to make him operational.

He was excused from giving further evidence. But that was later …

Ha was an entrepreneur, an investment broker with a PhD in economics, and involved in the high fashion world. Independent police investigations have shown she would feature in any Australian rich list if her assets were publicly known.

Brother Phuc would not have needed to see a balance sheet to know Ha was wealthy. She was to spend about a month in the Regent Hotel and another month at the Hyatt in 1996. Being rich was to become a fatal liability for her eldest son.

The trouble was, an international businesswoman would be a handy ally for *The Brotherhood*. The theory being that using her clothing business as a cover she could move money out of the country, and bring drugs in.

Brother Phuc went to see Ha in the Regent Hotel on March 16, 1996. He proposed a partnership to import clothing. He believed it would be an offer too good to refuse.

At the meeting Brother Phuc said the real deal was to import drugs and Ha was later to tell police she refused the proposition immediately. He told her to think about it for a few days and not to dismiss it out of hand.

At the meeting Truong made a cryptic and, as it turned out, blood-chilling comment. He said that if Ha was difficult that the 'consequences for her family would not be good'.

For hundreds of years Asian organised crime groups have demanded compliance from others with a single threat: fail us and we will kidnap and kill your eldest child. It created fear in enemies and blood loyalty from subordinates who knew their own families were not beyond reach.

What was going through Truong's mind as he boarded the Cathay Pacific flight CX 104 to Hong Kong three days after the meeting will never be known.

He might have believed he could force a partnership on the rich businesswoman, or he might already have been considering extortion.

Certainly, he already had details on Ha's son, including his address in a nondescript house in Glen Waverley, and his movements in Melbourne.

When Truong landed in Hong Kong he rang Ha for an answer.

He didn't like what he heard. Stung by the rebuff, he demanded $400,000 as compensation for her stubbornness.

The threat didn't go away. On March 23, Ha was visited again by a female associate of *The Brotherhood*, and told to pay the money. Five days later her son, Le, received a fax at his home for his mother from the 'Happy Excel International' in Hong Kong. It was an unlisted fax number but Brother Phuc had no problems obtaining it. The document contained details on how the money should be transferred in $100,000 lots to four accounts in the Hong Kong and Shanghai Bank.

On the same day a Melbourne man arrived at Tullamarine on a Qantas flight from Saigon. He would soon learn that he had been selected as the driver of the kidnap team.

Within a week police seized heroin valued at $3million in Canberra. The package contained the address of the 'Happy Excel International Limited'.

By April 10 *The Brotherhood* was losing patience and the woman left a letter at the Regent for Ha. 'Sister Mai. I went to your place and waited from 3.30 for a few hours and you have not returned yet. You have told me to come to your place to pick up the money to give the other man but you did not phone me for the entire evening ... I have wasted too much time. Whenever you return phone me immediately, I have no more time to wait for you.'

Ha instructed her son to withdraw $20,000 to give to an agent for Brother Phuc. But it was like tossing a fish finger to a circling shark.

THE kidnap victim, Le Anh Tuan, 21, was born in Hanoi in 1977 and moved to Russia with his family after he finished primary school. He lived in a rented home in Moscow and, because his mother was already making big money through her businesses, educated at home by a private tutor. He went to Moscow University to study linguistics before he decided to migrate to Australia.

He married as a teenager and fathered a daughter but the relationship broke up by the time he was twenty. In early 1996 Le was unemployed but had plans to use some of his mother's money to set up a clothing business. His girlfriend was pregnant when he was abducted. He was dead by the time the baby boy was born.

Late in April a woman went to visit Le at his Glen Waverley home and asked him and his pregnant girlfriend to go to Hong Kong for a business deal, but his mother told him she feared it was a trap to abduct him. But *The Brotherhood* could reach out, virtually anywhere in the world. Later, Le found that a spare key he kept in a rice container had gone missing.

It was never found.

If Le feared he could be the target of a kidnap plot he did nothing to protect himself. If he had gone to the police at this time it might have been enough to frighten off the circling vultures, but by the time police were aware of what was happening, it was already too late.

Around 11am on April 29, Le went to his new house in Fiona Court to allow an electrician to install light fittings. The tradesman didn't turn up so Le went back to his Regal Court home to ring him. Just over an hour later a neighbour looked out his bedroom window to see two Asian men chasing a third down the street. A green car reversed up the street and the man was bundled into the boot before the car sped off.

At the same time another neighbour looked out of her kitchen window. She saw two men punching a third who 'appeared to be pleading for help and seemed distressed'.

She watched as the victim 'put his hands together as if he was praying, begging for mercy, crying and shaking his head'. He was thrown into the boot and it was slammed shut.

Both witnesses called the police. By 12.35 the Glen Waverley divisional van pulled into Regal Court and Senior Constable Mark Standish walked up the drive to find the house locked.

When police went into the house they found a note in Vietnamese. 'You call mother to tell her that I have gone with the guys from Brother Phuc's company ... those guys said to give mother 72 hours to pay the money.'

The deadline was set at midday on May 2.

Who knows what would have happened if the neighbours had not called the police? It is possible, perhaps likely, that the money would have been paid and no-one would have known.

When police checked the scene there was little to indicate who the abductors were. But, as Senior Constable Standish walked up the drive, he noticed something on the ground.

It was a black Marlboro baseball cap ... one of the two given to a passenger who had bought duty-free cigarettes in the Los Angeles airport nine days earlier.

POLICE now know that three men, including the American hit men, the Bui brothers, went to Regal Court just before midday. The driver left the brothers, who used the key stolen from the rice container to enter the house and ransack it, looking for money.

When Le returned, the brothers grabbed and beat him before forcing him to write the note.

They rang the driver on a mobile phone and ordered him to return. As they went down the drive Le momentarily broke away, knocking the cap off the head of one of the hit men.

That night Mrs Ha called Brother Phuc from the criminal investigation office of the Glen Waverley police. There was no point in long discussions. The man who had organised the kidnapping said, 'You have three days to transfer the money to Hong Kong, if no money, everything happen to Ang' (her son). In another phone call nearly 30 minutes later he said, 'Look, I have told you already I can do whatever I want. When you have the money prepared, ring me'.

Time was already running out.

Day one (April 30): The kidnap victim is being held in a house in Glendale Road, Springvale. The kidnappers use four public telephones in Springvale to make nine calls to mobile phones used by members of *The Brotherhood*. Police believe they are given instructions and regular updates on the progress of their ransom demands. Police go to the Federal Court to get warrants to start monitoring suspects' mobile phones.

The phone taps provide vital evidence but, ultimately, they do not help the victim. The tapes provide a chilling record, as the chances of Le living through the ordeal slip away. Like a black box in the cockpit of a doomed aircraft, the tapes were to show what went wrong and when – pinpointing when danger turned to disaster.

Day two (May 1): Brother Phuc calls the victim's mother, Mrs Ha. She pleads for her son, but he makes it clear that paying the money is just the first step in any negotiations. He says: 'Now, I am sorting things out with you now, and that is you owe me money. Are you going to pay or not? You tell me. Do not discuss any other matter. Everything has its place. You must sort out one thing first before you can go on to the next.The $400,000 – are you going to pay me or not?

'You play games and there will be nothing good in it for you. Do you understand? You know my personality. You understand that? He will always stick to his principles, he won't cheat anyone, but no-one should cheat him.

'You better understand. There are still many games. I am not saying that it will be such and such. Do you understand? But with you playing games you have overstepped the mark a little.

'I have misjudged you. You are too low. I accept that I am stupid. I do not blame you any longer.'

The mother senses that the chances of her son being returned alive are ebbing away and she starts playing for time. 'I am only thinking of my child. But the time before I have already said to you to allow me until the end of May. But you did not understand me and did that thing.'

Brother Phuc remains unmoved. 'Why did you allow it to reach that stage?'

Day three (May 2): Brother Phuc calls Ha Que Thi Mai at 10.45am. He says, '(For) the matter to be resolved between you and I if you want to be happy it will be joyous and if you want to be unhappy then it will be sad.'

There are further calls and threats at 10.57am then, two minutes later, he extends the deadline until that night. Later he again extends the time limit.

'There will be someone coming to collect the money. But if something should happen to my people coming to collect the money, then you will accept full responsibility. Everything is caused by you. You have brought everything about by yourself. Therefore you have to accept the consequences. No matter how tough things get, you will have to bear the responsibilities … You have played one game after the next. In short, you can't win.'

Ha asks if her son is alive. Phuc replies, 'Now, you do not mention that matter too early, okay. This matter, you sort out my money, that amount of money for me, okay. After it is done then I speak to you … I promise you that I will take care of it properly for you. With my character of paying back in kind both vengeance and debt, do you understand? There … that is my only request. If you do that to my satisfaction then there is no problem … the money, if I collect it in full, all matters shall be happy … Whether you pay me or not is determined by your conscience. Everything, family happiness and the like is up to you to decide. I have told you many times, not just today.'

Day four (May 3): Brother Phuc extends the deadline until midday. When the money is not moved to the four Hong Kong bank accounts Le Anh Tuan, a young man about to buy a house and have a family, is killed on the orders of a man he has never met.

In the days Le is held in the Springvale house he refuses to eat. Finally, his kidnappers feed him sedatives and he is shot dead while sleeping. He is shot in the right side of the head – execution-style – and dies instantly.

His body is dumped in an aqueduct in Mile Creek, Noble Park, close to Springvale.

At 2.25pm, Bui Tan Huu, the executioner from Long Beach, rings the kidnap driver from Melbourne Airport. Bui and his brother fly to Sydney that afternoon. Their work in Melbourne is done.

But Brother Phuc is still determined to get 'his money' and continues to talk to Mrs Ha. In one phone call the mother tries to draw him into incriminating statements. 'I am telling you the person coming to pick up the money is only a black pawn. You should remember that. The person is totally not privy to anything, okay? I have already told you that I am not going to say anything over the phone … apart from the matter of asking you to repay the money … Now, you do not have to talk to me on the phone any more. That's all.'

He starts refusing to take her calls. She rings and another man answers the phone, telling her brusquely, 'You do not talk over the phone. You cannot solve anything. Don't treat us like children. We are not children. You must understand, this is not Vietnam where you can trick people. Don't think like that'.

Later, she rings again. The man, believed to be Truong's brother-in-law, says, 'If you intend to play with the big brothers then you go ahead … There are people keeping an eye on you. You are not playing fair. That is why they do not want to phone you yet … There is someone keeping an eye on your every move. Don't think that things are so simple. You do not have to worry about anything. If you play fair then nothing will happen. It will be beautiful forever. That is all'.

Day five (May 4): Even though Le is already dead, Brother Phuc continues to demand the money. The following day the three 'black pawns' are ordered to collect the ransom at Spencer Street railway station.

Two of the men, including a former captain in the North Vietnamese Army, fly from Sydney to pick up the money.

Brother Phuc has some of his men watching the drop-off point and they identify some of the police waiting. The man in Hong Kong is prepared to sacrifice his collectors in the hope they can still get the money.

At 9.28am, 10.26am, 11.07am, 11.25am and 11.40am Ha receives phone calls from *The Brotherhood* in Hong Kong and is told to bring $400,000 to Spencer Street. She is told to take the money to bus stop 31, and to hand it over to the 'black pawns'. But at 11.54am she receives another call. 'You do not have to come. The way you play is pretty ordinary. You don't have to come … There is also someone standing there waiting for us already. You stay there. If you feel like playing games, then you go ahead.

'On your side, every move you make, we know. There are people there already … They have been keeping watch since this morning.

'You have been talking on the phone for a long time and they know what you are talking about. They have been listening on your phone. Happy or sad, it's up to you.'

When police move in to make the arrests at 11.59am the former army captain is on his mobile phone talking to his controllers in Hong Kong. The three collectors are taken to the St Kilda Road police station. Police then notice a bulge in the captain's mouth. He was attempting to swallow a list of phone numbers including Brother Phuc's Hong Kong mobile number.

Hours after the arrests in Melbourne, Brother Phuc flies out of Hong Kong to Vietnam and then back to his base in London.

At 12.57pm Brother Phuc rings the executioner in Sydney and in a three-minute call tells him they have been betrayed. In the next few weeks both American hit men slip out of Australia to Vietnam.

After the arrests at Spencer Street Station, the Royal Hong Kong Police Force Organised Crime and Triad Bureau hits five homes and offices identified as connected with *The Brotherhood* through international bank records.

At one of the flats in Kowloon there are two men. One is Nguyen Hoa Ngoc – the man who got the Marlboro promotional cap and flew with one of the Bui brothers from the US on April 20.

During the search, investigators find the original fax message demanding $400,000 from Ha. They also find a novel called *Until Proven Guilty*. Written inside it were two telephone numbers. One was the Sydney motel where the Bui brothers stayed from May 3 to 5 and the other was the Los Angeles home of the hit men's parents.

Fingerprints on the fax also matched those of the person who mailed 1.3kg of heroin to the Australian Capital Territory in April 1996.

On June 7 the body was found in the Noble Park drain and police knew they faced an international murder investigation. Senior Detective Steve Tragardh of the homicide squad had a contact in a tobacco company who was able to provide information on the US Marlboro promotional caps. This breakthrough took the investigation to Los Angeles.

Detectives were able to identify six people involved in the kidnapping – two from Melbourne, two from London working from Hong Kong and two from the United States.

The old mates' network proved effective. A Victorian police inspector rang a friend from the Hong Kong force and asked for help. An Australian Federal Police agent in California used personal contacts to get local detectives to help find one of the kidnappers. A Melbourne policeman rang a friend at New Scotland Yard and the Flying Squad began searching for Brother Phuc.

Crooks aren't the only ones with long distance contacts.

On June 17, 1997, Officer Zbigniew Hojlo from the Oakland Police Department and Sergeant Frank Sierras from the Emeryville Police Department flew from San Francisco and then drove to the Long Beach City College, where a man called Bui Quang Chuong was studying history. They said they wanted to talk to him over local extortion and fraud crimes. The nervous Bui puffed on cigarettes during the interview. One friendly policeman leant over and told him that while the office was officially non-smoking he could drag away freely as long as he made sure he put them out. Just to make sure, the police-man added, could he spit on the lit end of each butt to make sure they were out? The suspect was happy to oblige.

The kidnapper was relieved he was not asked any questions about Australia and left believing he was in the clear.

What he didn't know was the police were carefully putting the three butts into a special exhibit container filled with a bag of dry ice, ready for Hojlo to fly it to Melbourne to be DNA tested.

The tests established that Bui was likely to have once worn the baseball cap found in the Glen Waverley driveway. While the evidence wasn't enough to extradite Bui from the US, it showed police they were on the right track.

The investigations finally identified the suspects in the US, Hong Kong, Vietnam, Australia and Britain.

ABOUT 90 minutes out of Hanoi, in the Ha Tay Province of Vietnam, the Ministry of Public Security has built the Provisional Detention Centre. The jail is so remote that many of the inmates – and most of the guards – have rarely seen a white face.

When Steve Tragardh of the Victorian homicide squad and federal agents Stewart Williams and Laurie Grey headed from the Australian Embassy through Hanoi's chaotic streets on their way to the jail they knew they would have only one chance to talk to the man who, they believed, had killed Le in Springvale.

The investigators were tied to a strict timetable. They could interview Bui Tai Huu, the executioner who had flown to Australia from California to kill, but only from 9.30 to midday and again from 2pm until 4pm. Midday to 2pm had been reserved for lunch with the prison chiefs, as the guest of one Colonel Nam. Tragardh had so many questions that he requested to skip lunch. He was told this would be an insult – no lunch, no interview.

They arrived at the sprawling, single-storey prison, were taken to a room and sat at a table. Bui was ushered in. There were no shackles or handcuffs. There was no need. There was nowhere to run. Bui seemed relaxed, despite being interviewed for a murder that would earn him a hefty jail term in Australia. He refused to make admissions on tape but chatted amicably with Tragardh 'off the record'.

Before they were well into the story guards stopped the interview. It was time for lunch with the Colonel.

It was a banquet of pond fish, dogmeat, rice and jail-made brandy. Colonel Nam sat between Tragardh, whom he nicknamed 'The Strong One' and Williams, 'The Handsome One'. He grabbed at the blond hairs on Tragardh's arms and head, saying he had not seen a fair-haired person before.

He told the Australians that all the food and brandy had been prepared by inmates. Tragardh told him that wouldn't happen in Australia for fear that the prisoners would adulterate the food. Nam smiled when the statement was translated to him. He then explained it was not a problem here because if a prisoner tried that … the remainder of the explanation did not need to be translated, as the prison chief slowly ran his finger over his throat.

After lunch Tragardh was able to share a beer with Bui. Then he played his best card. Bui, the executioner, was in jail because he had been arrested with a kilogram of heroin in Vietnam. If he stayed he faced certain execution, but if he gave evidence in Australia he would serve a sentence in Melbourne and leave jail alive.

But there was no deal. Bui said he wouldn't be going back to Australia with the visiting detectives. As Bui saw it he had no choice but to stay and be executed on the heroin charge. If he gave evidence about the syndicate in Australia it might save his life by keeping him in an Australian jail – but all his family in the United States would be murdered.

That was the power of Brother Phuc. According to the executioner, Truong could order an innocent family in America to be slaughtered from his jail cell in Melbourne, and would do it without hesitation. For the man who had executed other people himself, it was a case of 'if you live by the sword, you die by the sword'.

WHEN Brother Phuc was finally escorted onto the British Airways 747 at Heathrow by extradition squad detectives from New Scotland Yard, few on the packed flight knew he was a murder suspect heading to Melbourne for a Supreme Court trial.

Truong was brought in before any other passengers were allowed on the flight. He was handcuffed to Steve Tragardh and they sat in the last row of three seats in economy. Their handcuffed hands were hidden discreetly under a jumper.

The prisoner was wedged in the window seat, next to him was Tragardh and in the aisle seat was the head of the homicide squad, Detective Chief Inspector Rod Collins.

For security reasons, the two detectives and the suspect were allocated their own toilet, which remained locked. The reason was simple. Police feared another passenger could plant a weapon in the toilet for Truong to grab.

Tragardh told the man he had hunted around the world that they could all relax and enjoy the flight if he understood that he no longer gave the orders. On this trip he had to remember at all times that he was a prisoner and not a passenger.

Truong nodded in agreement. He had one request. 'Please,

could you put a handkerchief under the handcuffs?' The Victorian policeman asked why. The prisoner indicated he was concerned the chunky metal cuffs could scratch his gold watch. It was a Gucci, worth more than a month's pay for a policeman. During the flight the handcuffs were removed and the suspect was allowed to scan the menu.

A flight attendant asked if he wanted a drink. He automatically answered, 'red wine', the habit of dozens of first class trips. Tragardh reminded him that this was not a pleasure flight. He settled for Coca-Cola. If Brother Phuc was worried about the court battle ahead it didn't affect his appetite. He ate Moroccan chicken, Italian salad, a cheese and tomato omelette, stir fried chicken with black bean sauce, pickled vegetables and a chocolate dessert.

After one meal he leant over to Tragardh and said with a smile, 'Better than prison food'. Which, of course, is a matter of opinion.

Truong later said that he had difficulty understanding English. The problem was so great that the courts would later order that transcripts of the committal evidence should be translated to Vietnamese at a cost of $60,000.

But his language problems did not seem to worry him on the flight. He managed to kill time on the plane listening to the comedy channel – in English. And he laughed at the right places.

IN the Melbourne Supreme Court, Justice Frank 'The Tank' Vincent sentenced Brother Phuc to an effective 25 years in jail for kidnapping and murder. For the sentencing, all visitors to the court were searched and checked with metal detectors because of fears of a plot to free Truong. He stood in the dock as Justice Vincent's remarks were translated to him. At the end the accused, neatly dressed in a blue shirt and pressed slacks, bowed to the judge and his legal team. He then turned to the body of a court and began passing instructions to a group of Asian men and women.

He put his hand to his mouth in a gesture to his supporters that they should immediately start making phone calls. He was now a prisoner, but he still called the shots.

POSTSCRIPT: Mrs Ha is a devout Buddhist. She has decided to move to Melbourne because she wants to be near the spirit of her son.

Brother Phuc appealed his conviction. He lost.

Bui was executed in his Vietnamese prison. He refused to talk of The Brotherhood to the end. A second member of the gang was also executed in China. The gang is still active.

CHAPTER 7

THE FACE OF EVIL

His face was chilling. He was enjoying every minute of it.

LATE in the afternoon of June 29, 1991, Margaret Hobbs was turning her car into Springvale Road from Burwood Highway in Melbourne's eastern suburbs when she heard the radio news: a little girl had been abducted at Rosebud.

She felt sick. 'I thought, "It's Robert Lowe",' she was to recall. 'I knew he had a unit at Rosebud. And I knew he'd been building up to it.'

Three and a half years on, the shock of that moment still registered on her face as she talked about a crime that wrecked so many lives.

By the time Hobbs heard the news that winter day, Sheree Beasley, the six-year-old girl, was dead, her tiny body defiled and hidden in a concrete pipe. But Sheree Beasley, the case, was just beginning.

That case ended, legally, at the Supreme Court, when Robert Arthur Selby Lowe was sentenced to life in prison for kidnapping and murdering little Sheree.

Margaret Hobbs had known killers, rapists and compulsive offenders of all sorts in the previous 25 years, first as a parole officer, later as a psychotherapist in private practice. But none affected her the same way as the mild-mannered, middle-aged, middle-class salesman who revealed himself to her as a secret monster.

The first time she saw Robert Lowe was in 1984, when he was 47. He had been referred by his lawyers, who wanted a report to present to Springvale Magistrate's Court. He had been charged with exposing himself to schoolgirls at Glen Waverley shopping centre.

At first, Lowe appeared to be just another client undergoing therapy for compulsive behaviour – in his case, exhibitionism.

He was placed on a good-behaviour bond for a year on the obscene exposure charge. A condition was that he went to Margaret Hobbs for therapy over that period. He did. It became another habit he found hard to break.

Lowe was always punctual, always polite. But, as Hobbs sensed, never genuine. She realised she was dealing with more than just another 'flasher'.

Lowe was a neat and well-spoken man. Tall, thin, with curling fair to grey hair (and, later, a beard), he wore fine-rimmed glasses that lent a prim, bookish look in keeping with his standing as a church elder and Sunday school teacher.

This mild exterior concealed a calculating, intelligent deviate who told Hobbs he often exposed himself to young girls, sometimes first placing pornography (invariably stolen) where they were likely to see it.

As she spoke about the man she had grown to loathe, Hobbs

sat uneasily in a blue easy chair in the pleasant room where she has heard so many unpleasant things.

'He was the complete Jekyll and Hyde character,' she began. 'I knew the bad one, the Mr Hyde bit, that was hidden from his wife, family and friends.

'He would sit here very attentively and take copious notes but he wouldn't enter into any sort of meaningful therapy. He pretended to be in therapy but he wasn't trying. I told him it wasn't any good, that he had to be completely honest or I couldn't help him give up obsessive behaviours … but he enjoyed it too much to give it up.'

At first, Lowe admitted only one previous conviction for obscene exposure but later acknowledged being in trouble often. In fact, he had a record of sex offences spanning three decades but had dodged many convictions through his deceit. Hobbs described him as a skilled and habitual liar who thought he could 'run rings around police', which he often did until he came up against the homicide squad.

'He is clever and enjoys the excitement of jousting with police,' she said. 'He is a sophist that is, he is a skilful arguer who will mount a clever but fallacious argument to rationalise his behaviour.

'And he is a specific liar. If you ask him if he has a blue car he will say, "Certainly not". If you change the question slightly and ask him if he drives a blue car, he will say, "Yes", but point out that he doesn't own it.'

Lowe saw Hobbs intermittently after his bond expired in 1985, and often called her. He was still offending, and appeared in court for wilful and obscene exposure, offensive behaviour and theft.

It was a disturbing pattern, although not yet sinister. According to Hobbs, that changed in April 1990, when Lowe complained to her that police had spoken to his then employer after questioning him about approaching a girl in Yarraville. Although nothing came of the incident, it rang warning bells for Hobbs because it meant he was willing to accost a child rather than just expose himself.

'When he told me he'd been spoken to by the police about the incident with the young girl at Yarraville, I got very worried,' she was to recall. 'It was an escalation. He was getting bolder and the targets were getting younger.'

Soon afterwards, he approached some girls on Flinders Street station. 'They were holding some balloons. He said something like one of the balloons looked like "a big dick" and made a sexual suggestion.

'The girls were frightened and ran out and spoke to a traffic policeman, who tackled him. He got charged and pleaded not guilty.'

By this time, Lowe had upset Hobbs' professional detachment. 'He came and told me all this very blandly, as if it was the most natural thing in the world. I told him to leave my rooms. I opened my door and ordered him out. I refused to support a not-guilty plea.

'He said, "You can't do this to me." But he went. I was worried about this escalation.'

Lowe brought his wife Lorraine with him to see Hobbs soon after the Flinders Street incident. Lorraine Lowe was distraught and at one point demanded of her husband, 'Why don't you just stop it?' To which he had replied coolly, 'Because it gives me too much pleasure.'

At that moment, Hobbs judged, he unmasked himself. 'Lorraine went pale. She realised her husband had built a cardboard cut-out life for her.'

Lowe's solicitor asked Hobbs to write a court report to verify that he had been seeking therapy. She felt the first pangs of a looming crisis. Trapped between professional obligations to a client and personal feelings about his actions, she feared what he might do.

She wrote a court report, which, she says, was a warning. 'I said this man had to be shown he couldn't do this sort of thing without being punished. I meant that he should be locked up.'

But the court judged otherwise. 'He was only fined $750,' Hobbs said bleakly. 'Six months later, Sheree Beasley disappears.'

On July 25 – 26 days after Sheree's abduction – Lowe went to Hobbs' office in Fitzroy. He was, ostensibly, querying an account but was agitated and refused to leave for hours. Hobbs said: 'At 5pm I walked downstairs to my (barrister) son-in-law's office and said, "I reckon Robert Lowe took Sheree Beasley. I wonder what sort of car he's driving." There'd been publicity about the suspect driving a blue hatchback.

'I asked the office girls if they'd noticed his car. None of them had. But next day one of them told me she'd seen him drive past later … in a blue hatchback.'

Meanwhile, the police had reached the same conclusion. The same week, Detective Senior Constable Andrew Gustke, of the Zenith task force set up to investigate the abduction, identified Lowe as the driver of a blue Corolla similar to the car at the crime scene.

He made a routine call to Lowe and was immediately suspicious because Lowe conjured up an instant alibi and vehemently denied being near Rosebud on June 29.

The hunt was on. The police brought Lowe in for questioning on August 13, and did their homework, discovering his long history of sex offences.

On September 26, Sheree's remains were found in a pipe near

the Mornington-Flinders Road at Red Hill. Soon afterwards, the homicide squad secretly approached Hobbs and placed intercepts in her rooms without her knowledge to tape Lowe's conversations with her.

It was then that a homicide sergeant, Alex Bartsch, struck up a rapport with Hobbs that was vital to the ultimate success of the case.

In the following months, she was to have more than 100 contacts with Lowe, in person or on the telephone. Each word was taped and transcribed into thousands of pages of what became known as the 'Fitzroy tapes'.

It was a cruel experience for the psychotherapist. A mother and grandmother herself, she had to make the crucial decision that her commitment to the community was more important than confidentiality to a client.

Lowe, by this time rejected by his wife and two sons, used his interviews with her to start a bizarre ritual of dropping clues that he was the killer. It was an extension, she said, of his exhibitionism.

'He would come in here and say, "Margaret, would you tell my wife that I didn't put this girl in the car for sexual purposes". He was an arch-teaser. A shocker. He has absolutely no remorse, no sense of culpability. It was like *Silence of the Lambs.*' The reference to the chilling film is not fanciful. Hobbs shuddered as she relived a scene she could never blot from her mind.

'One day, after the body was found, he brought in a rucksack and a plastic bag and put them down each side of his chair. He looked at me and said, "Margaret, do you really think I could bury a child in a drain to be eaten by maggots?"'

'His face was chilling. He was enjoying every minute of it. As he was speaking, I noticed something white on the back of his chair. I thought it was a piece of cotton. Then I saw it was crawling. I thought it was a caterpillar. I took a piece of paper and walked over. It was a maggot. There were hundreds of them, crawling over the chair, across the floor, up the wall.

'I screamed at him, told him to get out, and to take his filthy bag with him. He took the rucksack but left the plastic bag, and that's where the maggots were coming from. I wrapped it up and ran downstairs and threw it in the bin. I didn't want to know what was in it.'

Other scenes from those nightmare months were branded into her memory. Once she steeled herself to drive around Red Hill (where Sheree's body was found) with Lowe on the pretext it would help him build a case for manslaughter rather than murder.

'As we drove, he's telling me this dreadful story of putting her in the drain face up … I had to turn my face away so he couldn't see the tears on my cheeks.'

Then, in early May 1992, Lowe handed Hobbs a written 'confession' admitting Sheree had died after he had abducted her, but claiming that she had accidentally choked. Shaken, she managed to copy the document and hand it to police a few days later, the same day Lowe was picked up shoplifting with the original confession in his bag.

He was finally arrested in March 1993, when police decided they had overwhelming evidence.

Afterwards, Margaret Hobbs stripped her consulting rooms to exorcise every trace of Robert Arthur Selby Lowe. She threw out the desk, couch and easy chairs, the carpet, even the pictures on the walls.

Everything but the clock. But she could never rid herself of the memories. She took them to her grave. She died in a car accident in January 1996.

POLICE interest in Lowe didn't finish with his conviction. An unsolved murder, which had played on detectives' minds since 1984, had many disturbing similarities with the Beasley case.

Kylie Maybury was six when she was abducted, sexually assaulted and murdered on Melbourne Cup day, 1984. Like Sheree, Kylie was grabbed on her way to a shop. Her body was dumped in a drain in Preston.

Old murder cases are never closed, although the reality is that they are rarely solved. The Maybury case was destined to remain a tragic mystery. But during the investigation into Lowe over the Beasley case, police were able to track him back to Preston in 1984.

Shortly before Kylie Maybury was murdered, Lowe was interviewed by police over offensive behaviour involving three young girls in Preston, only one kilometre from where Kylie would later be kidnapped. He was a travelling salesman whose work often took him to the area.

He had made sexual suggestions to the girls, and a neighbour took the registration number of his car.

Police did not prosecute him because of lack of corroboration. His name was not passed on to detectives working on the Maybury case.

Significantly, perhaps, Lowe first went to Margaret Hobbs weeks after the Maybury murder. Privately, she always suspected he could have been the killer of the young Preston girl. After some years he drifted away but returned to therapy two weeks after the Beasley killing.

There were many similarities between the cases. The girls were the same age and were abducted while on errands for their mothers on a day when Lowe was not working.

Hobbs said Lowe was fascinated by pink. Kylie carried a pink strawberry shortcake bag and Sheree was dressed in pink. The bag was later recovered near Ferntree Gully Road. Lowe lived off the same main road.

More in hope than expectation, one of the original investigators, Glenn Woolfe, later a detective inspector, ordered that Kylie's clothes, which had been kept as a possible court exhibit since the murder, be tested to see if modern DNA technology could help identify the killer.

The answer came back. It could be done.

The Victorian Government had passed legislation to demand blood samples for a DNA bank from convicted sex criminals and murderers where the crime had a sexual motive. Lowe provided an ideal example of the need for such legislation. This would prove, one way or the other, whether the former church elder was a double killer.

Lowe decided to fight the order. The man who said he would take a lie detector test to prove he was not a murderer became surprisingly coy about the DNA test.

The Office of Public Prosecutions found a possible loophole in the law through which Lowe could wriggle. Lawyers withdrew the case. But police ultimately secretly gathered a sample to be tested.

Despite the strong circumstantial case the tests proved negative. Whatever else he had done Lowe was not Kylie Maybury's killer.

CHAPTER 8

A WEB OF DECEIT

*'I don't love her, but I'm not
cold and heartless either.'*

THE crime he's accused of is not the only thing that shocks about the man in the dock. The first time we see him, there is the shock of recognition. He is so ordinary – so obviously one of us. A suburban husband and father, bland to the bone. Who could guess at the fatal fantasies hidden behind that mask?

Mark John Smith is 37 but looks younger, almost boyish. He's clean-shaven, and his dark hair is cut short and neat, with no sign of grey. Despite being held on remand in prison for months, his wiry frame is close to what it was when he trained regularly on his bicycle. His voice, heard in court only in taped interviews, is light and pleasant. And a touch too deferential, a juror might think, as if he's trying to be agreeable to police, when another man might be angry at being accused of such a crime.

Not quite handsome, not dashing, but trim and fit-looking, he wears square, fine-rimmed glasses and, even in a civilian suit, has a faintly military bearing that comes from being in the air force since high school.

A harmless nerd, some might assume. Others, stealing a look from jury box or press bench, might think his lips thin and mean, but that would be unfair. The fact is, he wouldn't look out of place in the jury box, press bench or bar table. He's the man next door. Even his name sounds like a furtive adulterer's lame alias in a hotel register. Which is ironic, because Smith's downfall, if you believe the police and the prosecution, began with his infatuation with another woman.

THE prosecution case against Smith, which reached court in late 2000, was forged from a chain of circumstantial evidence. But at its heart is a scenario as shocking as an axe murder.

To find him guilty, and not just seriously misunderstood, the jury had to believe that this mild-mannered, air force computer technician got up one morning, showered and dressed, took his baby son from a bassinette in another room and put him in bed next to his sleeping wife, soaked a handkerchief in ether (or a similar flammable anaesthetic), held it over her face until she lost consciousness, set fire to the bed and drove to work. Calmly planning, to borrow a prosecutor's bleak and carefully-chosen word, to 'delete' his family so that he could start a new life in a new country with a new woman and her child.

Unless a jury believed Smith capable of such chilling premeditation, the prosecution and police had wasted hundreds of thousands of dollars over several years, twisting together strands of evidence to form what the prosecutor described as 'an unbreakable rope'.

It is the web of circumstance – the 'timeline' of events, before and after the fire that killed Smith's son and maimed his wife –

that the prosecution relied on to show that murder, and not a tragic accident, unfolded at the unremarkable house at 7 Lorena Close, Hoppers Crossing, on the morning of October 4, 1995.

Investigators uncovered a lot about the accused man in the five years after the deadly fire, little of it in his favour, but they produced no 'smoking gun' – the alleged anaesthetic, a witness, or a confession – that would, itself, nail down charges of murder and attempted murder. The result is that Smith was charged and tried on the basis of a ghastly and compelling story – yet another variation of the ancient theme of sex, betrayal and death.

The question was whether a jury would buy it.

HIS Honour, Justice Frank Vincent, has seen a lot of accused murderers in his time. He defended dozens of them before rising from bar table to bench, and has sentenced plenty since. Each one different, but many of them classifiable into broad groups. There are the mad, the bad, the greedy and the pathetic – part of a vicious life cycle where violence begets violence. There are others caught in circumstances beyond their control that force them to lash out with fatal results.

But how do you classify Mark John Smith, who sat in the dock at the Supreme Court, facing Justice Vincent – and some disturbing questions – for a month?

Smith's defence counsel, Stratton Langslow, both inside and outside the court room depicted a mild and inoffensive man bewildered by the awful fix he was in. So bewildered, in fact, that the kindly Langslow didn't put him in the witness box to be exposed to robust cross-examination by the prosecution.

Langslow, a pipe-smoking, rumpled, Rumpolean figure, without benefit of script writers to ensure witty ripostes and happy endings, boxed on like the old trouper he is, reminding the jury at every chance that no matter what else it heard, no-one could prove absolutely that his client had used a bottle of ether and a box of matches instead of filing for divorce.

Smith sat stock still and silent, meanwhile, as a passing parade of witnesses – one by video link-up from America – dissected key parts of his private life in the past decade.

SMITH was not charged with contemplating or consummating an affair with the other woman, with sending her his entire superannuation and severance payout of $110,000, with buying her an expensive engagement ring and a cheap car, or with lying to cover up the above. But, in effect, those actions were put on trial. Because it is in the context of such behaviour that the fatal fire at Hoppers Crossing began to look sinister to police, who initially suspected no more than an accidental tragedy caused by an aromatherapy oil burner.

In his closing address the prosecutor, Bill Morgan-Payler, summarised the Crown case, detail by damning detail, to paint a picture of a man so obsessed with his lover and her baby (not his) that he would set up a fire to kill his wife and child.

Smith, bright younger son of a respectable Cobram dairy farming family, joined the air force as an apprentice in the early 1980s. He did well, and in 1991 was chosen in a team to go to the United States to work on new systems for F-111 fighter aircraft. The year before, he had met Nicole Taylor, a Queensland-born teacher, and they had become engaged. When the Florida posting was confirmed, they moved the wedding forward to marry before leaving.

The couple lived happily in Orlando, Florida, according to Nicole Taylor's later evidence, for more than two years. Smith's subsequent version of events was that he'd grown unhappy with the marriage – a claim dismissed by the prosecution as a ploy to explain his behaviour before and after the fire.

In early 1994, the RAAF project team was moved from Orlando to the Palm Bay area. The secretary at the new office was a local, Donna Wilkinson. Single, young, blonde, pretty and popular, she became friendly with several of the team, including Smith. She became pregnant at an office party later that year.

Nicole Taylor once called at the office to pick up her husband and found him washing Wilkinson's car, an incident she then ignored, but was later to recall in a harsher light. Taylor, who had feared infertility for medical reasons, also fell pregnant in late 1994. This, she believed at the time, made her husband happy, although they had an argument when he told her he had accompanied Wilkinson to the doctor's when she'd (Wilkinson) had an ultrasound scan. In the heat of the moment, Taylor accused him of being the baby's father (not true; another Australian was) but the argument blew over.

They returned to Australia around Christmas, 1994, and moved to Hoppers Crossing, near Werribee, in the new year. Adrian Kingsley Smith was born on July 25, 1995. Smith seemed delighted. But he kept in touch with Wilkinson who, meanwhile, arranged a sham marriage with another Australian airman, so that she could come to Australia in early 1995 in time for the birth of her daughter, Melissa. She stayed in a rented unit in Queanbeyan, near Canberra, where she knew other members of the RAAF project team she had met in Florida. This seemed an odd arrangement, and not one that was explained in court.

There was no evidence that Wilkinson travelled to Australia to see Smith, nor that he visited her in the first months of her stay. But on September 3, he went to Canberra for a conference, leaving his wife and six-week-old son home for several days. It was then, the prosecution later argued, that Smith's private 'obsession' with the American woman turned fatal.

The jury was to hear that the accused wore a white tuxedo to accompany Donna 'in an evening gown' to a dinner. Later they, with others, shared a spa at the hotel where Smith was staying.

Back home in Hoppers Crossing, strange things started happening. Two weeks after the conference, on September 17, Nicole Taylor noticed a smell of gas in the house. A plumber found an unexplained leak near the main stop-cock and mended it. On September 22, Smith's 32nd birthday, Wilkinson returned to the US. Four days later, late at night, there was a mysterious fire in the Smiths' kitchen rubbish bin.

Taylor's recollection of the incident was that she was woken by a smoke alarm and went to the kitchen, where her husband was standing over the burning bin with a fire-extinguisher. His version was that he woke to find Taylor at the burning bin with the fire-extinguisher. Morgan-Payler said the jury should believe Taylor, that the fire was a 'dry run' by Smith.

The next day, September 27, Smith signed discharge papers – but didn't tell his wife. When police later asked about this, Smith claimed that filing the papers didn't mean he had to leave the air force when his three months' notice ran out, because the papers could be held by his immediate superiors as long as he wanted, and be sent to Canberra for approval only when he found an outside job.

However, on October 3, Smith's superior officer noted that he 'can't be talked out of leaving' the air force, apparently indicating that Smith firmly intended, at that point, to resign.

On October 4, the second mysterious fire in eight days struck the Smith house, but this time there was no extinguisher. Some time between 7.20am and 7.30am a neighbour heard a smoke alarm, and saw smoke coming from the house. She woke her husband and ran next door, where she found Taylor slumped on the patio, half in a doorway. Her hair was burned off, and her right arm badly burned, the charred skin peeling off. Taylor was conscious and distressed. 'My baby's in there,' she moaned.

The neighbour's husband went into the house several times, but couldn't find the baby near the bassinette in the living room, where the distraught mother told him he should be. He wrapped a wet towel around his face and fought his way through smoke to the bedroom door, which was hot to the touch. He was too late. When he opened it, he saw the baby's body burning on the bed.

Outside, he could not tell Taylor her baby was dead. He rang Smith at the Laverton air base, about ten minutes drive away, and told him his son was missing and his wife had been taken to hospital by ambulance.

Smith drove straight to the hospital rather than going home to find baby Adrian – indicating, the prosecution contended, that he was worried by what Taylor might remember about how the fire started. When Taylor was transferred to the Alfred Hospital by helicopter, air force colleagues drove him there, and he spent several days at her bedside.

Smith's barrister said this was the act of a devoted husband whose wife had lost her baby and an arm. The prosecution said he wanted to find out – and cover up – what she remembered about the fire. That Smith was already planning to leave her while she was in hospital somewhat weakened the devoted husband theory, the prosecution argues.

What the unfortunate woman remembered was enough, ultimately, to swing suspicion towards her husband. She recalled having something held over her face against her will and smelling a pungent chemical odour she associated with dental surgeries. She did not recall asking Smith to get the aromatherapy burner she had bought, put it on her bedside table and light it. Nor did she support Smith's explanation that, because she had a cold, he had put Vicks Vaporub on a handkerchief and put it over her face as she slept, accidentally scaring her so that she reared up, throwing him across the bed.

They did have Vicks Vaporub in the house, but he had never before put it on a handkerchief over her face. Smith concocted the Vaporub story to explain his wife's increasingly dangerous recollections, Morgan-Payler argued. The defence countered that Taylor's memory was suspect and that her sensory perceptions were disturbed by her ordeal, and so couldn't be relied on – especially in view of her subsequent separation from her husband, which would make her hostile and vengeful.

There were other holes in Smith's story, according to the prosecution. Although the baby had often been in bed with both parents, Smith had never before fetched him from his bassinette and put him in bed with Taylor when he left for work.

Smith made a statement to a detective called Andrew Bona, then of the arson squad, a week after the fire. For Bona, it was the beginning of a long and complex investigation, complicated by the need to interview witnesses interstate and in the US, which he was to visit twice in compiling the brief of evidence against Smith. As, bit by bit, he learnt more of Smith's behaviour, he and other police grew increasingly suspicious.

A WEEK after the fatal fire and three days after his child's funeral, Smith wrote to Wilkinson: 'Hi Donna, I was worried you wouldn't be able to read my writing. But then I remembered that you had to interpret my scribbles back at Harris.

'As you can see, here is another cheque. I've put it in your mum's name so she can easily put it in her account. I checked out a few things yesterday, about Nicci. All her expenses are paid by Medicare, and she will be entitled to a disability pension. I think I was a bit worried about that. I don't love her, but I'm not cold and heartless either.

'I am looking forward to so many different things when we get started in the US. I can't remember if I said this, but any amount of money I send over can be used for whatever purpose you see fit. (Including your personal loan). You would manage money better than me anyhow. Give Melissa a kiss for me, and say hi to your mum and dad. Talk to you soon.'

On November 22, seven weeks after the fire, he paid for a one-way ticket to Florida – a reservation he'd made weeks before, and wrote a letter which included the line: 'Yay! One month and one week to go.' He also sent $2000 (not the first time he'd sent money) and asked for the address of 'our place'. Two days later he opened a separate bank account in which to deposit some $110,000 in superannuation and severance pay.

Three days later, on November 27, he told Taylor – still in hospital – that he was leaving his job and their marriage. He didn't tell her he would soon be transferring almost all their money to Florida.

'And on 27 December,' said prosecutor Morgan-Payler grimly to the jury, 'he flies out … three months to the day after lodging his resignation papers. He never once wavered in his intention of going to Florida to join Donna Wilkinson.'

It is a terrible story. The defence case, of course, was that it missed a vital passage on which everything hinges. No-one could prove that Smith obtained ether or a similar volatile liquid and used it to knock out his wife. Nor could they prove that the fire, despite all the expert evidence suggesting otherwise, wasn't accidental. It just looked that way. But the jury found otherwise.

JUSTICE Vincent gave no clues of what he thought of the evidence until the jury had returned its verdict, but, weeks later, when sentencing Smith, he was free to speak his mind.

'You placed a cloth impregnated with a volatile anaesthetic, possibly ether, over the face of your sleeping wife. She awoke and struggled as she inhaled its acrid fumes, but you held her down until she lost consciousness. You then took Adrian from the bassinette, in which he had been placed by Nicole in the lounge room after he had been fed at about 5am, and put him into the bed beside her. Then, using an aromatherapy burner that had been purchased only a few days earlier, you staged a setting, designed to indicate that an accidental fire had occurred and set fire to the bed. You left the house and went to work as if nothing abnormal had happened.

'After considering the substantial body of evidence adduced in the trial, including the letters set out, and having observed you over a period of several weeks in this court, I have concluded that you are a self-centred individual who, lacking any sense of compassion for your wife and child, and possessing a great deal of confidence in his own capacities, simply decided that the deaths of your wife and child in an "accidental" fire would resolve all such issues and leave you completely free.

'Your action in attempting to conceal the money that you received when you resigned from the air force is consistent with this approach. More significant in the same context, is the creation by you, at some stage, of a family tree in which Donna Wilkinson appeared as your wife and her child, Melissa, as your natural child, with no reference to Nicole and your own child, Adrian. They were disregarded as if they had never existed.

'You are, I consider, a calculating individual who, having decided what he wanted, was prepared to let nothing stand in the way of the achievement of his desires, not the life of his child and certainly not that of a wife of whom he had grown tired.'

Justice Vincent sentenced Smith to a minimum of 22 years. Smith still says he didn't do it. It is unlikely Donna Wilkinson will be waiting when he finally gets out.

CHAPTER 9

THE SCENT OF A KILLER

*Only then, after nineteen years of evading detection,
did the wanted man blunder into police hands.*

THE best welder in Pentridge's J Division finally blotted his copybook in 1992. After six years of faultless behaviour, Raymond 'Mr Stinky' Edmunds – rapist, murderer and model prisoner – made a break for it.

And the quiet man with the loud nickname came within a sniff of getting away. The official line was that he was foiled only by the keen nose of a prison dog that led officers to find him hidden in a metal cabinet on a truck moving goods from the prison industries yard where he voluntarily worked seven days a week. There were persistent rumours, however, that the authorities had information and knew exactly when and where to have a dog when Edmunds made his move. With an inmate nicknamed Stinky it couldn't have been a hard task for a trained sniffer dog.

After his attempted jailbreak, Edmunds, then 48, was moved to maximum security to spend his days with a neo-Nazi, a mass killer and serial murderer. He was not out of place in a mess room of monsters.

Unlike many notorious inmates, Edmunds was prepared to bide his time and wait until the time was ripe for his carefully planned bid for freedom. But his aborted escape has added more headlines to one of Australia's most notorious and long-running crime stories, one that has inspired extraordinary public fascination, a best-selling book and film negotiations. For all his infamy, Edmunds is a nobody: an introspective, hard-working man whose very 'ordinariness' let him get away with murder and serial rape for nearly twenty years. Profoundly average – although far from normal – the adopted son of a farmer who became a peeping tom, child molester, killer and rapist, is in himself of little more interest than the dingo in the Azaria Chamberlain saga.

But as with the dingo, Edmunds' acts of random violence have had a seismic effect: ruining many lives, affecting scores of others. To those people belongs the real story.

That story began in February, 1966: the week decimal currency was introduced, Sir Robert Menzies announced his retirement from Parliament and a young batsman called Doug Walters was picked to play Test cricket.

Australia, already shocked by the Beaumont children's disappearance in Adelaide a few weeks before, was confronted by another chilling crime.

On Thursday February 10, two teenagers disappeared from a pop concert at Shepparton's new civic centre: Garry Heywood, eighteen, a gangly apprentice panel beater with a touch of the lair about him, and Abina Madill, sixteen, extroverted and only a few weeks out of school.

At first the police assumed the pair had run away, but when Garry's immaculate, dark green, FJ Holden was found in Shepparton's main street next morning, his family and friends feared the worst. They knew what the detectives didn't, that young Heywood would never willingly abandon his car. Later, police accounted for every fingerprint found on the vehicle except one found on the driver's door, a fact they kept secret for sixteen years.

The homicide squad was called in, and the town turned out to search, but nothing was found until sixteen days later, when two youths stumbled on the missing girl's half-naked body in a paddock at Murchison East, 37 kilometres south of Shepparton. Heywood's body was nearby, a .22 calibre bullet hole through his skull.

In the months that followed, Shepparton became a town of stares, whispers and ugly rumour. Hub of a giant orchard area, the district population swelled each summer with the annual invasion of itinerant fruit pickers.

Young, and free with their money and their fists, they flocked into town at night; looking for a good time, often finding trouble. Trouble, after the bodies were found, meant being questioned about the murders.

But there were too many potential suspects, and so the investigation narrowed to a few – to Abina's former boyfriend, a young mechanic called Ian Urquhart, and his friends. Urquhart's movements on the night of the murder didn't really tally with his being the killer, but he was the only person with an apparent motive, that of jealousy.

The investigation wrecked Urquhart's life. Bashed and hounded by a couple of rogue police, he left Shepparton and, eventually, Australia, only to be killed in a speeding sports car in Singapore on the sixth anniversary of the murders, a haunting postscript to the murder story that still hangs over the district almost 40 year later.

Urquhart's best friend, Peter Hazelman, also left town, eventually moving to Darwin to escape gossip and unhappy memories.

Abina's friend Jan Frost and her boyfriend (later husband) Max Hart were questioned repeatedly and roughly because they had been among the last to see Abina and Garry alive. They, too, left Australia for several years and even now choose not to live in their hometown.

Inevitably, given the profusion of potential leads, police made other mistakes. Forensic experts quickly determined that a relatively rare Mossberg .22 rifle was the murder weapon. But despite a nationwide 'search', detectives failed to check all available gun shop records, which was why they did not find that a Myrtleford sports store had sold a Mossberg years before to a farmer called Harold Edmunds, Raymond's adoptive father.

A few months after the murder a policeman came to the Gawne family's dairy farm at Ardmona, near Shepparton. He asked to speak to a 'Raymond Edmunds'. Edmunds, who had been on the farm for two years had moved a few weeks earlier to Finley, near NSW. The policeman said he would follow it up.

He didn't. If he had, it would have saved a lot more suffering.

Meanwhile, the two faint prints from Garry Heywood's car were to sit in a drawer of the fingerprint bureau in Melbourne for sixteen years.

For almost a decade in the 1970s and early 1980s, Melbourne's eastern suburbs were terrorised by a callous attacker known to police as 'the Donvale rapist'. The man – pudgy but strong, with sandy hair, a potbelly and soft hands – preyed on shiftworkers' wives at home alone with small children. He often raped women with their children present.

The most chilling thing about the rapist was that it was obvious he watched families for weeks before striking, once even hiding under the floor of a house so he could hear their conversations.

He carried a knife, was usually barefoot and, according to a handful of his many victims, had a peculiar body odour, a fact which led a *Sunday Press* sub-editor to dub him 'Mr Stinky'.

As with the Heywood-Madill murders of the 1960s, police investigating the rapes got nowhere. The only clues were prints from some of the rape scenes, but these did not seem to match anything held on record ... until the day in June 1982, that a young fingerprint expert called Andy Wall recognised that the rapist's prints resembled the mystery print taken from Garry Heywood's car sixteen years before.

It was a marvellous feat of forensic work. Police now knew that the Melbourne rapist was almost certainly the Shepparton killer of 1966, but they still had no idea who he was.

A task force was set up. Two years of painstaking detective work followed. Thousands of hours and millions of dollars later, hundreds of men had been eliminated from suspicion, but little else was achieved.

Eventually, in early 1985, the task force was wound up. Only then, after nineteen years of evading detection, did the wanted man blunder into police hands. He was picked up for indecently exposing himself in Albury on March 16, 1985.

Because of tougher fingerprint laws in NSW, Edmunds was routinely fingerprinted. From that moment it was only a matter of time.

When the fingerprint reached the central bureau in Sydney five days later it was instantly matched with the 'Mr Stinky' print at the top of the wanted list of unidentified prints. The case was all over bar a small formality: the arrest.

Shepparton detectives did that next day, March 22, at the

factory where Edmunds worked in the Melbourne suburb of Highett.

Edmunds was subsequently convicted of the Madill-Heywood murders and five sex attacks, but because of limits to questioning under the since-abandoned six-hour rule he was not interviewed about dozens more rapes. Tracing Edmunds's life, detectives uncovered the story of an outwardly ordinary working man who was a secret monster – a violent sexual deviant who had beaten and raped his first wife, molested his daughters, and once beat a cow with a shovel for minutes on end.

Some police still want to talk to Edmunds about unsolved crimes, but cannot while he is in jail unless he invites them to. At least, they believe, he owes it to his victims to confirm exactly which rapes he is responsible for.

It is true that Edmunds pleaded guilty to the crimes for which he was convicted. But the belief that he ever truly repented seems hollow after his escape attempt six years later.

Has the last chapter of the 'Mr Stinky' story been written?

Who knows? Edmunds has many years left to wait and watch for his next chance. Some day, when the events of 1992 are just a hazy memory and he has long returned to the mainstream prison on a lower security rating, he will make another move.

Never trust a caged dingo.

CHAPTER 10

PERSISTENCE PAYS

'Tell the police that Lucifer was here.'

WHEN senior police want results they usually turn to their most experienced detectives. Men who understand what questions need to be asked and have the criminal contacts to know where to get them answered.

But when Detective Inspector Paul Sheridan was given the hardest job in policing – to catch the killers of police officers Gary Silk and Rod Miller – he resisted the temptation to use veterans.

Lack of evidence and of any obvious suspects led police to believe they might be facing a lengthy investigation. The then head of the homicide squad, Rod Collins, told Gary Silk's relatives that if there was not a breakthrough in the first two weeks it could take two years to solve the case.

He was one day off.

The final arrest – that of apprentice builder Jason Joseph Roberts – was on August 15, 2000. It was the day before the second anniversary of the murders.

Sheridan, an experienced homicide squad investigator and a graduate of the FBI Academy, set himself for a marathon from the beginning. While he hoped for an early lead, he knew of similar overseas cases that had run five years.

As second in charge of the homicide squad, it would be his job to run the investigation. His deputy would be Detective Senior Sergeant Graeme Collins, also from the homicide squad. On the night of the murders, Collins was not supposed to work but the on-call crew had been assigned a suspicious death in suburban Melbourne. Collins and his crew were then moved up to on-call status.

The suspicious death turned out not to be a murder, but by then, the back-up team was already at the scene of the police double killing. Sheridan had seen Collins work at close quarters and was happy to have the experienced homicide man take a pivotal role. For Collins, a family man with a ready laugh and a thick moustache, the Silk-Miller murders would consume him for more than four years.

To try to keep some balance in his life, he would goal umpire for his son's junior football side every Sunday. Few at the suburban grounds knew that the man in the battered white coat had been assigned one of the most important jobs in policing. But junior football wasn't his only respite from the drama and drudgery of the long-term investigation.

An art lover, Collins took watercolour-painting classes throughout the investigation. Yet after the job was finished and the task force disbanded, he would find it difficult to pick up his artist's brushes again.

Sheridan is no stereotype career policeman, either. A team

man who still likes to be an individual, he favours a dapper sports coat to the mandatory dark suits that tend to be the unofficial plain-clothes uniform of the modern detective. Not particularly big in a profession still dominated by large-framed men, he demands respect through intellect and logic rather than size and bluff. An original thinker, where some prefer to follow well-worn paths, he can be determined to the point of stubbornness.

When Sheridan set up the task force, many advised him to rely on detectives who had proved themselves under pressure. But Sheridan wanted young guns, not old hands.

He reasoned that if the investigation were to run for months and years, energy and stamina would be more valuable than experience and rat-cunning. Old detectives might have contacts but they are set in their ways. He wanted police who could think laterally. In football terms, young players chase hard while old players sometimes look for easy kicks. If his team took short cuts, he reasoned, the odds of solving the case would plummet.

There was no shortage of volunteers. Hundreds of police wanted to help catch the killers. In the first few days, highly trained members of the Special Operations Group turned up at the office just to answer the phones. They would have a more important and dangerous role to play much later.

From the beginning there was pressure on Sheridan to 'make a statement': to launch a series of raids on known criminals to show that police would not accept the killing of two of their own.

But he was more the chess player than the prize fighter and, as such, the right man for a job in which the criminals were not known. The only statement he wanted to make was one under oath in front of a Supreme Court jury after his team had found the offenders.

From the beginning, the investigation had two main arms.

The two police had been murdered on stakeout duty outside the Silky Emperor Restaurant in Moorabbin as part of an operation to catch two prolific bandits.

Logic suggested that Silk and Miller had pulled over the armed men as they were about to commit the robbery and were shot dead to avoid arrest.

It seemed simple.

Find the bandits, who were suspected of being linked to an estimated 38 robberies since 1991, and you would find the killers.

Sheridan mostly selected young investigators with homicide experience but, suspecting that his targets were also bandits, he also recruited a team of armed robbery squad detectives, under the dogged Detective Sergeant Mark Butterworth, to join the task force, which was codenamed *Lorimer*.

But the armed robbery squad had been frustrated for months in their hunt for the stick-up team. Habitual bandits are usually career criminals, yet no police recognised the distinctive methods of the wanted men. If, as the theory had it, the killers were also robbers, then it looked as if they were not from known gangs. This turned up the degree of difficulty several notches.

For a start, underworld informers usually point towards likely suspects, but no-one knew who was doing the robberies.

This led the police to profile the robbers as the type that were the most difficult to identify – an independent crime cell, a self-sufficient team of 'loners' who did not associate with other criminals and lived seemingly normal lives in mainstream society.

The profile indicated they probably worked in regular jobs and were not even suspected by their neighbours of being dangerous. Nearly all the robberies were in Melbourne's outer east, leading police to suspect the men lived in the area, possibly in the region of Dandenong, Cranbourne and Narre Warren.

But who were they?

The second lead was glass at the scene found to be a match of a rear windscreen of a Hyundai five- or three-door Excel. Police believed it had been shot out during the murderous confrontation with the two police.

After visiting the car manufacturer in Korea, forensic experts were able to narrow the number of potentially suspect cars in Australia from 35,000 to 2808.

And that was the second arm of the investigation. It appeared to be simple: find the car and you had the killers. But where was it?

Almost a year after the murders, an Australia-wide search had failed to identify the suspect car. Even though the task force had followed nearly 2000 separate leads, investigators were no closer to identifying the armed robbers who were likely to have killed Silk and Miller.

Despite attempts to remain positive, the investigation was in danger of stalling. Sheridan, a keen Carlton supporter who could see the parallels between team sport and task force policing, used former AFL premiership coach (and respected policeman) Alan Jeans to speak to *Lorimer* staff at a motivational breakfast. Jeans told them to believe in their methods and their colleagues and to persist. He told them in his trademark whisper-then-yell style that fear of failure was the rust that eroded commitment and endeavour. That once a team starts to think they can lose, it becomes self-fulfilling. He said the breakthrough would come not through luck or inspiration, but only through hard work.

Sheridan personally contacted the families of the victims every two weeks to keep them updated, but the reality was there had been little to say for a long time. There had been too many leads that had turned into dead ends. Task Force *Lorimer* was running out of time and information. In the previous months, investigators had gathered enough intelligence against six strong suspects to convince courts they should be allowed to bug telephones and plant listening devices.

But in each case, initial excitement gave way to disappointment. Police had checked every Hyundai in Victoria but could not find a match with the rear windscreen glass found at the crime scene at Cochranes Road, Moorabbin, on August 16, 1998.

Publicly, senior police remained supportive but, behind the scenes, some were losing faith, confidence and patience.

There was another, unspoken pressure on the *Lorimer* task force that was always just under the surface. Almost exactly ten years before the events of Moorabbin – on October 12, 1988 – two police constables, Steven Tynan and Damian Eyre, were ambushed and murdered while checking a stolen car in Walsh Street, South Yarra. Despite a massive investigation and a complex prosecution, the four men charged with the murders were acquitted in court. All young recruits at the police academy are told about the murders of Tynan and Eyre and the events of Walsh Street remain deeply ingrained in the collective psyche of the force.

To all members, from chief commissioner to junior constable, the thought of another double police murder for which the offenders escaped conviction was the stuff of nightmares.

There was talk of scaling down *Lorimer* or changing tack to introduce a 'harder edge'.

Sheridan's ideas might have looked cute on paper, but some

thought it was time to kick down a few doors and loosen a few tongues in the old-fashioned way.

Chief Commissioner Neil Comrie had his critics in the job and was in an open war with the police association, but he never wavered over the Silk-Miller investigation. He refused to listen to those who entertained doubts and decided to press on, backing the task force against backstage critics and backdoor snipers.

In July 1999, Sheridan ordered a review of all material held by the task force. In effect, he was prepared to begin again.

One of the most obvious steps was to review the phone records of all 'persons of interest'.

One of those was Bandali Debs, a self-employed tiler from Cranbourne, who was identified as a promising suspect just ten days after the murders.

Debs had come under notice after police notified car-part suppliers and wreckers that they wished to speak to anyone who wanted a replacement rear windscreen for a Hyundai. On August 26, eight days after the shootings, a couple went to Grant Walker Parts in Bayswater to buy just such a window. The salesman jotted down the registration number of the Mazda they were driving. The car's owner was Joanne Debs, Bandali's daughter.

Further checks showed that his eldest daughter, Nicole, owned a Hyundai in the suspect class.

When police asked Nicole about the windscreen the following day she had first denied it had been broken. Later, she explained she lied because she didn't want to get her father in trouble.

A car and a lie – it was a start, but only that. A seemingly relaxed Debs explained to police he had broken the window when he slammed the hatch shut on some of his tiling equipment. Forensic tests carried out three months later showed the car did not provide a match to the glass from the crime scene.

What's more, police surveillance in the same month showed Debs was a hard worker who was up early every morning heading for work – not a lazy crook who did his best work at night.

Although Debs had a minor criminal record, police concluded he was a family man with five children just trying to make a living.

But the *Lorimer* review of Debs' telephone records showed a tenuous link to the series of unsolved armed robberies, and that made him a suspect, of a sort, in the Silk-Miller murders.

Police believed two bandits, a middle-aged man with a younger assistant, had robbed 28 targets between 1991 and 1994. All the robberies occurred in Melbourne's outer east and, in most cases, the victims were tied up.

But on the pair's last job, on October 9, 1994, at the Palm Beach Restaurant in Patterson Lakes, they had too many victims – seventeen diners and three staff – to tie them all up.

One of the diners was able to follow the gunmen and spotted the getaway car. Although he was menaced with a gun for his trouble, he was later able to provide police with a strong lead.

But an armed robbery operation, codenamed *Pigout*, failed to identify the bandits and, after the close shave at Patterson Lakes, the bandits appeared to retire – for more than three years.

In 1998, there were ten stick-ups that, to armed robbery squad detectives, appeared disturbingly similar to the Pigout raids. But police noticed one big difference. The older gunman seemed the same but his partner was cooler and more aggressive.

They speculated that the original younger robber had been scared off when he was nearly caught after the Palm Beach Restaurant raid and that the older man had recruited a fresh partner. A cocky one.

A new investigation, codenamed *Hamada*, was launched into the 1998 robberies and police identified a list of 60 possible targets, with ten highlighted as the most likely. The Silky Emperor on Warrigal Road was in the top ten. Gary Silk and Rod Miller were on stakeout duty as part of *Operation Hamada* when they were murdered.

Now, during the review of information by the *Lorimer* task force, police found a possible link via phone calls between Debs and a suspect for the early spate of robberies, tagged the 'Pigout raids' by police.

It was enough to warrant another look at Debs, the hard-working tiler.

Police had five separate target investigations into suspects identified by *Lorimer*. They were codenamed *Crystal, Crimea, Doren, John* and *Pole*. Now they had a sixth – *Operation Solly*.

According to Sheridan, the information was promising 'but we weren't too excited; we had seen strong leads before that had led nowhere'.

In November 1999, police planted listening devices in Debs' house in Springfield Drive, Narre Warren; in his Commodore station wagon; and in his daughter's Hyundai coupe.

Within weeks, police found that the seemingly honest trades-man was a habitual and opportunistic thief. He stole anything that wasn't nailed down, and sometimes things that were. He would loot building sites where he worked – taking cement, tiles, nails, and buckets, even hot water systems. If he couldn't steal something at the time, he would return at night to finish the job.

This was interesting, because the armed robbers the police were looking for were also opportunists. In one robbery on an Endeavour Hills chicken shop on September 27, 1992, a customer walked in with a late-night order. The two bandits tied him up with duct tape and stole $10. As well as taking money, they stole wallets, credit cards, mobile phones and cheap jewellery. At licensed restaurants they would take ouzo, whisky, Bacardi, Midori and Malibu, Cointreau, Jim Beam bourbon and beer. It was another possible link.

Police knew that Debs was a thief, but was he a cold-blooded killer?

It was not so much that Debs was dishonest that interested *Lorimer* detectives. His foul and violent language suggested the tiler was living a double life.

Further telephone record checks showed that Debs had called a man in Ballarat on August 16, 1998 – just hours after the murders. The man in Ballarat had placed an advertisement in *The Age* and the *Trading Post* offering Hyundai parts for sale.

This didn't tally. Because, according to Debs when police first approached him on August 27, he had smashed the rear window of the car with his tiling equipment on August 19 – three days after the murders.

There was enough new evidence for *Lorimer* investigators to ask forensic experts to re-analyse glass taken from the car. This time the results found that the glass 'could not be excluded' as the same type found in Cochranes Road.

So why the initial confusion?

After losing the first rear windscreen Debs had fitted a replacement that had blown out, requiring yet a third window. It was later found that glass shards from the two broken windscreens had been collected for examination, creating the initial false results.

This first window was clear, as were the pieces found near the Silky Emperor, while the first replacement was tinted. The initial tests, by pure fluke, contained fragments from only the tinted glass and gave a negative result. The second set of tests put Debs squarely back in the frame.

Debs bought the dark blue coupe as an 18th birthday present, in June 1997, for his eldest daughter Nicole, who was living with Jason Joseph Roberts in Merrijig Drive, Cranbourne.

In October 1999, task force armed robbery specialist, Detective Sergeant Mark Butterworth spotted a photograph of Roberts in the *Lorimer* office as part of a cluster of pictures of Debs and associates. He immediately saw striking similarities with a face image from the robbery of the Sportsmart shop in Noble Park on Sunday, March 29, 1998.

In that robbery, right on closing time, the older gunman yelled, 'I'll kill if I have to' and then, with a reference to a US school shooting in which five people had died four days earlier, he said: 'I'll make Arkansas look like a picnic'.

One customer had her two-year-old daughter with her. The bandits made the mother lie on the floor and trussed her up with the child in her embrace, immobilising both of them.

But one woman in the robbery felt she could pick the younger robber. Olivia Coffman worked at the shop and told police that when she had gone outside to move her car she had seen the younger gunman before he had put on his disguise. She had assumed he was a customer but when she returned and walked in on the robbery he was wearing a stocking mask so sheer she could still see his face. She told police that despite the seriousness of the situation she felt like laughing at the comical Woody Allen nature of the stick-up.

She helped produced a police impression of the bandit. It was this likeness that struck Butterworth as being a match with

Roberts. He compiled a photo board of pictures of young men that included the driver's licence of the suspect. Coffman picked Roberts without hesitation.

Now detectives had a link between Debs and a suspect from the first set of robberies and Roberts, now a suspect for the 1998 raids. Debs and Roberts also lived in the Narre Warren area; right where police profiling had indicated the robbers probably lived.

DETECTIVES constantly fight for resources. There is never enough time, staff or equipment. Police learn early in their careers to make do.

The armed robbery squad sometimes takes perverse pleasure in managing to get by and do their investigations without assistance. Sometimes when a job is running hot they can't wait for surveillance units or the Special Operations Group to be available. Over the years they have become adept at DIY policing.

In 1998, two armed robbers began raiding smaller targets in Melbourne's east. Their pattern was strikingly similar to the team that had struck 28 times from 1991 to 1994.

The *Hamada* investigation into the 1998 robberies began as just another job for the armed robbery squad but, as the bandits became more arrogant, they were soon high on the squad's list. In what would turn out to be their tenth and last armed robbery, the bandits hit the Green Papaya Chinese restaurant in Canterbury Road, Surrey Hills, on July 18.

This time they wore President Reagan and Nixon masks but the routine was the same: taping their victims and taking anything they could, including a $250 bag of coins and a six-pack of cold beer.

One turned to his tied-up victims and as he was about to leave left a message for the detectives who would soon arrive. 'Tell the police that Lucifer was here.'

It was an act of bravado that did not go down well with the armed robbery squad.

Ray Watson, then head of the 'Robbers', is renowned for his sense of humour, but he could see nothing funny in bandits with guns traumatising victims and taunting his detectives. He called his team together and told them in simple terms he expected these men to be caught. Soon.

Police had profiled the bandits as well as they could but there were glaring holes in the picture. They tried to work out where the bandits might strike next, using computer-enhanced geographic profiling. The plan was to beat them to the next target and catch them in the act.

The bandits liked to work in Melbourne's eastern suburbs, raiding restaurants and fast food chains around closing time and at weekends. They usually struck in areas close to main roads so they could make an easy escape.

For a few weekends after the Green Papaya raid police began to sit off likely targets but, while they did manage to arrest some would-be-bandits about to rob a Red Rooster outlet in Clayton, the *Hamada* gunmen remained free.

Senior police decided to enlarge the stakeout job – a 26 per cent jump in armed robberies on soft targets in just two years made it a priority. This time the 'Robbers' could not complain about lack of resources.

They asked local police to compile lists of likely targets and eventually settled on a list of 60. The Silky Emperor in Moorabbin was seen as particularly susceptible.

Isolated in an industrial estate, it was the only business in the area open at night. Sitting on busy Warrigal Road near Cochranes Road, it offered access to main roads and it had its own dimly lit off-street parking. It was a perfect *Hamada* target. But it was not the only one.

The bandits tended to strike every two to three weeks, so police believed the next armed robbery was likely to occur in early to mid-August.

Police planned to sit off all designated likely targets, a massive task involving five separate police districts.

On Friday, August 14, the huge static surveillance team was briefed at the Police Academy in Glen Waverley – the only police building in the area big enough to deal with the numbers needed for *Hamada*. While the police were ready, the bandits were not and, as on most police stakeout jobs, nothing happened.

The following night fresh police were called into the operation, including Sergeant Gary Silk, a popular career policeman whose larrikin streak, coupled with a dedication to duty, made him a favourite in any station where he had worked.

When 'Silky' was told he would be working stakeout duty as part of *Hamada* he declined the offer of extra staff to assist.

'I'll be right,' he told his then boss, Senior Sergeant Steve Beith. 'I'm working with Rod.'

Gary Silk and Rod Miller had not known each other long enough to become friends, but they had seen enough of each other's work to know they would team well.

Both had been seconded to work at the Elwood regional response unit. Silk was from St Kilda and Miller from Prahran. The RRU was seen as a bridge for young police to gain investigative experience before becoming detectives.

Silk, 34, was picked for the job because he was a trained detective with experience at St Kilda and the prison squad and could help mentor the staff. Miller was selected because he had already shown a flair for investigation.

'It was quite apparent that Rod would make a gun detective,' Beith would later say. 'Gary was quiet until he got to know you and was very good at his job.'

Police in the RRU wore scruffy clothes and did most of their work on drug crimes but, because it was necessary to cover nearly 60 potential armed robbery targets, they were called in to help.

Silk was the senior man, with thirteen years experience. Miller, an army veteran who was a year older than his sergeant, had graduated seven years and one day before the *Hamada* stakeout.

That Saturday night, August 15, Silk and Miller were assigned the Korean BBQ in North Road, East Bentleigh, and given the call sign Moorabbin 404.

It was a routine job. So routine that both men kept their bulky bullet-proof vests in the boot of their unmarked Commodore.

By 10.35pm the Korean BBQ had closed. Silk and Miller were told to cruise over to the Silky Emperor to back up Senior Constables Frank Bendeich and Darren Sherren in Moorabbin 403.

Silk and Miller parked in the underground car park of the restaurant while Bendeich and Sherren watched the target from a hardware shop across the road.

Just after 11pm a small car slipped into the car park and drove out again. Silk and Miller gave chase down Cochranes Road but lost the suspect at speeds well over 120km/h. Much later, police would find the driver was a small-time crook who broke into cars.

After losing the sedan, Moorabbin 404 cruised back into the hidden car park. Just after midnight, a dark Hyundai hatch travelled slowly into the car park and then drove out again, followed by Silk and Miller.

This time there was no high-speed chase. The hatch turned left into Cochranes Road, followed by the unmarked Commodore.

The police pulled over the car under a broken street light about 150 metres from the intersection. Silk and Miller would have been on guard, but not alarmed.

The driver of the car had pulled over soon after the police flashed the blue dome light. It was logical to think that if they were the robbers, surely they would have made a run for it. In America, police are quick to draw arms on suspects but in a quiet street in Melbourne there would have seemed no need for cowboy tactics.

Moorabbin 403 slipped past the two cars and parked about 200 metres away in Capella Court, with the headlights off. They could see Silk had approached the driver, who was standing passively at the door of the Hyundai. Miller was near the rear passenger side of the car. It looked, to an outsider, as if the police were conducting a routine car check.

Then Bendeich and Sherren saw the unmistakable muzzle flash of gunfire. As the shots were fired the Hyundai drove off. The two police in Capella Court could have given chase but their first duty was to assist their colleagues. They reported 'shots fired' and drove back to the Commodore.

They found Gary Silk already dead, lying on the ground. He had been shot three times, including once in the skull from point-blank range.

Rod Miller was missing.

When the call goes out 'Police in trouble', units come from everywhere. This time the message was 'One down, one missing'. The scene was organised chaos as police began to hunt for clues, killers and a colleague. Uniformed police, the dog squad, detectives and the police helicopter were called in.

Miller, fatally wounded but still alive, had managed to run, walk or crawl back to Warrigal Road near the Silky Emperor. As police were trying to contain the crime scene, they heard him call for help.

'Silky's dead, Silky's dead,' Miller told one of the first on the scene, Senior Constable Glenn Pullin. 'Help me, help me. Don't let me die.'

But as he thrashed and twitched in agony while fellow police provided basic first aid, he still tried to help the investigation. 'Two. One on foot … dark Hyundai … I'm fucked, I'm fucked … I'm having trouble breathing … get them.'

Miller had managed to fire four shots during the ambush but missed his killers although he might have left a telltale mark on the car that would be found years later. And evidence gathered from his jacket would posthumously help detectives find the gunmen. He was rushed to the Monash Medical Centre but died three hours later from a massive chest wound.

Police would later reconstruct the night as best they could. The most likely scenario was that Silk and Miller at first believed there was only one man in the car because the younger one was crouched down in the passenger seat. This would have made the policemen relax, as they knew the bandits they were looking for always worked as a pair. This lack of concern explains why they did not radio in the registration number of the car.

As they turned into Cochranes Road, Miller had activated the portable blue light in the unmarked police car. Silk, the senior man, pulled in behind the Hyundai.

Debs, the driver, hopped out and stood next to the door. His body language was non-threatening. He looked like a man expecting a ticket rather than questions over a series of armed robberies.

The policemen expected to chat to the driver for a minute or two and let him go on his way. But, as they approached the car, they would have seen Roberts hunched in the front seat and, in a split second, everything would change. They would have realised there were two men who roughly fitted the *Hamada* profile.

Silk called on Roberts to get out of the car and moved him to a grassy verge on the side of the road. It was police procedure to get him out of earshot of the driver so that they could be questioned independently.

Both police still had their guns holstered and buttoned down. Silk stood about a metre from Roberts. He would have expected to ask a few questions as he had countless times before.

Miller began to head back to the police car to radio in the details of the Hyundai. If he made that call, Debs and Roberts were finished.

Roberts, still a teenager and the one, according to the police, who was supposed to be the less aggressive, stood there looking at Gary Silk, who was nearly twice his age.

As Supreme Court Judge, Justice Phil Cummins, was to say more than four years later: 'You knew that the time for stealth and cunning and bluff was over. You knew that imminently the two officers would search you and your vehicle, and would find the apparatus of the *Hamada* robbers: handguns, masks or means of disguise, and tape for binding your victims. You had a choice: apprehension or murder.

'You chose murder.'

Roberts fired from point-blank range with his .38 revolver, shooting Silk in the chest. Miller, caught between the two cars and lacking immediate cover, unbuttoned his revolver and fired at Roberts, but Debs had dived back into the car, grabbed his .357 Magnum and fired repeatedly through the rear hatch, shattering the glass and hitting Miller in the chest.

The policemen were no longer a threat, the road was clear and escape would have been easy, as Debs was already in, or near, the driver's seat. Instead, he walked around to Silk, who was lying on the ground with his gun still holstered, and shot him twice – first in the pelvis, smashing a vertebra, and then in the skull, killing him instantly. According to Justice Cummins: 'Then you both returned to your car and drove away. But not in panic. With deliberation. Slowly, so as not to attract attention'.

When homicide investigators arrived at the scene it appeared there would be no short-cut to the killers. As Miller and Silk had not radioed in the number of the suspect car there was no direct path to follow. Senior police at the scene were filled with anger and grief, but also with something even more debilitating – an overwhelming sense of pessimism. Seasoned and a realist, Sheridan fought against the tide to remain positive, hoping for a lucky break.

When Gary Silk's body was finally moved, hours later, Sheridan glanced at the palms of the dead policeman in the hope he had scrawled down the registration number of the car on his hand before he was ambushed. There was nothing.

But the seeds of the killers' eventual destruction were lying on the bitumen just metres from Silk's bloodied body.

In a crime scene devoid of many obvious clues, the shards of glass on Cochranes Road were the one meaningful lead.

An expert from Windscreens O'Brien looked at the glass and confirmed it was from a Korean car – the Hyundai driven by the killers. Forensic experts carefully collected the glass and sealed it in an evidence bag.

BANDALI Debs was born in Sydney on July 18, 1953, under the name Edmund Plancis.

His father, Silvester Weipnikowski, was just one of a series of live-in lovers and part-time partners for his mother, Helga Anna Rutherford. Edmund had a younger brother and sister.

As a teenager, he could not stand the men in his mother's life and started to run away from home. He found a father figure nearby in a man who ran a local boarding house, Michael Bandali Debs – known as Malik.

Eventually, the older man adopted Edmund Plancis, who changed his name to Bandali Michael Debs and became known as Ben.

He moved to Melbourne and, at 26, married Dorothy. They had three daughters and two sons – Nicole, Joanne, Kylie, Michael and Joseph.

Debs had been a labourer and cleaner but, after two years on unemployment benefits, he started his own tiling business, 'B&M Tiling', in 1995.

He had a reputation as a solid tradesman and was used by the KFC fast-food chain. He learnt the stores' operating system and when he and Roberts robbed the KFC store at Ashburton on July 5, 1998, senior staff suspected an inside job – but no-one thought of the contract tiler. Later, he was allowed to tile in one of the stores after hours, dropping the keys into the local police station for safekeeping. Police listening devices planted in his home would hear him talking to Roberts about being in the police station and seeing posters of 'our friends'.

In the Mooroolbark police station, where he dropped the keys, there were posters of the $500,000 reward for information leading to the arrest and conviction of the killers of Rod Miller and Gary Silk. Debs repaid the fast-food chain for the work by stealing frozen chickens just before Christmas, 1999.

Jason Joseph Roberts was ten when his father died. He was living at home with his mother and younger brother in Cranbourne when he met Nicole Debs while they were both learning karate. He was only seventeen when he became Nicole's partner. He spent weeknights at home and weekends with her.

He had drifted through the building industry, working as a junior glassmaker and labourer before becoming an apprentice builder.

When *Lorimer* police started to look at Debs a second time they were surprised at his close relationship with his daughter's live-in boyfriend.

They were constantly together at night. Surveillance showed they were involved in thefts and burglaries, stealing building materials and equipment.

They were observed casing possible targets and checking police movements, always looking for surveillance. Not once did they pick the police who were following them.

It is not unusual for entrenched criminals to recruit their sons for violent crime, but Debs freely confided in his daughters as well. He was no sexist – but he was an opportunist. On December 11, 1999, he spoke with his son, then 15, about the son's part-time work at Hungry Jack's at Cranbourne. It was not the usual father-son chat about work and life.

This father wanted to know the layout of the store, security and where the money was kept. He was using his youngest son as a forward scout for a robbery. He said if he robbed the store, staff could get hurt. The boy expressed his dislike for the manager. The caring father replied, 'I'll cut off his finger if you like … would you like me to do that?' The boy thought it was a fine idea.

If that wasn't enough, Debs suggested his son should be working at the store during the robbery. He would be made to lie on the floor and would be tied up. Then, the ever-helpful father said, the teenager could claim for crime compensation.

The conversation was a vital piece of intelligence. It showed Debs was more than a thief; he was a potential armed robber. He had access to a Hyundai, which was mysteriously damaged at the time of the murders, and he was a liar. The circumstantial evidence was such that even the conservative Sheridan was finally convinced they had found the killers. (In December 2003 the son, Joseph Debs, died of a drug overdose aged only nineteen.)

There was one other little sweetener. Debs, the opportunist, had once done a small tiling job, 'for a Chinese guy'. It was at the Silky Emperor.

Within days, four members of the task force went to the Silks' family home in Mount Waverley to see Gary's father, Morrie, who was dying of cancer.

Paul Sheridan went into the bedroom, knelt beside the bed and told him they had identified his son's killers. Morrie died soon after, on December 28.

Just before Christmas, the investigators also told Rod Miller's widow, Carmel, there had been a breakthrough.

Police recorded Jason Roberts talking of a robbery where one of the female victims thought it was a joke and refused to lie on the ground.

It matched – almost word for word – a statement from one of the victims of the armed robbery at the Green Papaya restaurant in Surrey Hills on July 18, 1998.

The listening devices showed how Debs was teaching his apprentice the lessons of crime. He told him to be aggressive on jobs and victims would 'drop like spaghetti'.

It confirmed the police belief that the two were responsible for the ten *Hamada* robberies and that the tiler was clearly the senior partner in all the jobs. It was a breakthrough, but the police case against the Debs and Roberts was still weak. They had a file full of intelligence connecting the men to the armed robberies but little to link them to the murders.

They had a few shards of windscreen glass that were not conclusive, no witnesses, and no inside sources. An undercover operation was unlikely to succeed because Debs confided only in family members – he would never talk to a stranger.

They needed evidence and the most telling would be from the mouths of the suspects themselves.

But how could they get them to talk?

IT was early in 2000 when Sheridan, the chess player, began to make moves designed to get his suspects to open up and talk so police could tape them. It would take more than six months to reach checkmate.

In February, task force police went to Debs' brother, Robert Rutherford, in Sydney, and told him they wanted to talk to him about the police murders in Melbourne.

They also visited his natural mother. Like fishermen, they were throwing berley in the water in the hope of getting a bite.

Rutherford rang his brother and left a message that Melbourne police had visited. He refused to trust the phones and would not give any further details, but Debs' sister-in-law rang and said 'get up here quick'.

The police ploy worked perfectly – almost too well.

In the kitchen of his Springfield Drive home, Debs had a frank and brutal conversation lasting nearly an hour with daughter Joanne.

He told her: 'Within the next six months, we're goin' to have to get rid of another two CPs (police) … to make the investigation spread … I think (the visit) is about the matter where two CPs have gone down. He (his brother) wouldn't ring me under any other circumstance.'

He then raised the possibility of killing Carmel Miller and her baby son. 'Seriously. Do you think I should get rid of the kid and the mother? ... So they try and get the investigation to think that it's drug related or anything like that.'

He referred to the guns being destroyed – one being cut up and the other being thrown in a lake. He said that at his mother's house, 'there's stuff in the ground but they won't find it'.

But they did.

Much later, police recovered jewellery stolen on June 8, 1998, from the Jumbo Restaurant in Blackburn, including a ring taken from the finger of one of the owners. A necklace and the ring were found buried in a builder's bucket under Debs' mother's house.

The dutiful daughter did not seem shocked and often gave rudimentary legal advice – information gleaned from her Year Eleven legal studies course at school.

She talked of police powers and correctly suggested that Victorian homicide squad detectives would not have jurisdiction in NSW.

She warned her father to be wary of police bugging equipment and advised him to use public phones or her sister's new mobile to avoid intercepts.

Police were to say she became her father's legal adviser and when she applied to work in the police department, Debs thought it was a good idea: it could be useful for the family, especially if she got access to confidential police files.

They discussed the idea that if Debs went ahead with his plan to kill two more police he should take back roads rather than the CityLink tollway to avoid police checking e-tag records.

Debs: 'But I'm telling you now, if this continues like this on this matter, two CPs have got to go down somewhere, so the investigation goes stupid.'

Joanne: 'Yeah, but where? It's gotta be far, though.'

Debs: 'It's got to be out of this area.'

Joanne: 'Across the other side of the city.'

Debs: 'On the other side of the city.'

Joanne: 'That's where it's gotta be, though.'

The daughter told her father to wait. 'But I don't reckon there's goin' to be any need. Seriously, I don't reckon there will.'

What Debs was planning was to kill police in another region to damage the *Lorimer* theory that the murders of Silk and Miller were connected with the *Hamada* robberies, all committed exclusively in Melbourne's east.

Again, the theory of killing Carmel and the baby James was that it would skew the investigation away from the *Hamada* robberies link by suggesting that Rod Miller was a specific target rather than just a random policeman who had inadvertently run into robbers about to pull a job.

The father warned his trusted daughter: 'Don't say one word to your mother.'

Joanne: 'Why?'

Debs: 'Because your mother is fuckin' nosy.'

Wife Dorothy seemed to know she was not the chosen one. 'Oh yeah,' she complained to Debs, 'you talk to your daughter what's going on but you won't even fuckin' talk to your wife.'

Sheridan faced an immediate dilemma. He wanted to unsettle Debs and Roberts so they would talk but he could not risk pushing them to the point where they would kill more police.

He was not ready to move, but the killers could force his hand at any time.

The Special Operations Group was put on standby and a unit moved to the Police Academy in Glen Waverley. Debs and Roberts would not be able to head out of their region to ambush police. They were now being watched around the clock. Sheridan implored the specialists to make sure they took the men alive, but the SOG has not built its reputation by taking chances with armed police killers heading off to murder again.

At first, the fact that Debs and Roberts were insular made the investigation difficult. They did not talk to outsiders so police could not recruit informers on the fringe to infiltrate the group.

But the family's clan culture ultimately helped the investigation. Their conversations over the next weeks and months showed they were obsessed with the police shootings and they followed every development in the media.

This enabled Sheridan to manipulate them. In the months ahead the taciturn leader of *Lorimer* would go public. He would talk to the media in the hope of getting incriminating reactions from his suspects.

On February 12, Debs told his adoptive father, Malik Debs, who lived with the family, of his plan to kill more police: 'I'm telling ya, another two have to go,' but Debs senior disagreed.

'No, you don't go and do nothing.'

Three days later, he told Malik details of the double murder that only the killers could know: 'When we drove in just to quickly look, they seen us so they drove behind us and … they stopped us. Then, it's not good … A few shots. It's no worries, a little thing.'

Debs spoke of what could only have been Miller's actions after he was ambushed and shot that night. 'Next to it, he was on the ground, laying on the ground, firing in the air, he was on the ground.'

By February, Sheridan moved more of the *Lorimer* team onto the investigation of Debs and Roberts. But some had to keep working on other suspects even though it was now obvious they were not the killers. They had to tie up the loose ends so the defence would not be able to unpick them in front of a jury. It was not enough to prove who did it. They had to show who didn't. A brilliant Crown prosecutor, Jeremy Rapke QC, was called in to review the evidence as it was compiled. Sheridan didn't want to learn later of evidentiary problems when it could be too late.

While the case against Debs was looking stronger, they still needed more on Roberts. Sheridan used the media to try to divide the two men and isolate the master's apprentice.

On May 29, Sheridan held a press conference and said police had an anonymous tip on the younger offender's identity. 'This is the most significant lead we've had in twenty months, there's no doubt about that,' he said.

Two days later, a clearly puzzled Debs told Roberts, Joanne and Nicole Debs: 'No-one was there but us'.

Police prepared a face image of the younger suspect – suggesting they wanted to know the person's identity. In fact, the image was taken from Roberts' driver's licence. Sheridan released the image on July 16 – a quiet Sunday.

He had cancelled two previous press conferences because of competing news stories, including a coup in Fiji and the introduction of the Goods and Services Tax.

He was looking for maximum coverage to unsettle his targets and it worked. Immediately, Debs was recorded as saying police were trying to build up the pressure.

'All they're trying to do is, is whoever's done this photo bullshit, what they're trying to do is, they're trying to see if the people are scared.'

Debs had trained his younger partner to believe that police were like armed robbery victims – that if you confronted them they would eventually look away.

Eventually, Roberts decided to take the initiative and rang the task force to say: 'That's my picture, mate … It looks exactly like me'. He said that when he saw the picture in the paper he 'nearly had a fuckin' heart attack'. When police said they would make some checks and be in touch, he responded: 'Not a problem, matey'.

Often police try to deduce how a suspect will respond during an interview. In the Debs case it wasn't necessary. Listening devices picked up his conversation with his adoptive father in a virtual rehearsal of what would happen when he was finally arrested. He would feign that he couldn't remember.

'They don't like it when you talk tough to them … And when you say I dunno, I dunno – that one, they hate it. You know that one? I dunno. I'm not sure … Happened so long ago. I didn't take much notice.'

Debs knew he was the target of Australia's biggest investigation yet he still couldn't resist a little shoplifting on the side.

Shortly before his arrest he ran into Dean Thomas, one of the key *Lorimer* investigators, in an eastern suburban supermarket. Many times the task force had engineered chance meetings, but this one was a genuine accident.

Debs was shoplifting for a dinner party. He had already grabbed some kabana and then stuffed a tray of chicken valued at $15 up his jumper.

Most people would have panicked, or at least headed down another aisle, but Debs headed towards his enemy. He told his wife later that day that he said: 'How ya goin' mate? … Have you caught those pricks who … um … killed those cops?'

He thought meeting Thomas in the supermarket meant he lived in the area and this could lead to an opportunity. 'I'll have to get rid of him … find out where he lives and kill him.'

But his greatest concern was that because of the chance meeting he had to dump some of his shoplifted goods, including the kabana, although he was still able to steal the chicken. Debs loved nothing better than a free feed. He once demanded his wife rush home from visiting a sick relative recovering in hospital from a heart attack because he had been offered free Hungry Jacks' hamburgers at the store where their son worked part-time.

What he didn't know yet was that where he was going you didn't need to pay for food. On the other hand, the menu was limited.

On July 25, 2000, the Special Operations Group moved on Debs and Roberts at 7am and 7.20am respectively. Police were furious when a television news van turned up in Debs' street before the arrest, although the targets were still taken by surprise.

As he had rehearsed two days earlier, Debs stuck to his story and remained vague on detail.

Sheridan's plan was to let Roberts go unless the younger man confessed. He hoped a little time without his mentor would break his resolve.

But the more police learned of Roberts the more they realised he was no kid dragged into a situation not of his making. It was Roberts who fired the first shot, hitting Gary Silk, and it was Roberts who, in the weeks before his arrest, was laughing at the police investigation.

In the last weeks before the police raids, Debs started to show signs of concern while Roberts urged his older companion that it was time to start committing more armed robberies.

It was Debs who seemed to worry about how long the investigation could continue and who hoped police would eventually run out of resources, while Roberts referred to committing armed robberies as fun.

'It's time for a job, Ben,' he said, two months before the

arrests. It was Debs who counselled caution. 'I'd love to. But it's, it's so hot you wouldn't believe.'

When police left Roberts in the interview room, his head slumped on the table. Detectives thought this was the first sign of distress and possible remorse. They were wrong. He was trying to sleep. It had been a long day.

When he was finally released, he bragged he would sue the police after his robust, SOG-style arrest and 'make a fortune'. Even he must have known it was false bravado.

Police let him go to sweat for a few weeks, to give him a chance to consider making a statement against Debs. He chose to remain silent.

But the case did become stronger after the initial raids. While police were never to find the murder weapons, they found items stolen during the *Hamada* robberies.

They seized the Hyundai for exhaustive tests. This time, it was taken apart and examined piece by piece. The forensic experts found gunshot residue inside the cabin, the same type gathered on Rod Miller's jacket, and uncovered a handyman's attempt to repair damage made by a bullet. It may have been from one of the four shots fired by Miller in the ambush. The dead policeman had actually helped build the forensic case against his killers. Game over.

In the remand jail, Debs received a letter in the prison system internal mail. It was from Russell Street bomber Craig Minogue, who had left a car bomb outside the then police headquarters, killing policewoman Angela Taylor. In the note, Minogue gave Debs some free legal advice. He said not to trust anyone, including lawyers, and not to sign anything. Cop killers, apparently, seem to think they should stick together.

Roberts was finally charged on August 15. Sheridan had considered delaying the final act for a day, to coincide with the second anniversary of the shootings, but felt that would be too contrived. It was, however, two years to the day after Gary Silk and Rod Miller began their last shift on what was supposed to be a routine surveillance operation.

AFTER months of legal argument and delays that seem to have become accepted as part of the criminal justice system, the trial began in Court Twelve of the Supreme Court in front of Justice Phil Cummins. Exactly two years after Roberts' arrest, Jeremy Rapke was finally able to address the jury and outline the Crown case.

The modern-day metal detectors used to search people for weapons before they entered the secure court contrasted starkly with the historic setting of the nineteenth century law courts.

Unfailingly courteous to jury and witnesses, 'Fabulous Phil' Cummins made it clear if he felt a barrister was wasting his time. He seemed to save his most savage remarks for Debs' barrister, Chris Dane QC.

It is often said that a court room is just another venue for theatre – the murder trial was often as much about style as substance. Both sides tried to influence the jury with non-evidentiary tactics.

Dane and his legal team sat on a different table from Roberts' team, led by Ian Hill QC, to try to show they should not be seen as a joint ticket.

Debs and Roberts sat in the dock at the back of the court. They did not communicate in front of the jury, again to reinforce the view that they were standing trial as individuals, not as a pair. Debs' three daughters sat in the row in front of them.

Joanne, the part-time legal adviser, sat in front of her father, her black hair pulled back into a ponytail showing the rings in the pierced tops and lobes of her ears. She was stooped, with rounded shoulders. Next to her was Kylie with brown, highlighted hair, often wearing a blue jacket. Before the jury entered she would sit, smiling and apparently relaxed, given the gravity of her father's situation.

Next was Nicole, who sat virtually in front of her boyfriend Roberts, her black hair pulled back and often held with a red ribbon. Her body language changed only when she heard a police tape of her boyfriend and father discussing prostitutes.

The daughters would listen to the evidence, rarely looking around. Outside they could be mistaken for office workers on their way to city buildings, not daily visitors to the Supreme Court to hear their father accused of one of the worst crimes in Australia's history.

They would sit chatting and laughing less than two metres from the families who were also there every day, the Silks and Millers. Both camps learned to ignore each other like strangers on a train.

To the left of the judge and opposite the jury of nine women and six men were the families of Gary Silk and Rod Miller. Task force members sat in front of the families, always well dressed. Court staff nicknamed them the 'Eddie McGuires' because they always wore well-cut suits.

The positioning meant that when the jury looked at slides and graphics projected on to the wall of the court opposite them they looked directly over the heads of the Silk and Miller families. This meant the jury was constantly reminded of the loss in human terms.

Debs sat with a foolscap pad filled with handwritten notes. He looked straight ahead and tried to concentrate. It often looked as if it were a battle.

Roberts' interest ebbed and flowed. He seemed to spend more

time looking at people in the court than worrying about the damning testimony.

Both defendants were told by their lawyers to remain silent in court but at one point Roberts could not control his aggression, saying to Justice Cummins: 'One question – are you prosecuting, or are you the judge?' Cummins did not respond. He knew he would have the last word. Judges always do.

Even the way the Debs girls sat looked as if they had been coached. It was as if they were waiting to be asked to dance at a debutantes' ball. Only once did their emotions betray them.

They were caught rolling their eyes during one witness's evidence. Justice Cummins sat quietly during this display, but when the jury was excused he told them, 'Do that one more time and you're out for the trial'. Both defence teams chose to keep their clients out of the witness box. The defences were left with no alternative but to counterpunch, to try to somehow damage the prosecution case without leaving themselves open to rigorous examination. The prosecution called 157 witnesses, the defence just four. Even when they tried to respond, it did not go according to plan.

One of the most damning pieces of evidence against Roberts was a bugged conversation when the younger suspect says, 'I kill Ds'. The Crown alleged Roberts was talking of detectives or plain-clothes police, with the relevance being that Silk and Miller were in plain clothes when they were murdered.

Ian Hill QC, for Roberts, called a speech expert to dispute the police version of the tape. The original questioning of the expert seemed to go well, but then it was prosecutor Jeremy Rapke's turn. Quietly, he took the expert though his testimony. Again and again he played the tape in front of the jury. Ultimately the men and women who would judge Debs and Roberts heard the chilling words, 'I kill Ds' twenty times. Each repetition underlined its real meaning. It was a master stroke by Rapke.

The daughters learnt court procedure and would bow to the judge when they left court. But if the impression was to create an image of a caring family it was shattered when taped conversations were played for the jury. The language, the undertone of dishonesty and violence, and the family's complicity in the murders made them objects of curiosity and contempt rather than of sympathy.

The trial lasted 113 days and the jury heard evidence for 87 of them. Finally the jury was culled by ballot from fifteen to the traditional twelve. The extra numbers had originally been included to ensure against a mistrial because of illness. They were sent out to consider their verdict over the Christmas break. Many observers had thought it would be quick and so began to imagine problems as time dragged on but, after seven days, at 10.40am, they returned to open court. It was the last day of 2002.

Family members and friends of the two dead police cried and clapped as the jury announced that the two men in the dock were guilty of the murders. Debs and Roberts sat impassively. They must have known after hearing the evidence that it was inevitable.

FOR the Silk family, the four-month trial was the end of an exhausting journey that began when Gary was shot on August 16, 1998. Gary's mother, Val, went to the Supreme Court nearly every day, even though she sometimes ended in tears.

She heard the D24 tape recorded when her son's body was being discovered. She heard the strained voices of the police as they searched for the gunmen. Then she heard the bugged conversations of the suspects as they calmly talked about how they murdered the two police and were prepared to kill more. But she had been briefed by the police task force on what to expect, so there were no surprises. But while it was no longer a shock for her it would always be shocking. Behind her, on the court wall, they projected a picture of her son, lying dead in the grass next to Cochranes Road with a bullet in his head.

During the weeks and months of mundane evidence there were moments that will stay with Mrs Silk for life. Such as when they played one of the incriminating tapes catching the two killers talking about what they had done.

Mrs Silk says Roberts used his left hand to conceal his face from the jury, not because he wanted to hide any expression of guilt from the people who would ultimately judge him, but because he was trying not to laugh. 'His face was red with the effort. He was nearly hysterical.'

Despite the trauma, she went every day. 'I'm here as a mother. It is the last thing as a mother I can do for my son. I want the jury to see that he had a family.'

Ian and Peter, her two surviving sons, sat with her. Peter took the time off to be there and Ian worked through lunches and nights to keep up with his job as the chief executive of one of Australia's biggest superannuation funds.

But Gary's father, Morrie, who so desperately wanted to see his son's killers caught and convicted, couldn't. He died from cancer on December 28, 1999, seven months before Debs was arrested.

'They killed two members of my family that night. Morrie was diagnosed with lymphoma six months after Gary was shot. The doctors said it was the stress that brought it on,' Val Silk was to say.

In court, she always wore a small pin on her lapel. On its face was the logo of the Special Operations Group, the police who arrested Debs and Roberts. It was at a wake for her son that a friend of Gary's, a member of the SOG, gave her the pin. 'I was given it to wear on special occasions, I wear it every August 16 (the anniversary of her son's murder) and at court.'

In the sunroom of her neat suburban house there are photographs of the type seen in most family homes. On the television set is a picture of Gary in his police uniform. On the table are pictures of the three Silk boys, smiling at Ian's wedding.

On the wall is a group photo of nearly 100 people standing on the steps of the Esplanade Hotel in St Kilda – all wearing a special dark tie with the initials GMS – Gary Michael Silk. It was his wake and Val and Morrie are there, wearing the tie like all the others.

On the first day of the trial, Ian and Peter and a group of Gary's closest police friends wore their ties. It was a small statement of solidarity.

For the last few months of the trial, Mrs Silk was desperate for the jury to return their verdict. 'I want my two remaining boys to get on with their lives. And I want the task force team who worked on the case to be able to get on with theirs, too.'

She knew of one investigator who asked his wife to have a caesarean birth so he could be back at work the next day. 'They have worked so hard for so long.'

Mrs Silk wanted her son's killers caught but she was always concerned that the investigators who worked thousands of hours trying to find them may have been damaged in the effort. She would ring Paul Sheridan, to make sure he had given his team days such as Christmas off and that they were not becoming burned out. 'She was a bit like a mother to us all,' Sheridan says affectionately.

Mrs Silk always knew her Gary would be a policeman. Even

in high school, he wrote that one day he would join the force. A senior officer, a friend of the family, sat down and told him all the drawbacks of policing. When it was clear Gary would not change his mind, the officer told him that if he insisted on joining he would make friends that would last a lifetime. He was not to know how short that lifetime would be.

He joined at the age of 21 and, although quiet by nature, became one of the most popular members stationed at St Kilda. Everyone had a story about Silky.

But he was more than just a man in a blue uniform. His mother says: 'Gary had another life. He was very close to his family. He adored his nieces and nephews. When we came home from holidays there would be flowers at home to welcome us back.'

The jury's verdict was a message to all criminals, she says. 'If you kill police, you will get caught.'

CARMEL MILLER spent all day writing thankyou notes to the 90 friends and relatives who had sent cards welcoming the birth of their first child.

But she didn't seal the envelopes – she wanted her husband, Rod, to sign them before they were posted.

Even though he was tired from a Friday afternoon shift, Rod Miller sat up to finish the letters. It was no chore; they had tried so hard to have a baby that the birth of James, just seven weeks earlier, still seemed like a minor miracle.

The letters were posted the next day before Rod returned to work for a night of watching eastern suburban restaurants.

By the time the letters arrived on Monday, Miller was already dead. Shot by strangers in a nondescript street in Moorabbin.

On the night of the murders Carmel was staying with her brother, Brendan, as they planned to go to the airport in the morning to farewell their sister, Michelle, who was flying to Hong Kong. At 2am, police knocked on the door. They told Carmel her husband had been shot but the initial reports were that he was not badly injured.

On the way to hospital she tried to remain positive. 'I was on maternity leave and I thought if he had to be shot it was the best time, because I would be there to look after him.'

She asked a policeman at the hospital: 'Why was he alone? Where was his sergeant? What happened to Gary?'

The policeman answered: 'Don't you know? Gary's dead.'

Even then she couldn't comprehend that her husband was losing his fight for survival. 'He was always larger than life. I could never imagine him being badly hurt.'

Then a surgeon told her that his major organs were ruptured by the gunman's bullet and they were desperately battling to save his life.

'I had a seven-week-old baby, I told him to go back and save him. Twenty minutes later he came out … I knew Rod was gone.'

Rod Miller had just left the army when he met Carmel at a wedding in Melbourne in 1989. She refused his first invitation for a date but he persisted and she later weakened.

They went out only twice before he flew overseas on a backpacker's holiday. He wanted a break before joining the police force. They wrote regularly and when he returned they became an item.

He joined the police force and graduated in August 1991. They married three years later.

Carmel Miller just happened to fall in love with a man who wanted to be a policeman.

'He loved his work but he was able to leave it at the door when he came home. We would go to art galleries; he was interested in pottery and classical music. Most of his mates didn't see that side of him.'

Carmel had her own career as a talented interior designer. Together they had meticulously renovated a bayside house.

She talks about her life with Rod with love and warmth and refuses to let the injustice of his loss poison her memories.

'I look at the life I had with Roddy and I don't have any regrets. There are no "if onlys".

'It doesn't mean I accept what happened. There is not a day that goes by when I don't think of him.'

Just days before his death they sat together in their home and talked of how life seemed so perfect. They had the careers they loved, a healthy, happy baby and the home they had built. She asked him if he thought the bubble would ever burst. He responded by telling her not to be negative and enjoy the moment. Two weeks later he was dead.

Rod had been back at work only a week after taking six weeks leave. On the day he was due to start stakeout duty, Carmel bought him a Timberland jacket as an impromptu present. He was wearing the jacket when he was shot the next night.

In that jacket police found slivers of glass and gunshot residue that were eventually traced back to the Hyundai and the two killers.

She buried him, not in his police uniform, but in the casual clothes he loved, including his favourite Mambo shirt and odd socks.

For the first week she couldn't sleep and for the first year she was consumed with grief. But even at her lowest she always believed her husband's killers would be caught. 'There has never been any doubts in my mind. Paul (Sheridan) made me believe. He told me it's going to be a long road and there would be frustrating periods, but we would get there.'

Carmel's faith in the taskforce was tested in February 2000, when detectives monitored Debs discussing murdering her and James.

Three days later, Sheridan called and asked: 'Where does Jimmy go to kinder?' Carmel sensed something wrong and asked 'Are we safe?'

He told her of the overheard threats. She asked 'Will we be fine?' Sheridan said, 'Absolutely.' She believed him.

She had tried to shield James from the details of his father's death. She could protect him from the media – but not from kindergarten talk. She was pulling into their driveway one day when James asked, 'Did someone kill my Dad?' He was three years old.

Carmel Miller spent much of the trial within metres of her husband's killers. She listened as tapes were played of the murderers gloating and plotting.

She sat an arm's length from Debs' three daughters, and heard their recorded conversations planning ways to thwart the investigation.

'I feel nothing for them. I have never let them inside my thoughts. To me they are just nameless, faceless people. I don't want to feel any emotion,' Carmel said later.

She went to the trial to support her husband's memory – and the taskforce. 'But I also went because I wanted to know what happened and I wanted the jury to know he had a wife and son.'

After the trial, Carmel moved house, put James in a new school and started again.

'We just want to be normal. Someone told me of a saying, "I didn't choose to be a victim but I sure as hell won't remain one".'

In 2004 Carmel Miller was appointed to the Victorian Government's new sentencing advisory council. Bandali Debs was sentenced to life with no minimum, Jason Roberts to life with a 35-year minimum. Both appealed against conviction. They lost.

CHAPTER 11

OUTGUNNED

*At least twelve shots hit them, indicating that up
to 108 lead balls were in the two shattered bodies.*

IN underworld parlance, Paul Ronald Skews was running red
hot. Skews, 35, was granted parole and released from Morwell
River Prison Farm on January 5, 1994, after serving just two
and a half years of a seven-year term for armed robbery and
attempted armed robbery.

Sometimes, Parole Board members release inmates hoping
they have learned a lesson. Sometimes they even believe they
will never see them again. But there are some who are released
because the system has no choice. Overcrowded prisons
combined with a revolving door policy on sentencing led to
many in the 1980s and 90s being freed when everyone – police,
prison guards, lawyers and parole officers – knew they would
be back sooner or later.

Few were optimistic about Skews. But when he told the

Parole Board he believed he had learned from his mistakes he was not lying. What he meant was that he believed he had learned enough not to get caught again.

He was, it was soon to be found, fatally overconfident. Police would soon shoot holes in his case.

Police say that within weeks of his release Skews was talking like an A-grade gangster and was trying to recruit others to commit armed robberies. He had big criminal ambitions and a raging drug habit. It was a recipe for disaster.

Detectives had been told that Skews, who had also been acquitted of a 1991 murder, had bragged he would shoot it out rather than go back to jail. His criminal record went back to 1973 and included firearms offences, stealing cars, escape, burglaries and intentionally causing serious injury. He knew nothing but crime and wasn't that flash at his chosen profession.

Within weeks of release, Skews was picked up by police with amphetamines in the vehicle. Despite his record and his probable breach of parole, Skews was bailed to appear in the Oakleigh Magistrates Court on May 27. As an added precaution, he had to report to the Springvale police station daily.

If he had been denied bail perhaps he would have lived to finally give up crime. But the criminal justice system managed to kill Skews with kindness. Being charged with a criminal offence did nothing to slow down the drug-addicted fringe dweller who wanted to be a mobster, but lacked the brains and contacts to be anything but a reckless fool. While on bail and facing another jail stint Skews, armed with a sawn-off shotgun, robbed a butcher on April 22, 1994.

The butcher, Brian Craik, was about to load his refrigerated truck to deliver to a supermarket. He had just hopped into the van when he was confronted by a man wearing a black balaclava, a blue loose-fitting jumper and carrying a shotgun.

'He shoved the gun through the window and put it to my head. He said, "Give us the money",' Craik said later. Told there was no money in the van, the gunman and his unarmed accomplice ran off. 'He was very cool and not really aggressive. He didn't appear to be excitable and wasn't worried. The gun didn't shake at all,' Craik said.

The butcher said he recognised the jumper worn by the man who threatened him as the same type worn by one of the balaclava-wearing men shot dead by police weeks later. 'I saw a picture of him on the ground in the newspaper and it looked very, very similar,' he said.

About seven hours after attempting to rob the butcher, someone rather like Skews robbed an Ampol service station in Springvale Road armed with a shotgun. The gunman grabbed the attendant and demanded money. 'He had a shotty and stuck it up his nose,' the proprietor said later. The attendant gave the bandit around $200 and a few phone cards. The gunman was chased by two customers who saw him get into a nearby car driven by a second man.

The proprietor said he recognised Skews from pictures in newspapers as a regular customer. 'He lives around here and I know the face.'

If Skews thought he could keep his plans secret he was wrong, for he was a man with few friends but many enemies. He was desperate to recruit an offsider for further armed robberies, but the more people he spoke to, the more people chatted to the police.

The armed robbery squad targeted Skews, after being tipped off that he was planning to hit a $50,000 payroll from one of several factories in Blissington Street, Springvale, on May 12. As part of *Operation Short Time*, members of the squad were given permission to enlist the surveillance police and the heavily armed Special Operations Group, to try to trap Skews. Eight days before the robbery was expected police watched Skews hide a plastic bag containing thirteen twelve-gauge shotgun cartridges in a stormwater drain. They knew he had a sawn-off single barrel shotgun and a .44 magnum revolver.

They found a stolen car nearby, at the corner of Nash and Sullivan Streets, which they assumed was the getaway car. And they had information that he was ready. On May 12, Skews drove up Blissington Street with an unidentified man in another car. But it was a dry run. He didn't stop. Police were later told the job had been delayed a week.

Detectives believed they did not have enough evidence to arrest Skews and ordered 24-hour surveillance. But hours later they lost him. He was sleeping at different locations in the Springvale area and he eluded them.

Skews was about to pull a big job, but he also needed cash immediately. He owed $4500 to drug dealers and he was not sure if they would wait a week. People have been killed for smaller drug debts.

The following evening, about 6.30, he surfaced again. He was held by former policeman and part-time security guard, Jim Sheerin, 65, after he smashed the window of the Trewarne Antique Jewellery shop in Macedon Road, Lower Templestowe. He allegedly grabbed gold chains and diamonds valued at $25,000, which would net him about $8000 and clear his debts.

Travis Trewarne was in the shop with four other people when he heard the front window smash. 'He was still plucking things from the window when Jim got to him,' he said.

Sheerin, who had retired from the police force in 1986, chased Skews down a laneway into a carpark, and then grabbed him. 'He was puffing when I was on top of him. He said he did the smash-grab because he owed about $4000 for drugs. He said he had received threatening phone calls and needed the money. He said he had been told about the shop and how to do it.'

Skews was charged with burglary and theft and bailed from the Doncaster police station less than four hours later. 'The funny thing was that he was out before me,' Sheerin said. 'By the time I finished my statement it was about ten o'clock. He was walking up and down outside the station waiting for a lift.'

For the second time since his release from prison, police had their man, but he was released on bail. The coroner, Graeme Johnstone, was concerned at the way Skews was given bail while he was running red hot. He said he understood why the armed robbery squad wanted to keep the operation a secret but he felt that the police officer, Sergeant Michael Pearcy, who granted Skews bail, might have acted differently if he had been briefed by the squad. 'Had Pearcy been given (full) information, his investigatory and decision-making process would have been different.

'Skews, having been granted bail, within a short period of time completed his plans and the end result is known. Whether a bail hearing by an agency independent of the police would have actually changed the events or merely put off the fatal day is a matter of conjecture. Had bail been refused and Skews sentenced he would not have been in a position to undertake the robbery on the 16th. It is a moot point as to whether he would have continued with his plans after his eventual release.

'It must be recognised this situation is a dilemma for police concerned with the overall safety of the public. However, that is a regular difficulty managed by police working within our legal system when dealing with potentially dangerous and violent criminals like Skews. The real problem in this case is that appropriate procedures in the circumstances were not taken. The consequences of that failure are unknown.'

Detectives wanted to gather more evidence and, they hoped, catch him in the act of committing an armed robbery. But the risks were great. What if he avoided police surveillance? What if he struck before police were ready? What if he took hostages or killed witnesses? This may have seemed to be a game of cat and mouse but in this case the mouse was fuelled on amphetamines and armed with a shotgun and a magnum. That made him more like a rat – dangerous when cornered.

Skews became suspicious when he went to Springvale police to report on bail and noticed his picture had been removed from his file. Police made up an excuse so that he didn't realise it had been sent to the armed robbery squad.

The Templestowe arrest had not slowed him down. He cased a video shop and two service stations as possible robbery targets. At one point he returned his hire car and borrowed different vehicles, making it difficult for surveillance police. Detectives countered by getting a friend of the target to lend him a known car so he could be easily identified and followed.

On Sunday May 15, the informer, codenamed 'Mr Smith', rang police and said Skews was going to hit a real estate agency the following day, but he didn't know which one. At 9.30am the next day 'Mr Smith' rang and said it was Deacon Real Estate in Dingley. The office was also an agency for the Bank of Melbourne at the time, which made it a lucrative target. The SOG went to the scene and quietly checked the area, working out the best spot to grab the gunman. A few hours later they were confident that all was set. It had been done so quietly that the estate agent, Jim Farrell, said later he did not notice any police in the area that day.

At 11.45 'Mr Smith' rang and said Skews had just stolen a car from the Hallam railway station. Everything was going to plan. Five minutes later they got the call to say a robber had shot three members of the public during a raid on an Armaguard van at the Hoyts Cinema Complex in Chadstone Shopping Centre. It was not related to Skews, but it meant the armed robbery squad's resources were going to be stretched that day.

At 12.40pm 'Mr Smith' rang again and said the robbery had been switched to Finnings, a real estate office in Somerville Road, Hampton Park.

The plan had always been to intercept Skews before the job, but now time was running against the police. The SOG had to move to an area they had not checked. They had just over an hour to get everything set for an ambush. The job was a rush.

Surveillance police swept the area, looking for a getaway car. They found a stolen Falcon parked in Hallam, and sat off it. It had been stolen from Hallam railway station earlier that day.

Police knew there would be a second man with Skews. They did not know who he was, but had been told Skews would have a shotgun and the second man a heavy-calibre handgun. Detectives didn't know then that Skews had recruited Stephen Raymond Crome, 18, for the robbery. Crome had convictions for burglary, theft, possessing drugs of dependence and assaulting police. In June 1993, he was driving a stolen car that crashed and killed his passenger, Ricky Carpando. Crome had suffered serious head injuries and walked with a limp afterwards. He was a loser and a drifter who was fatally drifting into a police trap

At 1.56pm Skews and Crome approached the stolen car and drove off. Surveillance police notified the SOG that the job was on. The surveillance police, known as 'the dogs', kept a loose tail on the two, who doubled back and drove up side streets to check if they were being followed.

Police were told the job was to be between 2pm and 2.30pm. About 1.45pm, two members of the SOG arrived and cleared two staff out of the building and took them out a rear door. Minutes later, the arrest team of six arrived in a van and the driver also joined the group at the rear, along with another office worker from the agency.

Five SOG members, led by a sergeant and armed with five- and seven-shot shotguns, stayed in the back of the van.

The two bandits pulled up in Lakeview Drive and changed into blue overalls and put balaclavas on their heads to look like beanies. At 2.19pm, they arrived outside the agency and ran towards the building. According to police, the five SOG members attempted to intercept them, yelling: 'Police, don't move!'

They claim Skews turned and pointed his gun at the police. Crome, who was unarmed, allegedly had his hand in a blue linen sack. Four of the five police fired a total of seventeen shots. They were using heavy SG cartridges, each of which contains nine heavy balls the size of a revolver slug. The member who did not fire his gun was the last out of the van and believed the threat was over. The shooting took less than five seconds.

Skews and Crome were both shot in the head, body and legs. At least twelve shots hit them, indicating that up to 108 lead balls were in the two shattered bodies.

One SOG member fired three times; the second fired seven, the third five times and the fourth, once. The two were dead when they hit the ground. Crome's hand was near the bag. Skews's single-barrelled shotgun was loaded and he had spare ammunition. By luck, no members of the public were hurt.

The homicide squad and the then coroner, Hal Hallenstein, were called to the scene. The SOG members were separated, their guns seized and the area cordoned off.

They were tested for gunshot residue on their hands and clothes. They all made statements after being advised by Police Association lawyer, Tony Hargreaves, who was called to the scene to act for the police involved. But they refused to participate in a video reconstruction of the event on legal advice. All received psychological counselling on the night.

The death of the two bandits, while publicly defended by senior police, obviously created dissent behind the scenes. On October 31, 1994, the head of the state crime squads, Detective Superintendent Darryl Clarke, wrote to Detective Chief Inspector Ian Henderson, which stated in part: 'A question that may arise at the subsequent hearing is why Skews was on bail after being arrested on May 11 for drug offences and the May 13 for burglary and theft. On both occasions bail was on his own undertaking. An inference may be drawn that Skews was allowed bail in order to be permitted to commit an armed robbery and that the armed robbery squad influenced the decision on bail.'

Henderson's reply of November 1, also marked 'confidential', clearly showed the tension in the police hierarchy.

'The armed robbery squad did not request that Skews be granted bail for the smash-grab, nor did Detective Sergeant Watson nor any other member endeavour to influence that decision. The inference referred to in your report is totally incorrect and (I) have serious reservations as to the propriety of raising it in the current environment.'

Regardless of the rights and wrongs, police have been banned from using tactics such as those used in *Operation Short Time*. After years where Victoria Police killed more suspects than any other force in Australia, Coroner Hal Hallenstein, who reviewed a series of police killings, recommended a change in culture where the safety of police, suspects and the public were to be given paramount importance.

Under the safety first policies ushered in with *Operation Beacon*, police are banned from using prior knowledge of planned crimes to mount 'dead or alive' ambushes. The

Coroner, Graeme Johnstone, found: 'Skews and Crome contributed to their own deaths and to each other's death by attempting to undertake an armed robbery. Crome's contribution must also be seen in the context of him being young, probably immature, intellectually slow and 'led' by the far more mature and experienced career criminal, Skews. Although he was clearly aware of Skews' plans and ready to assist.

'Skews was affected by drugs and Crome may also have been affected. However, as to the latter comment there is no certainty that Crome was affected by drugs.

'The shootings by members of the Victorian Special Operations Group was lawful and justified in that all members fired after being put in reasonable fear that their own lives were at risk by Skews and Crome. The fact that Crome was later discovered not to be armed, does not, of itself, alter the view of the police response at the moment of the shooting.

'Skews and Crome, by attempting the armed robbery put themselves, the public and the police at considerable risk and the eventual consequences of their actions would have been foreseeable …

'In this case, whilst the management of the actual arrest situation was not unreasonable, it was the outcome that was not optimal. However, it must be remembered, the outcome was dictated primarily by the overt actions of Skews in presenting the shotgun in spite of police commands. In context of the management of an incident those commands inevitably occur rapidly with little opportunity for any rational thought by persons to whom they are directed. In that sense the potential for disaster is always present in the planned confrontation.

'No other person contributed to the death.'

In other words, it would seem, Skews and Crome had it coming.

CHAPTER 12

THE SEEDS OF DESTRUCTION

*Operation Phalanx was destined to bring
down Australia's biggest speed network, but
... it would also bring down the drug squad.*

WAYNE Strawhorn had more reasons than most to look
forward to his Christmas break in 1996. He and his team of
drug squad investigators had just smashed the syndicate responsible for more than half the amphetamines produced in Victoria
and snared the man alleged to have been the king of the trade
for more than a decade.

Now it was time to spend the summer holiday basking in the
success of a job well done.

Strawhorn had seen his star witness safely out of the country
and had a secure office filled with thousands of documents and
exhibits to be used to convict the man who had beaten the
National Crime Authority, Australian Federal Police and
Victoria Police since the mid-1980s.

His name was John William Samuel Higgs, and in the murky

world of amphetamine production, he was the main man. He was capable, according to police intelligence reports, of organising the production of illegal speed with a street value of $50million, had an Australia-wide network and could stockpile drugs to last years. Higgs' network was so large he cut out a layer between production and customer to form what conventional business calls a vertical monopoly.

His team would cut their 80 per cent pure drug, produced at one of more than twenty clandestine laboratory sites, and then cut it sixteen times down to one-pound lots of five per cent street speed. Each sold for $6000.

Higgs had a connection with a criminal figure, known as 'Kiwi Joe' Moran, who could provide the chemicals he needed and a New Zealand industrial chemist to control laboratory production.

For a long time it seemed to the convicted killer that his racket was as lucrative and nearly as foolproof as knowing the Tattslotto numbers a week in advance.

That is, until the drug squad's longest-ever operation, codenamed *Phalanx*, finally derailed his gravy train.

IN modern policing the cost of an operation is almost as important as the result. *Phalanx* proved to be an exception. A normal drug squad job is reviewed every 90 days to see if it should continue. *Phalanx* ran almost eight years.

It would ultimately result in the arrest of 135 suspects between August 1991, and August 1998, the seizure of $415,000 in counterfeit US currency, $371,500 in cash and eight tons of chemicals capable of producing amphetamines worth $200million.

Police would find fifteen amphetamine labs, seven previous sites, a chemical storage dump, cocaine, heroin, cannabis, explosives and weapons. And they would expose a national drug ring involving experienced criminals, a former star footballer, corrupt financial advisers and accountants – all part of a syndicate with links through Amsterdam, Hong Kong and Thailand.

The overall head of the investigation and officer in charge of the drug squad, Detective Chief Inspector John McKoy, said *Phalanx* broke the back of the amphetamine trade at a time when Victoria was the 'speed' capital of Australia.

Most successful drug squad operations result in screaming headlines, but make little practical difference to the flow of drugs on the street. *Phalanx* was different.

When the operation began, amphetamines were being sold at five per cent purity. But when it finished – arrests made and the drug stockpile seized – the purity on the street had dropped to between one and three per cent, proving that the amphetamine supply had been effectively halved.

Operation Phalanx was considered so important and complex the investigators were given a special evidence-preparation office, inside the electronically-protected drug squad floor at the St Kilda Road detective complex.

By mid-1996 the main evidence had been gathered. Now it was only a matter of collating the material so it could be presented in court.

The adrenalin-pumping part of the investigation was over. The *Phalanx* team had made the main arrests before its informer was identified. This was vital, because Higgs had threatened to kill anybody found talking to the police.

The investigators seized drugs and chemicals, had hundreds of hours of secret tapes, and were completing complex financial audit trails to uncover where Higgs and his network had invested the millions of dollars they had made.

The police were confident their case would withstand the inevitable legal buffeting it would receive from Higgs' defence lawyers during committal and trial hearings. A respected Office of Public Prosecutions barrister, Mark Rochford, had already reviewed their admissible evidence and declared it overwhelming. It was no wonder Wayne Strawhorn and his team believed the worst was behind them.

They were wrong.

SENIOR Detective Sharon Stone was first of the *Phalanx* task force back from Christmas leave. It was the morning of January 6, 1997. About 8.30am, after a cup of coffee at her desk, she unlocked the door of the preparation room. The evidence gathered over the previous five years was neatly stacked on 24 shelves in three steel grey bookcases.

Senior Detective Stone went to grab the three blue binders that held more than 100 statements from the star witness, a Melbourne businessman, who was given the code E2/92. They were not there. Micro tapes and other documents were also missing.

'I had this feeling of disbelief. I rang Wayne (Strawhorn) hoping he had taken them home. I knew he wouldn't have, but I was desperate,' she was to recall of that moment.

Strawhorn was later to tell the County Court: 'During the course of a Christmas break unlawful entry was made to that room and everything that had (the witness's) name on it, signature on it, or tape recording that had his name on it, or reference number on it was removed'.

THREE years earlier, E2/92 was a world away from drug squad investigations and the big players in Australia's underworld.

In his late 40s, married with teenage children, he was a

successful businessman with an annual income of $150,000 from his own company.

He had the knack of sniffing out business opportunities and moving quickly. His wife was successful in her own career. It was a good combination. Not intellectually brilliant, but street smart and a good mixer, he returned from bankruptcy in 1989 and within a few years his future seemed secure because of his skills in business.

But if he had a weakness it was a liking for playing cards, and through various games he had met men from the other side of the law. It was one of these who introduced him to a man who said he wanted business advice.

That man was John Higgs, a former member of the Black Uhlans motorcycle gang.

The two men sat and talked in an inner-suburban office and realised that perhaps they could make money together through several projects.

E2/92 had the business brains and Higgs had the cash … mountains of it.

Higgs was up front. He had a criminal record and had been involved with drugs, but he was beyond all that now and he wanted to 'go legit'.

He said he had been ripped off through a number of investments, including losing $600,000 on a rock concert that failed to get beyond the drawing board. He wanted to team up with someone he could trust.

The pair often talked. One day Higgs found out that his adviser had a friend who was a senior purchasing officer in a chemical company.

Higgs had just fallen out with 'Kiwi Joe', who had supplied him with chemicals for amphetamines production for years. Higgs refused to pay for some chemicals after a 'cook' failed, leaving Joe with a debt of $100,000. They no longer spoke. But here, it seemed, was the ideal replacement. Higgs made approaches through a third party to see if E2/92 could be enlisted to provide the chemicals.

On June 18, 1993, Higgs asked his card-playing friend to provide some chemicals, claiming he had already spent $350,000 on gear to make amphetamines and was set to produce drugs worth $5million.

The businessman went straight to a policeman he knew and explained what had happened. It happened just as Wayne Strawhorn was setting up an investigation into Higgs. The timing was perfect.

Three days later the card player was introduced to Strawhorn in a North Melbourne coffee shop. When the man started to talk, Strawhorn knew he could be the Trojan horse into Higgs' drug network.

Since July 1991, Strawhorn's attitude towards Higgs, who was notoriously difficult to target, had been that if any crime intelligence existed on him 'our aim was to obtain it'.

A break came while police were investigating a Melbourne criminal involved in amphetamine trafficking and dealing in counterfeit US currency.

They found that the criminal's supplier was Ronald Vincent Foster, known as 'The Strapper'. Foster lived at a horse property about 90 minutes drive from Melbourne. The stud was owned by Higgs.

It was there that police mounted an intense surveillance operation, which included hidden cameras, listening devices, tracking devices for vehicles and telephone intercepts.

Despite all the effort, it didn't work. Higgs trusted only his friends, so the introduction of an undercover policeman into the network was useless.

After more than 30 years in the underworld, Higgs knew as much about police methods as many detectives and appeared during some investigations to have benefited from inside information. Enter E2/92.

In a world where people are reluctant to stick their necks out, he had already done more than most by going to the police with the information that Higgs was in the market for amphetamine chemicals. But, for detectives desperate for a break, it wasn't enough. Strawhorn wanted more.

The detective asked Higgs' poker partner if he was willing to gather information for the police and he agreed. Over the next three years he became Australia's most important drug spy.

Strawhorn later explained in court that his star informer 'knew pretty well what the requirements were going to be and had the confidence and the abilities to go about that'.

Asked why the man was prepared to help, Strawhorn said: 'That came up more than once, and on every occasion it was that he had a hatred, for want of a better word, of drug trafficking and drugs in the community. He did have young children and swore that this was something that he could do to try and do something about that'.

The police provided chemicals for E2/92 to supply to Higgs's syndicate. The method, known as controlled deliveries or drug diversion, was a tactic used by the drug squad for about ten years. It resulted in a large number of convictions but it was a high-risk endeavour.

Many times the drugs could not be followed and the drug dealers were able to use them to produce amphetamines. The drug squad was to become a major supplier of the chemicals for the trade in a bid to catch the main players.

The squad bought the chemicals at the usual wholesale rate and sold them at the wildly inflated prices that drug dealers were able to pay. The massive profits were concealed in a secret bank account.

Eventually the system would go horribly wrong – but that would be years into the future. At this stage, E2/92 had virtually unlimited access to chemicals supplied by police to trap Higgs and his crew. It was to be claimed in court that he was told he should tell Higgs – who had offered him $100,000 including bonuses – that he had 'the keys to the lolly shop'.

Higgs asked for, and was given by the police spy, various chemicals crucial for amphetamine production, including mono methylamine, acetic anhydride and hydriodic acid.

Once, when E2/92 rang Strawhorn, who pretended to be his chemical contact, Higgs pressed his ear to the phone to listen, and on another occasion the card player bluffed by threatening to punch Higgs during an argument over prices.

Every meeting the witness had with Higgs and his associates was documented. His dangerous double-life ultimately resulted in 600 intelligence reports, sixteen separate police task force operations and the arrest of more than 100 people.

Virtually every day for three years he would speak to Strawhorn. He wore a small tape recorder to many meetings with Higgs, even though its discovery could have meant death.

Police say he did not tell his family what he was doing, believing that after Higgs and his gang were arrested his life would return to normal.

He was later to find that life would never be normal again.

There would be no massive climax to *Operation Phalanx*. Police would arrest offenders, release them and continue building the case. It was to be a war of attrition rather than a firefight. In November 1994 Higgs gave his chemical contact a bag containing $25,000 for five drums of chemicals. It was time to move.

Detectives knew that West Australian police would soon have to disclose phone tap details over the arrest of Jimmy Krakouer in January. Those transcripts would show Higgs he was a major police target.

More than 60 police, using drug sniffer dogs, raided the country properties of Higgs and his brother-in-law David McLennan. They found incriminating evidence, including explosives.

According to police, Higgs behaved calmly during the raid. To him, it was an occupational hazard.

He was arrested again in October the following year for conspiracy to pervert the course of justice over perjury allegations. And in April 1997 he was charged with drug conspiracy between 1989 and 1997.

By 1996 it was obvious that E2/92 would be identified as the man inside Higgs' operation. He was then asked if he would take the next step and give evidence. According to Detective Senior Sergeant Strawhorn, the insider asked only one question: 'Will Higgs be convicted if I don't?' The answer was no.

'He agreed without any great delays,' Strawhorn said.

A police threat assessment on the star witness was bleak. Higgs had an Australia-wide network that could reach almost anyone, anywhere, any time.

Arrangements were made for the first time in Australia's history to relocate an informer overseas.

According to police he had to go to his family to tell them he had lived a double life working as a police agent. They were now all in real danger and their lives would never be the same again.

Even then he didn't tell them the whole story, trying to shield them from the realities of what he had done. He said he had helped the police and was in some danger but he painted a picture of a great overseas adventure with new opportunities for all of them.

If he believed what he was saying he was being blindly optimistic.

It was only after the drug squad burglary that his wife started to comprehend how important E2/92 had become to the operation. One policeman says he thinks the witness will never tell his family all he has been through.

During the ordeal of secretly preparing to flee the country with his family, he completed 100 formal statements to be used in evidence in court.

Almost all protected witnesses used in Australia are criminals who have cut deals to save themselves from jail – co-offenders motivated by self-preservation and greed rather than community spirit.

This one was different because he had lost money working for the police and, according to Strawhorn, was motivated to act because he genuinely wanted something done about the drug problem. 'He was unique. He was prepared to put his hand up out of a community spirit. I am unaware of any other instance where a family has given up so much for no other reason than the interests of the community.'

IT WAS supposed to be a straightforward armed robbery for the young John Higgs and his three mates. The target was a poultry farmer called Vincent Dugan, whose small property was at Westmeadows on Melbourne's north-western suburban fringe.

The gang surprised the farmer outside his home around 9.50pm on the first day of autumn and marched him into the hallway of his house. Why one of them panicked and shot Dugan dead with a .22 rifle will never be known, but when he did Higgs graduated from robber to killer.

In the eyes of the law, although he did not fire the fatal shot, Higgs was guilty of manslaughter. He was sentenced to twelve years with a minimum of ten. That was in 1970.

Higgs was born in November 1946, and like so many youngsters who become heavy criminals, he was in constant trouble with the police as a teenager, with his first conviction recorded at the age of thirteen, around the time he left school. Police records show he has convictions for theft, stealing cars, assaults, manslaughter, assaulting police, resisting arrest, possession of cannabis and firearms offences.

He was also charged with the illegal possession of a stuffed possum.

His string of juvenile offences was only an apprenticeship for the budding career gangster. He was to learn that drug trafficking was the growth industry in his line of work.

He was a founding member of the Black Uhlans motorcycle gang, declared by police to be heavily involved in amphetamine distribution for many years. Police reports show that Higgs gave the gang its Melbourne clubhouse and that he is a life member of the club.

He was released from prison in 1978 after serving more than eight years of his manslaughter sentence and began to live with his girlfriend, Karen McLennan. They had two children.

He became close to her brother, David McLennan, who became his right-hand man in the drug business and company director of the legitimate arm of the syndicate. In 1984 police started to receive a steady flow of intelligence that Higgs was becoming a major player in the drug industry. They were told he was involved in producing amphetamines and the importation of heroin, cocaine and hashish.

Police say Higgs was of a generation of Melbourne criminals who became the big players in the local drug scene. Many of them had convictions for street violence then moved on to armed robberies before making the jump to drug distribution.

Over the years they learned counter-surveillance tactics, rarely trusted telephones, spoke in code and trusted only fellow crims they had known for years.

Police knew that rather than being a strict hierarchy with a boss at the top, the Higgs group was a loose cartel, with individuals coming together to work and then splitting into different groups. They had a network of corrupt, seemingly legitimate experts, to advise them on how to stay ahead of investigators.

But the difference between knowing his involvement and proving it would turn out to be a fifteen-year battle. The National Crime Authority, the Federal and Victoria police tried to gather evidence on Higgs but after eight separate task force operations, he still remained the biggest amphetamine producer in the state.

By 1991 police knew he controlled the main syndicate but had not established the identity of his cook, where he produced his amphetamines, where he got his chemicals or the structure of the organisation.

There can be little doubt that Higgs, aged in his 50s, stayed in front of the posse with the help of some inside information. On August 20, 1993, he delayed an amphetamine 'cook' for more than two weeks after he was warned police were about to launch a blitz on the five biggest speed gangs in Victoria.

Police received information that Higgs took out an $80,000 contract on one Daniel Hacking who, he claimed, owed him $100,000. Hacking later fell from a boat in Caloundra in Queensland and drowned in mysterious circumstances in 1992.

Late in 1991 Higgs called in contractors to work on homes owned by him and David McLennan. He paid cash and bragged to the workers he needed to 'get rid' of $100,000. Police said he also bought harness horses to disguise his income.

As part one of the early operations police found the Higgs group was a loose cartel of criminals that would deal in anything they thought the market wanted. Cocaine was imported from America, cannabis from New Guinea, guns from the Philippines and amphetamines from Victoria.

'Evidence has been extremely difficult to obtain regarding Higgs. He has insulated himself through a number of companies and apparent legal businesses and controls a large number of other criminals in his illegal dealings.'

Police established that $1,773,491 went through Higgs' hands from 1982 to 1993. He bought a fish-processing plant and retail outlet in Geelong and an ocean-going trawler in Eden, NSW. Undercover police heard rumours he was a player in the lucrative abalone black market, buying the coveted shellfish from poachers to process for sale.

Higgs used a retired town planner to set up an excavating business, which helped remove soil for the construction of Crown Casino. Police claim corrupt local officials were used to obtain building permits for the company, run by a former member of the Black Uhlans.

Higgs tried unsuccessfully to organise a huge rock concert just outside Melbourne for Easter 1994. One fellow investor was former AFL star Jimmy Krakouer, who lost money and became an amphetamines courier.

In 1993 Higgs became a director of a business set up to export powdered milk to Vietnam and horse feed to Malaysia. On February 14 that year he flew to Asia for a month, visiting Malaysia, Vietnam and Thailand.

According to police, Higgs was going to set up a fake company in order to get federal government grants and a subsidy to export to Asia and at the same time use the business to import massive amounts of heroin.

Police say one of the group approached E2/92 and asked him whether he could launder $200,000 every three days through Hong Kong companies.

According to police, Higgs was also heavily involved in fixing harness races, including a failed bid to rig the Geelong Cup in 1992. David McLennan was rubbed out as a driver for pulling up a horse that year. Higgs was a registered stud master with the Harness Racing Board.

In February 1992, Higgs and four of his team booked into the Sheraton Hotel in Darwin and were noted as big spenders. Northern Territory drug detectives followed the five men to a remote seafood business where they stayed for days. After they left, the owner of the business was seen to be spending large amounts of money.

According to police one of Higgs's team later delivered two hovercrafts to the business. Police believe the hovercrafts were to be used to import cannabis from Papua New Guinea. Higgs was known to be able to supply hundreds of kilos of New Guinea cannabis on demand.

Police had information that Higgs moved $600,000 overseas through a corrupt lawyer's trust account. They were also told, though it could not be confirmed, that he has invested $18million in city real estate – and land in Queensland valued at $10million.

Police accept they will never know how much he made nor have any real chance of finding his hidden wealth.

In 1992 police intelligence claimed Higgs completed one 'cook' of amphetamines that had a street value of $48million and a wholesale value of $7.5million.

Higgs pleaded guilty to one charge of conspiracy to traffick methyl amphetamine between January 1, 1993, and June 30, 1996. Judge David Jones sentenced him to six years with a minimum of four years, and described him as the principal, key figure, driving force and mastermind of the conspiracy.

Judge Jones said the use by police of subterfuge and deceit against him and others was justified as 'this was not a case of police tempting, manipulating or harassing some vulnerable but otherwise law-abiding citizen'.

Described by his barrister, Roy Punshon, as a semi-literate 'wheeler and dealer', Higgs had discovered while previously in custody that there were opportunities to supply the private prison system with various items.

Punshon said a company of Higgs' had a contract to supply runners, tracksuits and soap powder to one prison.

THE insider known as E2/92 was accustomed to signing business contracts but this one was different. It was a formal agreement to join the witness protection program; in return he had to 'sever all ties with friends and business connections, assume a new identity and relocate overseas'.

It was, in the crime world, an offer too good to refuse.

It was the first time a Victorian witness was to be relocated overseas and it proved to be a nightmare. Promises were broken, documents delayed and the informer's family members left to fend for themselves when they were at their most vulnerable.

Because of the growing risks, the star witness decided to take his family overseas in July 1996, before the Federal Government had completed negotiations for him to move to a friendly country with a new identity.

He was determined to live as normally as possible, so his children were enrolled in schools in a friendly country and his wife was to restart her career. But because the government had not completed diplomatic negotiations for his new identity he was denied permission to enter the country and had to stay with relatives in another nation.

Friends of Higgs started looking for the poker player who knew when to walk away, both in Australia and overseas. Relatives of E2/92 in the Middle East received a visit from Australian criminals asking if they knew where the business-man was living.

Alphonse Gangitano, the notorious gangster executed in his own home in January 1998, began putting out feelers interstate about where he could find the main witness.

Yet although the risks were growing, his formal entry to his new country was still being blocked. According to police he was forced to live on the run, living for months in cheap hotels and backpacking hostels through Europe.

He finally moved to the country where he wanted to settle, so his children could begin study. But two months later he had to fly out and then return after diplomatic paperwork on his new identity was completed.

After almost six months it looked as if he could finally settle – until the Christmas drug squad break-in, which left him dangerously exposed.

Two months later he was flown to Bangkok where he was again interviewed by police, this time producing 200 statements.

Senior Detective Stone said he had aged considerably in the months he had been on the run. 'He was suffering from stress and needed medical attention for migraines.'

Police said they had no doubt a contract had been taken out on his life. After years of dreary paperwork, detectives tend to describe the most horrendous circumstances in clinical terms

He went shopping … then he got shopped.

Armed special operations police leap from an unmarked van to arrest one of 135 suspects during Australia's biggest amphetamines operation.

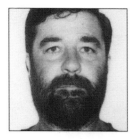

The boss ... speed king John Higgs.

The lieutenant ... Higgs's brother-in-law David McLennan.

The runner ... former AFL star Jimmy Krakouer was not a big fish.

The dealer ... Ronald 'Strapper' Foster.

The last convicted ... Les Burr.

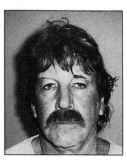

The importer ... Donald Royal Worcester.

Warning … bank patrons may be photographed. Worcester and Burr captured on a police surveillance camera.

The cook … Bruce Alexander Wilson, maverick chemist, bikie and thrillseeker.

The original supplier … 'Kiwi Joe' Moran.

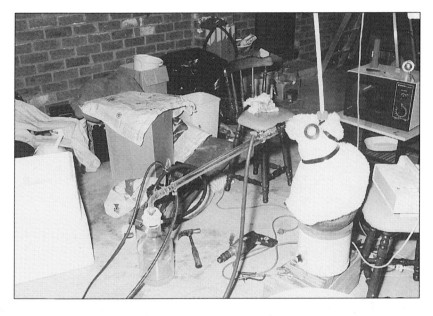

Drugs … produced by the unqualified in the unhygienic for the underworld to sell under the table to the unsuspecting.

The king and the cook ... Higgs and Wilson.

Strictly cash business ... why old crooks turn to new drugs.

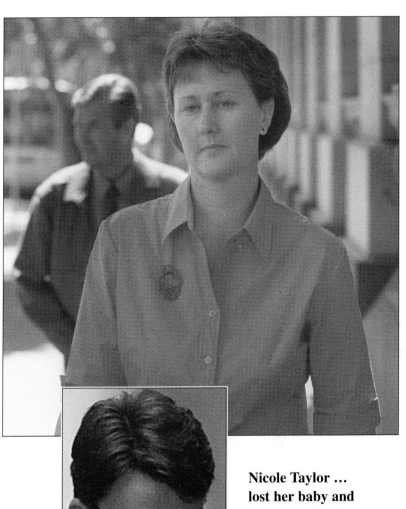

Nicole Taylor …
lost her baby and
right arm in a fire
set by her husband
Mark (left). He
was sentenced
to 22 years.

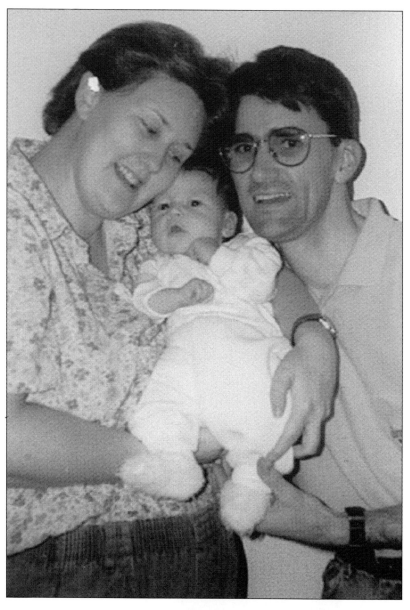

Mark John Smith, wife Nicole, baby Adrian. Happy families …

… and a bit on the side. Donna Wilkinson: a smile to kill for.

The victim, Johnny Moss … it took years to kill him.

**The investigator, Detective Senior Sergeant Jack Jacobs …
took years to catch the killer.**

Dennis William 'Fatty' Smith … proof that money can't buy class.

**A real underbelly crook … Smith and $320,000
worth of jewellery.**

Above: Attila Erdei … a millionaire drug dealer and killer who was unknown before *Operation Pipeline.* Sentenced: 22 years.

Bella Bernath … head of an elusive and established group supplying many substantial street dealers. Sentenced: Four years.

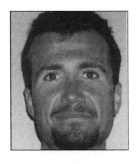

Manuel Veneris ... assets exceeding $800,000. Sold drugs valued at $1.2 million during the operation. Sentenced: Four years.

Paul Wooles ... involved in the distribution of heroin and amphetamines in prison. Sentenced: Six years with a minimum of two.

Peter Babes ... an associate of Leimonitis. Bragged of supplying pistols and machine guns. Sentenced: Two years.

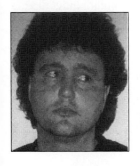

Anthony Hickey ... source of amphetamine.s Second in charge to Veneris. Sentenced: Six years, minimum of three.

John Falzon ... a millionaire who trafficked in amphetamines, heroin and hashish. Sentenced: Seven years with a minimum of five.

Theodore Leimonitis ... linked to an amphetamines laboratory of a hashish importer. Sentenced: Four years.

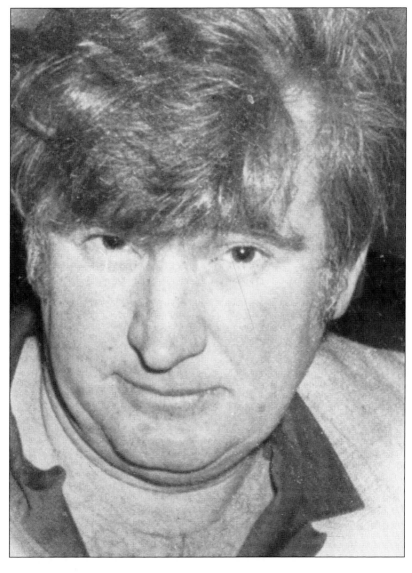

The killer … 'Deceptively ordinary-looking. He could be a labourer on a day-off, a farmer, salesman or small businessman. He wouldn't draw a second glance in a pub or in a church.'

when writing reports. But John McKoy, the head of the investigation, dropped the police-speak in one report as he tried desperately to show the urgency of the situation: 'Higgs will use his Australia-wide contacts to locate and kill E2/92. Therefore it is vital that the safety of E2/92 be given absolute priority'.

In 1997 he flew back to Australia in secret to give evidence in court. He went to Southbank, accompanied by witness protection police to have coffee with Strawhorn and Stone from *Operation Phalanx*.

Detectives believe a man, probably a private investigator, followed the detectives from the St Kilda Road drug squad offices to photograph the witness and the police at the informal meeting.

It was well-known that a plot to murder E2/92 had been developed for if he was required to appear at Melbourne Magistrate's Court to give evidence at Higgs's committal. The plan involved a painstaking study of the movement of police and security vehicles, to establish the pattern of the witness's movements at court.

The plot was for two motorcycle pillion passengers armed with shotguns to ride alongside the vehicle and shoot E2/92, a method often used in South America to silence witnesses in cocaine trials.

It is understood that an affidavit later presented to a senior magistrate detailing the police fears for the witness resulted in the arrangement for E2/92 to give evidence via a video-link from constantly changing locations in Victoria.

He was cross-examined by seven barristers from August 13, 1997, until mid-September. He left Australia but had to return in October for another week of gruelling evidence.

His Melbourne solicitor, Paul Duggan, says many of those

who have already served their sentences 'are now free to conduct their lives in any way they wish, while my client and his family's lives have been seriously restricted for years and that is likely to continue for a longer period than those jailed and released'. Sharon Stone, who worked on *Phalanx* from the beginning, says E2/92 was treated disgracefully. 'He did everything we asked him to do. He was extremely honest and genuine.

'In some ways he has been left to fend for himself. He has lost all his money and is really struggling. All he ever tried to do was the right thing.

'He told me he has been the victim of broken promises. He is angry and disappointed with what has happened to him.'

She said the federal attorney-general's office had the request for E2/92's overseas relocation for nearly four months before it was signed, despite repeat requests for immediate action.

'Someone should be held accountable for this. We are talking about a real person who was just trying to do the right thing.'

She said the final documents for his relocation were sent to Canberra in September 1996, but not signed until January 6, 1997 – the day the break-in at the drug squad was discovered.

Stone resigned from the police force in August 1998, after fourteen years service. She said the treatment of E2/92 and the drug squad break-in were the main reasons she left.

The witness lost his annual income of $150,000 and had to sell his house at a loss. He was forced to use up his savings while on the run and his family began to fray under the pressure.

'I didn't know I would have to give up my home, my business and my country when I agreed to help police gather evidence,' he told Stone bitterly.

Detective Chief Inspector McKoy said *Operation Phalanx*

destroyed Victoria's biggest amphetamines syndicate and damaged a cartel of Australian-born criminals who had been heavily involved in organised crime for twenty years. Detectives from *Phalanx* had been offered bribes of $250,000 and jewellery to provide documents to scuttle key prosecutions, he said. The men who offered the bribes were arrested and convicted.

In February 1998, the Chief Commissioner, Neil Comrie, said an internal investigation, code-named *Sentinel*, had identified the police suspected of the drug squad break-in.

'I think we have a very strong idea of who is responsible for what took place and everything that can be done to bring those people before the courts will be done.'

The task force identified thirteen serving and former police, seven civilians and five *Phalanx* targets as suspects for the break-in.

The *Sentinel* team interviewed 286 people and found there was 'no apparent forced entry to the drug squad office nor to room 36'. The also found one unidentified fingerprint in the room. The investigation found that documents relating to four *Phalanx* targets, including Higgs, were taken in the burglary.

The final report of the task force found that there had been repeated warnings about the lack of security in the police complex. 'The investigation has revealed that security at the St Kilda Road complex leaves a great deal to be desired.'

Police, unsworn staff and a team of cleaners had access to the drug squad preparation room and electronic security was hopelessly inadequate.

The task force concluded: 'It is the belief of investigators that the most likely scenario is that between 26 December 1996 and 6 January 1997, the drug squad offices at the police complex, 412 St Kilda Road Melbourne were accessed by a member(s) of the police force, most probably by a current serving or ex-member(s) of the drug squad.

'While there is little doubt that the proceeds of the burglary have eventually been received by John Higgs and that a significant sum of money was paid to individuals responsible for the offence, at this stage of the enquiry, insufficient evidence exists to charge Higgs or effectively identify the others involved.'

• THE use of controlled deliveries in sting operation was to catch more than members of the Higgs syndicate. It would eventually bring down the drug squad itself.

Officially, the drug squad was supposed to buy amphetamine chemicals and sell them to specific targets in transactions authorised by a deputy commissioner, but eventually detectives began to stockpile supplies for future use.

'They were hidden in lockers and in store rooms,' recalled one drug squad detective who worked in the area. Another remembers opening a cupboard and hundreds of packets of Sudafed (a commercial cold tablet which can be used to make amphetamines) fell on the floor.

In 1999 a large amount of Sudafed was found in a raid in Sydney. The fingerprints of a now suspect drug squad detective were found on one of the boxes.

After a series of suspect purchases from the Sigma chemical company by a drug squad detective, an internal police investigation resulted in the arrest of several members of the squad.

Chief Commissioner Christine Nixon then ordered an immediate review of the efficiency and methods used by the squad. The officer in charge of the investigation, Superintendent Terry Purton, made 152 recommendations for change.

In 2001 Nixon banned the practice of controlled deliveries

and replaced the drug squad with the major drug investigation division.

A later review by the then Ombudsman, Doctor Barry Perry, was scathing of the drug diversion practice. He found that most of the chemicals used to try and trap drug dealers were 'lost' and later used in the production of amphetamines – in effect creating an 'elite group of drug manufacturers and suppliers'.

He found an estimated 40 to 80 per cent of the chemicals were never recovered. 'It is therefore reasonable to assume that the chemicals or drugs not recovered have been converted into amphetamines and illegally sold into the community.

'The scale and complexity of many of the transactions uncovered is beyond belief.'

The report said that although the practice had been in existence since 1992, financial records prior to 1996 were 'virtually non-existent'.

'The practice, in my opinion, has lacked accountability to an astonishing degree. There has been no accountability for drugs obtained, for drugs sold or for drugs recovered. There has been no accountability for monies received or paid.'

Police returned $281,416 to the state government when the drug squad secret controlled delivery account was finally closed in 2001. Because of lack of records no-one knows what happened to all the drugs and money used by the drug squad over a decade.

Doctor Perry described the controlled delivery policy as 'an unmitigated and foreseeable disaster'.

He also criticised the drug squad's use of 'unstructured, secretive, unaccountable and sometimes unprofessional methods in handling informers'.

In 2003 one of the police involved in the Higgs investigation was in jail waiting his own trial. The detective received a seemingly harmless card postmarked from the Gold Coast. It read: 'Remember what I said the last time we saw each other'. It was signed by John Higgs.

The last time the detective saw Higgs was in 1999, when the amphetamines dealer was being sentenced to jail. As he was led from the dock he told the detective, 'I'll get you'.

CHAPTER 13

THE NINE LIVES OF FATCAT

The body was said to have been fed into an industrial meat mincer and used in dim sims.

MOST average criminals learn during their apprenticeship that keeping a low profile is good for business – but Dennis 'Greedy' Smith is no average criminal.

Only Greedy would deal drugs out of the driver's window of his Rolls Royce in one of Melbourne's main streets during the afternoon lull.

And only Greedy would run a drug syndicate from a Carlton hotel and still find time to sell an undercover policeman a shoplifted shirt for $30.

There isn't an old-style criminal in Victoria who doesn't know Greedy Smith – also known by the less subtle moniker of 'Fatty' and a string of more conservative aliases.

Dennis William Smith, who was at one time supposed to be dying of cancer, finally pleaded guilty in the County Court to a series of drug charges in which he was described as being at the 'highest level of the hierarchy' in a sophisticated amphetamines syndicate.

The court was told he was battling melanoma – the disease that claimed his brother, diabetes and the after-effects of two strokes.

But Smith won't die in prison – at least not this time. In March 2002, he was sentenced to three years jail, with all but six months suspended. That meant Smith wintered in prison but was free for the football finals and the Spring Racing Carnival. It may not have matched a Pacific cruise but the wily old crook could do a few months in jail on the bit.

After years of overindulgence in Australia and South-East Asia it could be seen as a government-funded stint in a rather austere health farm.

Smith, 57 when sentenced, has dealt drugs and guns, moved stolen property, pretended to be the son of a war hero to get free air travel, smuggled prostitutes and once made three giant industrial diesel motors disappear for the insurance money.

He could get you a Queensland driver's licence, an Asian bride, a cheap air ticket or a hot credit card.

He has been an AFL football club sponsor, company director, hotel owner, gambling identity, railway worker, boner and butcher.

When asked his occupation in court he paused, as if momentarily confused, before replying 'labourer'. But few men who earn their living with a pick and shovel get to motor around in a Rolls Royce.

For a man called Greedy, he could be generous and has been known to hand over cash to people who were struggling. He has also been known to take some from those who are not.

Smith is rumoured to have laundered some of the proceeds

from the 1976 Great Bookie Robbery where six bandits, armed with sub-machineguns, grabbed 118 calico bags filled with cash, officially listed as containing $1.4 million but believed to have been filled with much more 'black' money because of unrecorded wagers, known in the game as betting 'on the nod'.

It was after the bookie robbery that Smith bought a sex bar in Manila that became an established offshore oasis for Australian criminals. He was beyond the reach of Australian police who could not trust Filipino officials to investigate his syndicate, and could not believe the reports they received from international intelligence sources.

Smith was one of the first Australian criminals to learn that by setting up his business offshore, he could operate outside the influence of Australian law enforcement.

When National Crime Authority officers secretly flew to Manila to gather evidence against Smith's syndicate, he had local investigators follow them.

Smith was surrounded by under-age bar dancers and prostitutes, but he was untouchable.

He organised international credit card frauds from Australia to Hong Kong. He protected criminals on the run from Australia, such as the notorious Russell 'Mad Dog' Cox, the only man to escape from NSW's maximum-security Katingal Division in Long Bay Jail.

Smith was a crime promoter. He could provide a woman for sex, drugs for profit, or guns for armed robberies and murder.

In 1983, Smith was the major target of a joint Victorian-Australian Police and Customs investigation, code-named *Spider*.

He was the prime target in three federal police investigations and figured in eight references from the Costigan Royal Commission to the National Crime Authority.

In 1985, his cousin, Morris James Smith, was arrested in Melbourne for the importation of 580 kilograms of cannabis and was sentenced to seventeen years jail.

Police were convinced Dennis Smith organised the importation from his bar in Manila but he remained out of their reach. He continued recruiting ship crewmen, who visited his bar, to smuggle drugs into Australia.

A bosun on one Australian ship was identified as regularly smuggling a kilogram of heroin inside containers for Smith. The sailor was later arrested with 24 kilograms of marijuana while driving a hire car from Sydney to Melbourne. For some reason, police did not believe the marijuana was for personal use.

Even though Smith was a known criminal, there was a large advertising hoarding for his Aussie Bar in a prominent position at the North Melbourne Football Club's home ground, Arden Street, in Melbourne.

Smith is rumoured to have helped a well-known player by paying out his gaming debts. The player didn't take advantage of this second chance and was eventually jailed for drug trafficking.

While still living in the Philippines, Smith owned ten harness horses in Victoria, including the aptly-named Holster.

When Holster was gelded the veterinary surgeon who did the operation inquired about payment. The trainer broke the news about who owned the horse and owed the money. The vet was advised he was welcome to take up the matter with Smith but that perhaps it would be easier to write off the debt unless he wanted to risk undergoing the same surgical procedure as had been performed on the horse. The vet did not pursue the matter.

Smith was listed as a director of Kerden Enterprises and when police raided the head office in Puckle Street, Moonee Ponds, sniffer dogs reacted to a section of the carpet there. Although no drugs were found, detectives believe the drugs in the office had been moved just before the raid.

Police intelligence reports show that Smith had a feud with a painter and docker but the docker lost interest after he was beaten with a lead-filled glove.

At his peak, Smith was seriously rich and made no effort to hide his fortune. He bought everything he wanted – except class.

He owned chunky gold jewellery – gaudy chains and big rings valued at $320,000 – and insisted on wearing them all at the same time, with jeans and an open-neck shirt.

Underworld folklore told that one of his rings was taken from a criminal murdered over a debt. The body was said to have been fed into an industrial meat mincer and used in dim sims.

Smith and his partner, Kerry Joseph Ashford, had every reason to feel secure in the Philippines. After all, they paid their dues … they had almost 50 officials on the payroll, including six immigration officials and 30 police.

Smith could afford the bribes. He told police he had bought the Aussie Bar for $25,000 and made $40,000 a month.

How he managed that profit from a shopfront bar defied even the most creative accounting. He was paid only a $12 fee when a patron took one of his 'girls' for sex. His main income came from other sources.

In 1986, the corrupt Marcos Government fell and for the first time in more than a decade, Smith was vulnerable.

One of his enemies sent a Melbourne newspaper an article exposing Smith's group to the Philippine Presidential Commission on Good Government. The local authorities began an investigation and asked for Australian police files on the group. It was enough – more than enough.

In the newspaper article he was referred to as a drugs 'fatcat'. The nickname 'Fatcat' became another one that stuck.

He was deported in August 1986. Back in Australia, the big man was no longer a protected species and he was immediately targeted by the National Crime Authority.

For more than ten years he had been untouchable but within weeks of moving his business back on-shore, he was arrested.

Smith, Ashford and another associate, Thomas Schievella, were arrested in October for dealing drugs out of a Campbellfield trucking yard.

One of his team, the son of a NSW judge, gave telling evidence and Smith was sentenced to eleven years with a minimum of nine for trafficking cocaine and marijuana valued at $500,000.

Ashford was sentenced to ten years with a minimum of eight. Schievella got eight years with a minimum of six.

When Smith was released, no-one seriously believed he was a reformed character and he was soon back in business.

Despite their extensive records, Smith and Ashford were easily able to set themselves up in the Hollyford Hotel in Elizabeth Street.

The pub soon became a meeting place for major criminals. Drugs, guns and stolen property were exchanged and bought inside the old-style pub.

Police would later describe it as a 'supermarket' for drugs.

MOST criminals do their best work at night – darkness is their protection – but Smith was different, doing his deals before lunch.

When on the move, which was often, he would leave the Rolls Royce at a car yard and use his battered blue Toyota Crown sedan to move his drugs to a network of sellers.

Smith worked on the theory that he was less likely to be pulled up in the morning by patrols, believing police were too busy chasing last night's crimes to worry about him.

By midday, Smith had almost always completed his on-the-road work and had settled into a bar seat. If you wanted Greedy after lunch, you would ring his mobile telephone or head for the Hollyford.

Many did; police were to monitor 2979 calls on his phone in just two months.

In May 1999, the Mill Park district support group began an investigation into the activities of a local woman who had become a prodigious amphetamine dealer.

Mary Gannon, 39, had turned drugs into her private cottage industry, selling speed from her home seven days a week, often using the family car to collect her supplies. Business was brisk in the suburbs. Police were to monitor 4500 calls on her mobile phone in two months – around 75 a day.

In a fluctuating industry controlled by supply and demand Mary Gannon had a reputation for reliability. The key to her success was that, unlike many drug dealers, she could provide what she promised.

While others had to worry about supply she was close to someone who had an apparently inexhaustible stockpile of drugs. His name was Dennis William Smith.

Once police knew the old Manila connection was back in business, the NCA joined the operation.

Mary Gannon had known Smith, Ashford and Stephen 'Fat Albert' Collins for twenty years and, although she was not a big client, Gannon was never allowed to run dry. Her network had grown to the point where she supplied her own group of sub-dealers, including one who ran a cafe in Collingwood. Gannon's business method was sort of Amway with attitude.

She was always keen to identify fresh markets and was quick to embrace Lewis Harley, a country dealer looking for a steady supply of speed. It would be months before syndicate members would learn he was an undercover detective.

Investigators were to buy amphetamines from the Smith network sixteen times over the next six months before conducting a series of raids in December 1999.

The myth is that drug dealers are cool business sharks, John Travolta types in expensive clothes who weigh the odds as calmly as they weigh their powders.

The reality is that most dealers almost always take ridiculous risks as they search for a win and Gannon was no exception.

On June 4, 1999, Harley went with Gannon to buy speed from a dealer they would meet at the Northland Shopping Centre in Preston. He handed over $2250 for her to buy the amphetamines. Instead of satisfying herself with a quick profit, she decided to embark on a shoplifting spree while she was there.

In a scene more fitting a Benny Hill skit than an NCA operation, she left the Rebel Sport store with the alarm ringing. Surveillance police watched as the drug dealer ran through the car park, throwing items of clothing away as she was chased by security guards.

She surrendered when she no longer had any shoplifted clothes left. Later she went on to meet her dealer to buy the drugs. To her it was all part of a day's work.

On September 3, Gannon and Harley drove to Carlton to buy amphetamines. Police watched as she walked up to Smith, who was about to drive from the Hollyford Hotel in his Rolls Royce. She went to the driver's window and returned with about thirteen grams of speed.

She confided to Harley that the 'fat guys' were harassing her over an old drug debt.

But Smith and Ashford were into more than just powders and were planning to grow a marijuana crop near Shepparton.

On October 18, police watched as they bought the necessary gear from a Kensington hydroponics wholesaler. The following day Ashford transported the gear in his gold Mercedes Benz.

Senior police doubted investigators would be able to gather enough evidence against Smith, Ashford, Collins and Dennis 'Wee-Wee' Baldwin, who had been a director of Kerden Enterprises with Smith fifteen years earlier.

But when Gannon was jailed over stealing cars, undercover detectives were able to move up the main players. Undercover policeman Harley persuaded Smith to sell directly to him. The street-smart 'Greedy' was too greedy to see that he was being set up.

During one deal, Collins went into the kitchen of the Hollyford and came out with a plastic bag filled with amphetamines. He put it under Harley's nose and bragged 'this will be the best stuff you have ever had'.

As usual, Fat Albert was exaggerating and although the undercover officer paid $3000 for the speed it was only twenty per cent pure.

Smith may have moved large amounts of drugs, but he was not too proud to make small deals. While he sold amphetamines to the undercover detectives for up to $11,000 at a time, he was also prepared to sell anything else that came to hand.

Harley was sitting in the hotel when Smith produced a long-sleeved Country Road shirt and asked if he wanted to buy it. While Greedy did not pretend to be a fashion expert, he knew a bargain when he saw one.

The shirt had been shoplifted from a Myer department store by a woman who always sold her stolen property in the pub. The price tag was $140. The undercover bought it for $30, along with $6000 worth of amphetamines. He also knew a bargain when he saw one.

Smith was monitored contacting associates and calling for a meeting at the 'headquarters'. Detectives were able to establish this was a house in Liverpool Street, Footscray. They observed Smith, Baldwin and Collins meeting at the house. And they watched as the crime team did reconnaissance on the Commonwealth Bank in Barkly Street and the Kealba View Hotel – both potential armed robbery targets.

At 7.43pm on December 21, about two hours before Smith was due to sell Harley $3000 worth of amphetamines, he started to have second thoughts. He called Gannon in prison and asked if Harley was a policeman. Gannon said she trusted him and told Smith the story of their meeting. Somewhat reassured, Smith went ahead with the deal. But he should have trusted his instincts.

On December 23, Harley bought amphetamines worth $11,500 at the hotel. He handed Smith a Richmond Football Club stubby holder containing $11,500 in cold cash. It would be the last buy before the raids 30 minutes later.

Police raided ten properties around Melbourne, including the headquarters, the Hollyford hotel and the marijuana crop near Shepparton.

They found drugs, guns, and fake documents, including drivers' licences, birth certificates, loan applications and passports. In the hotel, they found the storeroom had been turned into a drug warehouse with plastic bags and two sets of electric scales. Police found traces of amphetamines on one set.

During the raid on Collins' home police found 199 fake ecstasy tablets containing amphetamines. Collins had been selling the tablets for $23 each.

At Gannon's house they also found stolen property. In the raid on the Footscray 'headquarters' ammunition, balaclavas, gloves and two-way radios were found.

In the garage was a Lada Niva four-wheel-drive vehicle. Inside the car was a large metal ram adapted to attach to the bullbar for 'ram raids'. Police also found a loaded, sawn-off double-barrel shotgun, a .32 pistol and bolt-cutters.

The shotgun was tested and found to be the same weapon fired in a Moonee Ponds armed robbery four years earlier.

In the raid on the country cannabis property, police found fourteen guns, including two .22 rifles cut down into makeshift pistols.

In the front yard of the property they found explosives decomposing in a box. Experts had to detonate them at the scene.

DENNIS Smith looked at home as he sat in the County Court dock ready to plead guilty. It was more than two years after his arrest; he had already served 272 days in remand and knew he was not looking at another long stint inside.

Only a slight tic in his left eye betrayed any sign of stress. He was big and bald – perhaps not as big as he once was, but still big enough. And he was dressed in dark conservative clothes, with no sign of his trademark gold jewellery. Barristers aside, court is no place to show off ill-gotten wealth.

Police had in fact seized Smith's rings and chains but, as they could not prove these were proceeds of crime, they had to give them back.

His defence lawyer made a sensible plea to Judge Stott, concentrating on his client's ill health and sad family background without dwelling on the odds of rehabilitation.

'He is a sick man, there is no doubt about that,' he told the court.

He acknowledged his client's career criminal activities with practised understatement. 'He is not unfamiliar with the courts.' He did not need to mention the impressive list of 53 convictions gathered over almost 40 years.

Having been in the dock more than twenty times before, Greedy knew the game. He was even able to point out a prosecution mistake when they claimed he had committed his latest offences while on parole – and was able to produce the documents to prove he was right. After all, he had been committing crimes long before many in the court had left primary school.

Smith stood as Judge Stott passed sentence. They were two veterans of the system, each comfortable with his respective role in the game – like two tent boxers waiting for the bell.

Greedy's old loyal mate and partner in crime, Kerry Ashford, was sitting at the back of the court as Smith was sentenced to a further six months inside. When the judge finished, Smith walked briskly from the dock to the door and the waiting prison van. He didn't need to ask directions.

CHAPTER 14

DRAGNET

He wanted to be a policeman. He was too fat.

AN observant postal worker, an unexplained hand wound and a small crucifix combined to snare serial killer Paul Charles Denyer, who could spend the rest of his life in jail for the random killings of three women around the Melbourne bayside suburb of Frankston.

Early on Friday July 30, 1993, ten key investigators met at the Frankston police station to review information they had gathered since the killings began seven weeks earlier. The murderer had struck twice and the ferocity of the wounds and the manner of the murders led police to conclude that it was only a matter of time before the killer struck again.

And time was running out.

Nothing affects a community like a serial killer.

The random nature of the attacks and lack of any logical

reason for why victims are picked, spawns fear, bordering on panic.

There is a psychological tendency for people to 'blame' murder victims. If a victim is a criminal, a prostitute or a brawler the public attitude is that they in some way contributed to the crime. In just under a decade there were 33 underworld related murders in Victoria yet every independent study showed that the spate of killings did not increase the community's fear of crime. It was seen as just bad guy against bad guy and treated as a curiosity – almost a form of local entertainment.

The thinking is simple. It was the victims who put themselves at risk, so sensible, honest people need not worry. It would never happen to them.

But when a serial killer is on the loose then 'good' people are at risk. The next victim could be anyone.

The nature of homicide investigations is that police must try to get a breakthrough early or the case gets progressively harder. Police say the first 24 hours are crucial.

A homicide investigation usually has its own rhythm. The victim is not going anywhere, the crime scene is usually isolated and investigators take their time, slowly coming to conclusions, building a case, choosing their moment to interview witnesses, question suspects and finally lay charges.

But in Frankston, homicide investigators were in a deadly race. They knew that a serial killer usually continues until he is caught or dies. And, they had been told, the offender had probably fantasised for years about murder and now that he had moved from fantasy to reality the attacks would be more frequent and even more sadistic. Like wild dogs that have tasted blood, they learn to love the chase and the kill.

The pressure on the ten police in Frankston was intense. It was not so much that a killer could get away with murder but that one mistake, an unnecessary delay, a wrong conclusion, a false lead, could cost lives.

To leave a murder unsolved preys on the mind of a detective. Some retired police say they have never really recovered from failing to put all the pieces together. Long after they have retired some wonder if they could have done more – if they are to blame for not giving grieving relatives some resolution. But to allow a serial killer to continue killing can destroy the toughest investigator.

The Chief Commissioner at the time, Neil Comrie, a former homicide squad man himself, knew that nothing could destroy a community's confidence in itself like a serial killer. While remaining low key in public he made it clear inside police circles that everything else was to take a back seat to the investigation into a serial killer. The cases could not go unsolved.

Police had to go through thousands of pieces of information from the public. Well-meaning people provide little snippets of information that are nearly always rubbish. For the police it is like mining for gold. They had to be prepared to sift tonnes of slag to find a nugget.

Although more than 200 police had been involved in the seven-week hunt, detectives knew they were no closer to finding the killer of Elizabeth Stevens, 18, a student, who was stalked and killed on June 11, and Debra Fream, 22, a young mother who was abducted and murdered on July 8.

They checked criminal profiles and detailed forensic evidence, which was all logged on computer together with the tips and information provided by the community. But it was just a jumble of facts. There was no Eureka moment in sight, no Sherlock Holmes deduction. Just a hard slog when there was not time for a hard slog.

They knew that the killer would strike again – soon. The head of the investigation, Detective Senior Sergeant Rod Wilson, then of the homicide squad, says: 'In a case like that you are always aware that time is the enemy, but you have to try to remain objective and use the methods which have proven successful in the past'.

The detectives believed the killer would be local. They also knew that the first two murders had been committed during, or just after heavy rain. As the task force met that Friday, it began to rain – heavily.

Around the time police were meeting, 21-year-old Denyer drove a short distance from his Frankston home to Skye Road and cut three holes in a cyclone fence beside a bike track near John Paul College, a local secondary school. His aim was to ambush his victim and drag her into thick scrub away from potential witnesses.

It showed he was no impulse killer, not an offender who fought only to be overwhelmed with the desires to murder but a methodical beast, lacking mercy, compassion or a shred of decency.

Just after midday, he drove his yellow 1974 Toyota Corona to the Langwarrin Flora and Fauna Reserve. Police noticed the car in the reserve while they were on routine patrol at 12.10pm. Denyer later told detectives he had stopped to top up his leaking radiator but police had seen no signs of him near the vehicle.

They later established that Denyer had drawn detailed maps of tracks of the reserve, as part of his plan to abduct a young victim. They now believe he had been stalking a school group on an excursion in the park at the time, and would have abducted and killed one of the schoolgirls if he'd had the opportunity. He waited for a straggler to drop behind, but the children stayed in a bunch. Denyer moved on. He knew there would always be more opportunities for someone like him. After leaving the park, he drove back to Skye Road and sat in his car.

About 2.30pm, Vikki Collins, a postie, drove past Denyer on her motorbike. She had almost completed her daily round, when she saw a car parked in front of her and noticed it had no rear numberplate.

'I went past it and, while I delivered the mail at a house, I adjusted my mirror and saw there was no front numberplate on the car,' Collins recalled. The driver appeared to be deliberately slumped down, so that he was partly concealed by the steering wheel. Collins noticed a student walking near the car towards a bike track. It has now been established that the girl was Natalie Russell, a John Paul student.

For a moment Collins considered warning the teenager about the man in the car, but she worried that she would be told to mind her own business.

But rather than just drive on she decided to ring the police. She continued on her round until she found an occupied house, from where she phoned police and gave a detailed description of the car.

Seconds after the alert postal worker had noticed the car, Denyer got out, walked to the bike track, and ambushed and killed Natalie Russell.

Within fifteen minutes, two police units responded to the call. It proved the vital break in the investigation, even though it came too late to save the teenager.

When Denyer saw the seventeen-year-old heading to the track, which separates the Long Island Country Club from the Peninsula Country Golf Club, he positioned himself in one of his hiding spots, armed with a kitchen knife and a leather strap. As the girl passed by, he began to stalk her, ensuring he kept his hulking 120 kilogram frame on the wet grass so his victim would not hear his footsteps.

In the frenzied attack, he accidentally hacked his own hands, slicing flesh from one finger. As he left the scene he saw police checking his car, so he left it there and returned home, keeping his blood-soaked hands in the pockets of his jeans.

When Russell's body was discovered, police computer checks showed that Denyer's car had been parked at the scene of the murder.

For the first time, police knew they had a strong lead. Further checks revealed that Denyer had been seen at the Kananook railway station car park a week earlier and that he used to live in Long Street, the street where Elizabeth Stevens was grabbed.

Police could now place Denyer in the area where all three girls had disappeared. Investigators later learnt that, before the Russell murder, Denyer had rung Cranbourne police station, claiming to have been harassed by the homicide squad and wanting to know whether he was still a suspect.

At that time he had not been approached by homicide squad and was not on any short list. Looking back, it was the call of a worried man. Or a grossly disturbed one.

When police picked him up, at 5.28pm, he remained cool and denied any knowledge of the killings. He gave plausible reasons for being in the areas where he had been sighted.

As question followed question, he stonewalled. A homicide interview is not like a conversation or a debate. The questions are structured to block off escape routes before the suspect can see that his options are being whittled away. The target is not pulled up when he lies. He is allowed to wrap himself in the web of deceit he has constructed.

When the time was right Detective Senior Sergeant Wilson asked about the cuts on his hands, and Denyer responded without hesitation that he had hurt himself fixing the engine of his car.

The cut on his right thumb came from sharpening a knife in a scabbard, he said. He then helpfully acted out how he claimed to have done it. Both the police and Denyer seemed to realise at the same moment that the suspect had made a telling mistake.

He held the imaginary knife in his injured hand when he tried to show police how he had cut himself. It would have been impossible for him to have injured himself in the manner he claimed. He then tried to change hands to illustrate another version of how he got the injury.

It still wasn't possible.

It was then 10.19pm. Denyer knew he had been caught. Police knew they had the right man, but they also needed more information to mount a case. Further questioning elicited further lies.

After 1511 questions, police called a halt to proceedings so they could get a pathologist to try linking Denyer's hand wounds with evidence found at the scene.

During the break, Senior Detective Darren O'Loughlin, of Frankston, guarded Denyer. The policeman, who wore a crucifix under his business shirt, escorted Denyer to the toilet just after 12.45 Sunday morning.

Denyer professed a belief in God. He had decided to confess – not to his interrogators but to the quiet policeman wearing the crucifix.

Denyer said to him: 'I see you are wearing a cross under your shirt. Are you a Christian?' O'Loughlin said he was, and Denyer said: 'Okay, I killed them, all three of them'. It was now time to talk.

At 3.45am he began to make a videotaped confession to homicide squad detectives, answering their questions in a matter-of-fact way. He showed little emotion or remorse as he detailed how he had abducted and killed women who were strangers to him. He said he had wanted to kill since he was fourteen and had followed women since he was seventeen. He said he struck when it had rained or was wet, in the hope that the water would wash away blood and other evidence.

The warning signs that Denyer was evil had been present for years. His little sister's toy bear was found with its neck and torso repeatedly slashed, covered with cigarette burns and with the stuffing pulled out.

Fangs had been scrawled on its face. At the time the little girl was five; Denyer was ten. It was just one of many examples of unexplained violence that always pointed to the overweight, brooding loner.

Two years later a little kitten was found, with its throat slashed, hanging in a tree. Again, the finger was pointed at Denyer. He denied any involvement, but a relative checked his pocket-knife and found blood and flesh on the blade.

A local girl complained that she thought someone in the neighbourhood had been stalking her. Nothing came of that.

Denyer had few friends. He liked to frighten people. The psychologist would later say he had a personality disorder. In lay terms, he was a fat, apathetic, lazy bully – and increasingly weird. These were his good points, as it turned out.

He left school and had a series of jobs, which he lost through lack of interest or dishonesty. Being a lazy thief didn't help his employment record.

His last job was at the aluminium boat builders, Pro Marine, where his bosses found the same problem every other employer had found: he couldn't care less. He wouldn't finish even the most basic task. Asked to sweep the floors, he would wander off, leaving the job half finished. The only time he used energy was when he fashioned scrap metal into daggers. One of those was later used as a murder weapon.

Denyer taught himself to be a killer. Not only did he strike after rain in the hope that evidence would be washed away, but he used his bar radiator to change the pattern on the soles of his runners so they would not match imprints left at the crime scenes.

He had loved a horror movie called *The Stepfather* and delighted in turning up the volume to frighten his sister. But it was not just a scare tactic; Denyer used some of the methods from the movie when he progressed to murder. For years he had stalked women, looking for the chance to kill. In 1992 he decided to murder the sister of a neighbour. He went to the women's flat, but it was empty. He broke in and stabbed the women's cat and drowned three kittens in the bath. He smeared blood on the walls and wrote 'Donna and Robin – You're dead'. The girls were shattered. A few days later Denyer turned up and commented that he would love the chance to deal with the intruder.

When detectives arrived at the scene they should have known they were dealing with a potentially dangerous offender. He had slashed the victims' dresses, vowed to kill them and killed their cats. It was obvious the offender knew the women and that it was no random crime. There was another major clue. The offender had left bloody footprints from his Blundstone boots in the flat.

One of the girls nominated Denyer, who lived nearby, as a man who made her feel uneasy. But no-one went to interview him and the boots that would have proved a match stayed in his cupboard. If police had knocked on his door perhaps Denyer would not have got the chance to kill months later. Certainly he would have been recorded as a potential suspect after the first murder and might have been arrested before he had killed three times.

When he was finally grabbed, the boots were still in his wardrobe.

During his homicide interview he told police he killed because he hated women. In his flat, unemotional tone he explained how his last victim, Natalie Russell, obviously knowing from the moment she was grabbed that this man was the serial killer who had murdered two young women, had begged and tried to negotiate for her life.

'She said disgusting things,' he told police. This from a man who delighted in humiliating, torturing and slaughtering young women.

The quirks of a random killer are hard to fathom. Denyer followed hundreds of girls for years, but left most untouched. On July 8 he attacked Roszsa Toth, 41, outside the Seaford railway station. He jumped out of the bushes and grabbed her, sticking a fake wooden gun into her side and warning her not to fight. He put his hand over her mouth and she responded by biting him and breaking free. She ran out onto the road and stopped a woman motorist for help. Denyer hid in a park, then boarded a train and returned to Kananook.

Denyer walked for hours looking for a victim. He saw Debbie Fream pull up at a milk bar to get some milk, eggs and a block of chocolate. She had given birth to her son, Jake, only twelve days earlier. She left the car unlocked and he slipped into the car and hid in the back seat, grabbing her when she returned.

The day after his last murder, police waited for him to return to his Dandenong-Frankston Road flat to question him over three murders but it could easily have been four. As police were waiting Denyer was preparing to grab another victim.

A group of four women had gone to the Langwarrin Shopping

Centre but one, Vicki Cooper, was asleep in the car, so the other three left her snoozing in the car park. They left the car unlocked.

About 40 minutes later the group returned. Parked right next to their car was an unregistered yellow Toyota. It was Denyer's. The car park was almost empty, yet the cars were side by side.

Denyer had the bonnet of his car raised and was looking at the motor. Police said he had used that tactic when stalking a victim.

One of the women, Wendy Halemba, said she saw a man between the two cars and recognised Denyer as a former neighbour. She greeted him, but noticed that he seemed to be behaving strangely.

One of the women on the shopping trip was Mrs Halemba's daughter, Tamara. Denyer had once asked her out and she had refused. A short time later the family disturbed a prowler in the backyard, near the bungalow where Tamara slept. They found a screwdriver near the sleep-out. Then the family's chickens were found hacked to death.

Cooper said that when she was dozing she felt there was someone else in the car, but assumed it was her friends returning from shopping.

Denyer, thwarted, drove home. The police were waiting. It was to be the beginning of the end.

After the long interview he was prepared to co-operate fully. He returned to the murder scenes and calmly acted out his crimes for the police video camera. He even tried to joke with stone-faced detectives.

Later in a police cell he told his girlfriend, Sharon, that he was the killer. When she asked what evidence the police had to link him to the crimes, he replied: 'My hands.'

'I'm a serial killer, I've got a problem,' he said.

In many ways Denyer was the classic serial killer. FBI crime profilers are taught to look for key signs in a suspect's past. One obvious signpost is cruelty to animals. As a child he attacked soft toys then progressed to killing pets and domestic small animals. His parents must have thought he would grow out of it. Sadly, he did – graduating to humans.

World expert and former FBI profiler John Douglas says that rather than hiding, serial killers often stay close to the investigation, wanting to see how police are progressing. 'Now, because of what we we've learned, we routinely consider the likelihood that a subject will attempt to insinuate himself into the investigation.'

There was the occasion Denyer contacted Cranbourne police to ask if he was considered a suspect. On another he drove past a task force caravan which was parked at one of the crime scenes to take information from the public. Denyer was later able to tell one of the homicide squad detectives that he recognised him from seeing him standing outside the caravan.

According to one member of the task force, 'He revelled in it. He drove around Frankston; he saw the newspaper posters about the serial killer. He knew the fear in the area. And he had the secret. He was the only person who knew it was him.'

Douglas also found that for serial killers, 'It isn't surprising that one of their main fantasy occupations is police officer'.

Denyer had applied to join the police force but had been rejected.

He was too fat.

Denyer was sentenced to life with no minimum, but on appeal was given a minimum of 30 years.

The sadist, the stalker, the peeping tom, the cat killer, the man who wanted to humiliate his victims, was put in jail with hardened criminals. He spends his days in protective custody.

Years after he was sentenced the man who waged his own private war against females, decided he wanted to become one and tried to change his name by deed poll to Paula – a move blocked by the state government.

Denyer was never an attractive man, but he made an even worse looking drag queen when he decided to become a cross-dresser after years in jail.

In prison Denyer tried bodybuilding, Christianity and even flirted with becoming a Muslim before deciding he was a woman trapped in a man's body.

In June 2004 it was revealed that Denyer had been assessed in jail as a possible candidate for a sex change operation. He was rejected and told he was not eligible for gender reassignment surgery and he also lost a legal battle to be allowed to wear makeup in prison.

In a series of letters to a transsexual inmate published in the *Herald Sun* newspaper Denyer wrote: 'This year, I've looked back over my life and I'm convinced that I should have been born female. What lays ahead of me is the will to fix things.

'I feel like shutting myself away a lot. Staying in my room with a friend.

But I'm a sun-loving summer girl. I want to work on my tan as much as I can. I committed those disgusting crimes Jayne, not because I ever hated womankind, but because I have never really felt that I was male. Which leaves female, the other side of the human race.

'Unfortunately for me, I used the word "hate" when the police interviewed me. Because hate was the only emotion I thought I could correctly identify with my confused identity.

'Well, I must go, must get to sleep, rise when the sun does, doll myself up, put on some tight clothes, prance about the unit, … tease all the closets. Same shit different day I guess.

'I'm only 32, and I'm living like an old lady.'

Denyer will be 51 when he is eligible for release in 2023.

Then it will be up to the Parole Board to decide whether he can return to the society he terrorised 30 year earlier.

CHAPTER 15

HEAT

'When there is the slightest doubt, walk away.
These blokes let greed colour their judgment.'

IT was the perfect night for the crime of the decade. The filthy weather meant nosy joggers would stay indoors, while the blinding hail cut visibility to a few metres and would wash clues away long before the scam was discovered.

The six-man team was confident, even a little cocky. They had done their homework – checking six potential targets in Victoria and South Australia – before settling on a factory in Melbourne's south-east.

They had broken into the sprawling complex more than twenty times to plan every tiny detail and prepare for every possible contingency. They had practised disabling the electronic security system and brought a truck-load of sophisti-cated equipment with them to ensure nothing could go wrong.

After more than nine months of research and training, plus

investing $30,000 in equipment, it would only be a few more hours before they were all millionaires – never having to work, or steal, again.

Inside the safe they were about to drill was a product more valuable than gold – pure amphetamines and chemical by-products – produced not by some motorbike gang in the filthy kitchen of a rented house, but by one of Australia's most respected pharmaceutical companies in state-of-the-art laboratories.

Behind the huge metal door was $166,754,940 worth of amphetamines and related products, enough to make more than 3300 kilograms of street drugs. They would be able to flood Australia with the paranoia-inducing 'speed', considered one of the most dangerous of the illegal drug group.

To the firm that produced the drugs for legal purposes, such as providing medication for children with Attention Deficit Disorder, it was valued at a mere $113,000 – but on the street it was worth 1400 times more.

THERE isn't much Geoff Williams (not his real name) doesn't know about safes. He has been in the industry for 23 years and is acknowledged as one of the best in a game where all the experts know each other. He is a self-motivated businessman who carries a mobile phone everywhere and is available any time.

He sees each call as an opportunity rather than a distraction and when his home phone rang on the evening of August 22, 1996, Smith answered with his usual polite, businesslike voice.

He was mildly surprised to find the caller was an old acquaintance, George Ernest Lipp, a man he had last seen in 1982. 'We were never really mates,' Williams was to recall. 'We shared an interest in GT Falcons. He was just a local hood – a friend of a friend.'

A safe expert has to know everything about the different metal boxes that are supposed to be thief proof. He studies them to find their strengths and weaknesses. Eventually he knows what keeps them shut and, more importantly, what makes them open.

Lipp chatted with Williams about the old days but, after a few minutes of mandatory small talk, he revealed the reason for his call. He knew his old acquaintance was in the security industry and he wondered if he could help with a safe. Lipp said his mother was suffering from Alzheimer's disease and could not remember where she had hidden the key to her small home safe. Could Williams pop over to the family home in Greensborough and give it a tweak?

The expert said he would be free in about two weeks. When he arrived he gave the safe, positioned in an alcove near the lounge, a cursory glance. It was the type that might deter a sneak burglar but was no problem to an expert. He opened it in seconds.

Lipp seemed impressed. He took him into the kitchen and while he made cups of coffee he explained that he had another, more difficult problem. He slipped over a polaroid photo of a huge, industrial vault door. Could Williams open that one?

The safe man looked silently at the photo in front of him. He knew immediately what he was being asked and he also knew whose vault he was being asked to crack. The poisons code on the front was only on safes in two pharmaceutical companies in Melbourne.

Lipp led with his chin and made an offer. There would be $100,000 in cash for him if he could open the safe.

Lipp didn't wait for an answer but let his plans spill out. It was the safe at the Sigma chemical company's Croydon plant. Lipp was part of a team that planned to raid the two Sigma factories at Croydon and Clayton on the same night.

The team knew the factories were to merge and they needed to move soon. To impress his potential recruit Lipp explained that his team had already broken into the Croydon plant to check the layout.

He bragged that the gang had developed a system to bypass the alarms and the seismic sensors. The team planned to knock out the telephone lines into the factory on the night of the job.

Lipp then started to quiz the expert on technical matters such as the use of thermal lances and core drills to break into the vault. He said his people were installing a pinhole camera in the ceiling of the factory to obtain the combination of the safe.

Williams, father of two, simply didn't know what to do. He was actually quoting for a security contract with Sigma – the firm he was now being asked to rob. For a moment, he thought he was being set up, that this was a form of integrity test organised by the company, but why would they use a half-baked mate he hadn't seen for fourteen years as the bait?

He needed to stall for time, to think of what to do next. 'I didn't want any part of this plot – but I didn't want George to think this at the time.' Then he saw that a pole photographed in front of the safe slightly obscured the picture of the safe door. 'I didn't really know what to say, so I said I would need a better picture of the door.'

He went home and the next day went to see one of the senior men at Chubb Security. When he told state manager Chris Gyngell what he had learned, Gyngell called the drug squad straight away.

Detective Sergeant Graeme Sayce of the drug squad listened to the story. He thought if Williams had the guts he might be prepared to introduce a police undercover man as a safebreaker and then police may be able to gather enough evidence to grab the offenders. It would be a big ask, but it had worked before.

Usually the go-between who introduces an undercover is an underworld informer who needs to curry favours from police. But Williams was just an ordinary man. Why should he voluntarily descend into the vipers' nest?

Yet he did not hesitate.

'I've got two kids myself and I don't like drugs. You can't leave this sort of thing to the next guy.'

He was introduced to 'Dave', a police undercover operative chosen for his ability to think on his feet and act a role to fit any investigation.

But this one would be more difficult than usual. This wasn't a case of tricking junkies or snowing the gullible. If the thieves had pictures of the safe door, police would have to work on the basis the gang knew what they were doing.

Dave would have to understand the safebreaking craft and to learn that he would have to go to the experts – fast. He was taken to a one student 'safe school' at Chubb and taught about timers, locks and security systems.

Williams helped train the policeman. 'He had to be able to talk the talk,' the expert would say of the safebreaking apprentice.

Dave would need to know all the terms because Lipp would not be easy to fool, as he had become a self-trained expert. For months he had been pretending to be a customer, walking into security companies, asking about safes – comparing one with another. He wanted to know their strengths … and weaknesses.

LIPP was the front man and one of the organisers of the scheme. His partner was Paul Geoffrey Elliott, whose uncle was the notorious convicted drug dealer, Dennis William 'Fatty' Smith. Elliott met Lipp when they were both in the paving and stone wall trade.

Both owned their own companies and while working on the Western Ring Road they recruited two men, Mark William Wills and Brian David Zerna, to help pull off what would have been Australia's biggest robbery.

The four were an unlikely safebreaking gang. They were all aged in their 30s, married with children, in regular employment and without extensive criminal records.

If they pulled off the job and kept their mouths shut, police would not immediately suspect them because of their background. The gear they were planning to steal could be sold on the black market for cash, and so not leave a money trail for investigators to follow. Drug dealers don't pay by bank cheque.

The four men knew they would probably have only one chance to pull off a crime of this size. They also knew Sigma was about to launch a major security upgrade. 'This is it. We can only do this once,' Lipp said in a conversation secretly recorded by police.

Police were later to estimate the gang had broken into the Croydon factory 25 times over the previous months. The would-be safebreakers were prepared to be patient because they knew if they got it right it would be the biggest theft in Australia's history. Lipp was to say he was willing to spend two years on the planning alone.

The gang had checked several factories. They decided to make Sigma Croydon their main project when they went through the industrial bins and found drums labelled 'Dexamphetamine'. For the prospecting burglars it was the mother lode – pure speed.

In one of the break-ins they checked the company's records to establish the amount of drugs kept in the safe. 'We went through all their manifests and the books,' Lipp boasted to Williams.

The records showed that huge quantities of dexamphetamine and pseudo-ephedrine were stored in the building.

The going rate for a 25-kilogram container of pseudo-ephedrine on the black market was $300,000. Little wonder, as half the drug is pure amphetamine. It could be cut and sold as powder or in designer pill form for a massive profit.

The Sigma factory in Croydon is a huge complex. Having gained access to the building, they needed to find the vault. Wandering through the facility, opening doors and looking for the giant vault would increase the risks of setting off alarms so one of the gang simply broke into the telephone control area and rang the extension marked 'safe room'. Then they just followed the ringing until they found the area. During the regular nightly visits they checked the alarm system and practised the best way to get the drugs out of the property. But the dry runs would be useless unless they knew they could get into the safe when the time was right.

And that is why they needed Geoff Williams.

GRAEME Sayce asked Williams to pretend to be interested in the scheme and to organise another meeting with Lipp. Williams rang Lipp at his home on September 7 but the once enthusiastic planner now seemed strangely reticent. He hung up but, a few minutes later, rang back from a public phone and this time he sounded keen and upbeat. Lipp was later to tell Williams not to ring his home again for fear of phone taps and listening devices.

They met at the Templestowe Hotel public bar about 8pm. Lipp walked in and immediately ordered Williams to remove the batteries from his mobile phone and place the phone on the ground.

He said he feared police would be able to activate the telephones through remote control and listen to nearby conversations.

The question remains as to how Lipp, an apparent crime novice, knew so much about police methods and seemed so well briefed on electronic surveillance.

At first it appeared that all Lipp wanted was some advice. He wanted an old vault door to practise safe-breaking techniques. He asked if Williams could get plans of the factory and he even suggested the safe man make a cardboard template of the Sigma door with instructions marked on it for Lipp to follow.

He wanted to know where he could buy a magnetic drill capable of piercing the safe. But as they chatted Williams realised he would be wanted for more than just technical advice. His old car buddy wanted him for a hands-on role.

'During the conversation George hinted on several occasions that perhaps I could come along with them and actually open the vaults for Lipp and his co-offenders. I tried to ignore the hints and really didn't commit one way or the other. Towards the end of the conversation he said we could team up and knock over many of these factories and make very large sums of money,' he said.

'George made a comment along the lines that with my skills I could become a millionaire.' During the meeting Lipp brought another one of his gang, Brian Zerna, who just sat and glared at Williams, trying to intimidate him. Lipp told Williams that if another man in the safe industry 'gave them up he'd be whacked'.

On September 11 Williams met Lipp again at the Templestowe Hotel. He was instructed by police to introduce the undercover agent Dave as a safe expert from Adelaide and then gracefully withdraw, leaving the detective to gather the incriminating information.

That was the plan, but undercover police operations have a life of their own and have to be continually refined, as the unexpected becomes the reality.

Lipp wanted Williams to be part of the team or the deal was off. Graeme Sayce was left with a black and white problem. If *Operation Baxley* was to continue Williams would have to go undercover for as long as it took. He would have to put his own business on hold in a bid to help police infiltrate a gang that had already said it would kill if needed.

Sayce put it to Williams to be the inside contact. This average man from middle Melbourne agreed – even though he knew there were real risks. It was to last nine weeks – 'It felt like a year' – although it took nearly two years before the final legal case was to be completed.

Williams and Dave met Lipp and secretly recorded incriminating conversations in Lower Plenty, the Templestowe Hotel, a Little Bourke Street restaurant and Hungry Jacks in Bulleen as they planned the job to the smallest detail.

They recorded Lipp's proposal: 'The money, look, the money's not a problem ... hundred (thousand) each. All right ... probably be paid 25 per cent up front and the balance a week later.'

They exposed the level of planning: 'We know all the entries and all the exits. Mate, we've been doing this for nine months,' Lipp said. They were confident they knew the security system. 'Put it this way, man, we've set the bugs (system) off on purpose, for two and a half hours, we couldn't be bothered hanging around,' he said.

Police set up a surveillance post near the Sigma factory and on Sunday September 15, Lipp, Zerna and two other men were spotted by drug squad detectives entering the site. At 9.07pm a detective monitoring secret cameras hidden in the vault room, watched as two men in dark clothing and wearing balaclavas methodically checked the room for nearly an hour.

The team's car was seen to leave the area around 10.50pm.

As the gang prepared to put in their own camera into the vault room they spotted the mini police system already installed. Instead of realising they were hot, cutting their losses and leaving, they attached their own camera into the police system and were able to see the vault room was being monitored.

Sayce was to find later that Lipp and his crew studied the Robert De Niro gangster movie *Heat* to pick up hints. 'But they failed to pick up the message from the criminal character that De Niro played. When there is the slightest doubt, walk away. These blokes let greed colour their judgment. Even after they found our camera they continued and talked themselves into believing the gear was there to find internal thefts.'

Lipp said: 'They could be checking staff … somethin' gone missin' too.'

He seemed upset that someone had beaten him to installing the camera. 'The staff don't know that, no-one knows about it except me and … hey, we had the same system … it was the same hole we were gonna go to and put ours in.'

According to Sayce, the criminals wanted to believe anything that would allow them to pull the raid. 'They had done so much planning they just couldn't let it go.'

Lipp answered the problem with typical bravado: 'Flash a brown eye at them … it was our idea to put a camera in anyway'. Even though the gang expected to become wealthy through the raid they still seemed to vastly underestimate what sort of money they could make.

Lipp: 'At Croydon they got dexamphetamine … pure … pick it up and walk out with a million bucks. Don't have to do nothin'. It's pure, they're the only ones that make it. The only place it's made in all of Australia is at Croydon, no-one else makes it and it's just sitting there … It's worth more than gold, apparently. Walk around this joint. It's potentially, I reckon, about two or three million dollars … How slack are they?'

Dave commented dryly, 'No wonder a hundred grand is no drama.'

As the night gets closer Lipp becomes more excited, saying there would be a bonus for the safe experts. 'We might turn around and say three hundred grand for youse.'

On the night of the raid Paul Elliott took over as the leader. He provided each of the six members of the team with a code number, a two-way radio and designated job.

They were also wearing stop watches – similar to those worn by the gang in *Heat*. When police asked them later why they had the stop watches they just shrugged. If it was good enough for De Niro …

Elliott gave the orders: 'Number one, he'll be watching the main gates, right. Number two here, he'll be on the roof … watching all the streets on the other side and number three, he'll be watching the paddocks.

'Make sure everything's sweet. All right. Then we'll call youse in, the gate'll be open for you by number one here. He'll open the gate for you. Brian knows where to drive the van he'll be directed anyway. He'll drive it around the back, reverse into the garage and then youse just sit tight until we've got past the bugs.

'Right, I've got hoods (balaclavas) for youse just in case you didn't bring any,' Elliott said. It was while sitting in the van that Williams noticed that Elliott had a .32 handgun. He didn't know that Elliott also had four loaded magazines for the weapon. 'I was shitting myself,' Williams said later.

He had good reason to doubt his decision to go undercover. He was going into a drug factory wearing overalls and a dark balaclava on a filthy night with armed offenders, knowing the Special Operations Group were planning an ambush.

'I was just praying they would know who were the good guys.'

Zerna drove the van and had stuck Telstra logos on the side to divert suspicion.

They had magnetic drills, police scanners, Telstra uniforms, communications gear, devices to cover the infra-red sensors, stop watches, torches, a generator and a roll-up ladder. They entered Sigma after Wills cut the bolt and chain on the gate. He then replaced it with one of their own so as not to create suspicion.

Lipp and Elliott were to break in. They would then come back to get Williams and Dave to make the final break into the vault. Dave then saw that Elliott was carrying the semi-automatic pistol.

After the two broke into the factory Dave saw Elliott in his black balaclava sprint back to the van to get more equipment. Lipp later came back and abused the safe experts because they had found another infra-red sensor on the vault. But even with the unexpected problem they were finally able to cripple the security system.

'Elliott also appeared excited and said that they'd done their bit and it was now up to us and all we had to do was walk straight up and drill it,' Dave later said.

'Elliott said that there was only twenty minutes to go and we could celebrate and "go get it" or similar.' They then carried the large safe drill into the factory. 'Elliott told me to go make him a millionaire.' Lipp kept telling the safe men to relax and not to stress. He said it was almost over. He was right, although his version of the conclusion was horribly wrong.

The break-in took hours longer than anticipated. Detectives sitting off the site wanted to avoid spooking the gang and so instructed police not to use their sirens. But fate played a hand. In the wet weather there was a bad car accident near the factory and police and ambulance vehicles arrived with emergency sirens blaring.

The gang stopped work and sat in silence until satisfied all was well before daring to move again. They were inside the premises for more than four hours.

Despite their caution they failed to spot more than 50 police, including drug squad, surveillance, Special Operation Group, air-wing members and uniformed members.

When the police moved in Wills made a run for it. But he wasn't as fast as the police dog that brought him to earth. Elliott was found hiding under some bushes in the sodden dirt.

One SOG man's position was in a small hollow in the ground. As it rained his hiding spot filled with water. He was within metres of the passing criminals and could not move even when the water had risen to nearly cover his face.

As they sat handcuffed in a police car, Wills complained that a police dog had savaged him. 'Yeah, well I was attacked by a bush,' Zerna said blackly, referring to the SOG man who came out of the shrubbery to take him down.

After their arrest Sayce walked up to Lipp and told him, poker faced: 'Your planning was excellent, full marks for the preparation, the execution was a bit slow – but your choice of staff was terrible.'

Williams, another citizen and four police later received a Chief Commissioner's commendation for their roles in

Operation Baxley. The then Chief Commissioner, Neil Comrie, said: 'The force has taken the rare step of awarding (Williams) a Citizen's Commendation because of the vital role he played in thwarting a very serious crime.

'His initiative and courage exposed him to potential danger and directly assisted in stopping a flood of drugs reaching our streets.

'As a result he has been recognised for "exemplary service to the community".'

In October 1998 all four suspects finally pleaded guilty in the County Court to burglary charges. Lipp was sentenced to six and a half years with a minimum of four, Elliott to five years with a minimum of three, Wills to one year's jail with two years suspended and Zerna to four years with a minimum of two and a half years. Police believe there may have been a fifth man, a financier, who was never caught. The planning seemed too good for gifted amateurs.

The police case was overwhelming but the burglars' decision to plead guilty means that many questions that would have been asked in open court remain unanswered.

For instance, how did four men with no major criminal experience get involved in such a complex plot?

Who told them of the massive amounts of amphetamines available in the company? Who financed the operation and who would have moved the drugs if they had got away with it?

Lipp's lawyer conceded in court that his client was an organiser of the scheme – but claimed he was 'not at the top of the tree'. The court was told Lipp's father died when he was eleven and after leaving school four years later he joined the family business of importing and selling chainsaws.

According to evidence given in court, he completed an apprenticeship at the business and ended up the service manager of a national company. But his real love was cars and at 23 he became a motor mechanic. Two years later he began his own construction business but interest rates of 21 per cent made it difficult, forcing him to sell his house. He was married with three children, one of whom had serious health problems. 'Despite having sold the family home and put the money into the business, the firm continued to lose money and so at the time of these offences my client was under huge financial stress,' his lawyer said.

Brian Zerna, the court was told, was 'a man of modest and sober habits'. He was married with three children, employed and described as extremely quiet and patient.

These are not master criminals. Police believe there was a major gangster behind the scheme, a man with the money to finance the operation and the contacts to move the drugs. Why he pulled out remains a mystery.

He is a man rumoured to have been involved in some of Australia's major crimes, including the Great Bookie Robbery in 1976.

But it is just that – a rumour. One thing is sure: he will never be charged for his alleged involvement in the Sigma safebreaking foiled by *Operation Baxley*.

Judge Campbell made a point of praising the police operation. 'Although it is not common to do so, I think special commendation should go to (Williams) and the undercover policeman. Without (Williams's) honesty and co-operation in harrowing and dangerous circumstances, the prisoners' plans might have had a very different outcome. The undercover policeman demonstrated great courage in carrying out his duties under the conditions and circumstances in which he found himself.

'This was a most audacious scheme which, had it succeeded, would have made the participants a great deal of money.'

The court was told that Elliott was making real attempts to rehabilitate himself and had worked while on bail.

He had, in fact, found employment with a security alarm company.

• IT was not the last time that the Sigma chemical company was to become unwittingly involved in major crime.

In 1996 – the same time as *Operation Baxley* – police began to buy chemicals from Sigma as part of so-called controlled delivery sting operations.

The chemicals, bought at heavily discounted wholesale prices were onsold through a network of informers and undercover operatives to amphetamines producers.

Police would then track the drugs to arrest the manufacturers. Police said the controlled deliveries resulted in a series of arrests but much of the chemicals were lost during the undercover projects.

The method became so popular that the Victoria police became Sigma's biggest national client and police made a massive profit – the money, more than $200,000, was kept in an undeclared bank account.

In 2001 Chief Commissioner Christine Nixon banned the method after allegations of corruption and lack of accountability and replaced the drug squad with the major drug investigation division.

Bandidos president Michael Kulakowski (left) … a former soldier and rodeo rider who drove a Mercedes. Shot dead at a Sydney nightclub.

'God forgives, Bandidos don't.'

Something to look up to … sons of Bandidos members with their fathers and friends.

A Harley Davidson bought by undercover police from the Bandidos for $17,000. 'We were ripped off.'

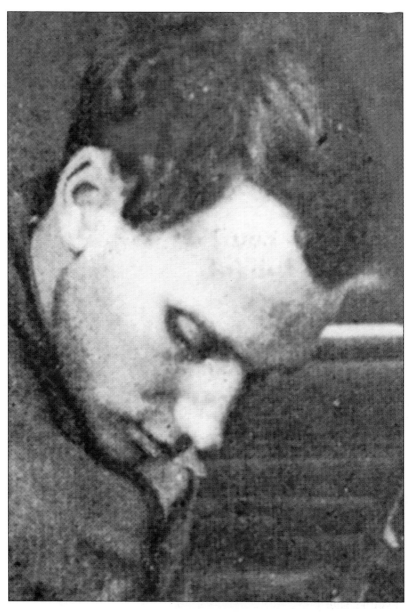

Derek Ernest Percy … bad, but not mad.

Yvonne Tuohy was murdered as a man called Armstrong was about to walk on the moon.

Shane Spiller ... took on a killer with his tomahawk, but it wasn't enough to save his friend. He is now missing and may be a murder victi.

Shane Spiller as a little boy ... a killer stole his childhood and destroyed his life.

The *Full Frontal* television dummy (above and right) used in an elaborate sting operation to catch corrupt lawyer Philip 'Mr Laundry' Peters (left). He wanted his enemy Peter Kypri drugged and murdered.

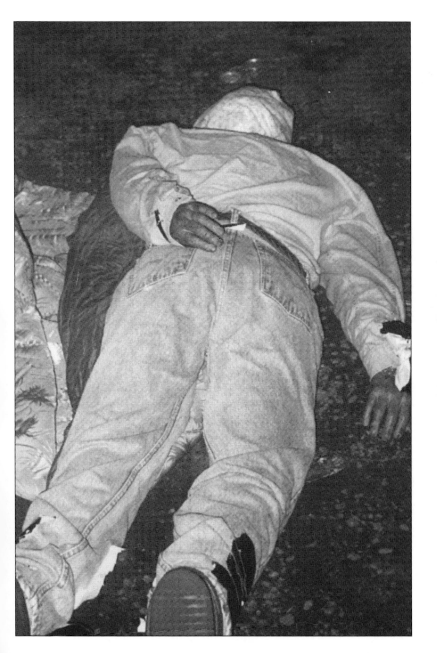

Jane Thurgood-Dove … the innocent victim of a mistaken identity hit.

Peter Kypri … a man they love to hate. Embroiled in three murder plots. LEFT: Kypri with his then lawyer Keith Allan.

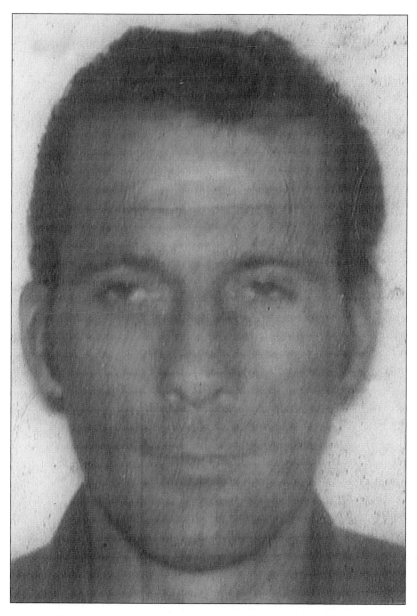

Ron Williams ... a battler taken in by a cold-blooded killer.

Alex MacDonald … murdered Williams to take his identity.

The Commonwealth Bank at Port Douglas ... MacDonald's hostage plan failed for the strangest reason.

The Chinese Vice Premier, Zhu Rongji, enjoyed Port Douglas.

Armed robber's kit ... number plates, cash and pain killers.

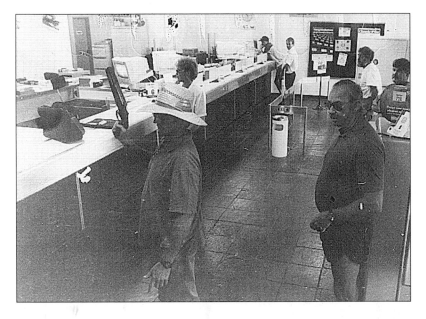

The cool cat in the hat … Alex MacDonald, wearing his distinctive hat, robs Airlie Beach bank in Queensland.

The moment of truth … video pictures capture the moment killer Paul Charles Denyer's story falls apart. He uses the wrong hand to describe how he cut his hand sharpening a knife, then realises his error. A fumbled explanation from Denyer prompts Detective Senior Sergeant Rod Wilson to remark in question 738: 'I don't think you're telling the truth.'

CHAPTER 16

A MAN'S BEST FRIEND

'He was well aware that one day he may die saving my life.'

PETER Cecil Reid was a real estate agent with a reputation in the industry as a deal closer. As he drove to a lunchtime meeting in the bayside Melbourne suburb of Brighton, he was confident this one would be no different.

His gut feeling was the punter he planned to meet was ready to settle and there would be no need for his well-practised sales pitch.

As Reid turned the wheel of his luxury coupe into a building site in Cadby Street at precisely 12.37pm, he could see promising signs. His man was already there waiting – a sure sign he was ready to be hooked. But Reid was more than a real estate salesman. As well as selling property, he had been developing a second lucrative line over the years. He was a drug-dealer – and a pretty cunning one at that.

But this time, the usually careful Reid was to allow love of money and hunger for a deal to blunt his sharp survival instinct. He was about to meet a client he knew only as John Brown – a man, he had been assured by a contact, who could supply large quantities of cannabis. Reid already had a buyer lined up and could see a big profit in being a middleman.

Brown looked the part – and so he should have. He was one of only a few undercover police trained to look and act like high-level drug dealers.

Brown gave Reid a heat-sealed bag containing almost a kilogram of top-quality cannabis. It was the first part of a proposed nine kilo shipment Reid wanted to sell on to a waiting client.

Reid put the package into his car boot and said he would take it to his customer and, if he were happy, he would buy the rest.

But the deal-closer couldn't leave it there. He wanted to sell as well as buy. Reid volunteered that he could supply any amount of heroin to Mr Brown and his friends.

He said he could supply heroin that 'had the edge taken off it' (diluted) for $6500 an ounce or heroin direct from the importer (the 'Rolls Royce') for $8500.

He took a small sample from a black screw-top container, the size of a lip balm holder, and gave it to his new contact. Brown immediately agreed to buy an ounce of the diluted heroin.

Reid called a paging service to leave a message for his heroin distributor – to contact him under the alias 'Ken'. Reid ordered one 'Mercedes' (one step down from a Rolls Royce) to be delivered later that day. It was as easy as ringing for a pizza.

Police would later find that 'Ken' was Mr X – a heavy heroin and cocaine trafficker.

The meeting ended with Brown and Reid agreeing to meet again later in the day. It was 12.52 on June 25, 1997. They had become business partners in just fifteen minutes. That's how it works for many drug dealers.

But, for police, it had taken years to build a dossier on Reid. He was one of hundreds who drift into major drug investigations without ever becoming prime targets.

His criminal history was minor. It included theft from a motor car, unlawful assault and cultivating a narcotic plant. He was also charged with owning an uncontrollable attack dog. Like most estate agents and drug traffickers, he always had his mobile phone on him – fearing he might miss a golden deal. He was once charged with using it while driving. He was a hands-on, not a hands-free, type of guy.

The drug and property dealer lived on his nerves – and it showed. It was noted on his police file that he 'appears rather highly strung'. Drugs can do that – for he was a ferocious user as well as a prodigious dealer.

Reid had been a target in Australian Federal Police and Victoria Police operations codenamed *Stealth* and *Sambuca*. Police believed he organised the sale of a house for a drug dealer who was in financial trouble.

According to police intelligence, 'Reid is heavily involved in heroin trafficking and has expressed interest in dealing in other drugs such as cannabis and cocaine. He has boasted of selling several pounds of cut and recompressed heroin on a weekly basis. He is looking to expand his market'.

In another report, detectives said: 'Reid was a wholesale source of supply of heroin and part of a well-organised heroin distribution syndicate, operating in Victoria, NSW and South Australia'.

While police knew plenty about the hyper deal-maker – even down to the birthmark on his left upper leg – they lacked an 'in' to gather evidence.

Enter Mr Brown.

Just over two hours after their building-site chat, the pair met again in the car park behind a real estate agency. Reid took a silver foil of rock heroin from his pocket. Mr Brown handed him $6500.

As they chatted, Reid couldn't resist another sales pitch. His syndicate, he said, imported five blocks of pure heroin at a time and if Brown were prepared to pay $400,000 for two he could have $25,000 discount. 'We wholesale, not retail,' he told the undercover officer.

Reid said he had another five ounces of diluted heroin available if Brown wanted it at $30,250. It was the hard sell for hard drugs. He added that if his customer was happy with the quality of Brown's cannabis, he would buy nine kilos every two weeks.

Brown looked around and spotted Mr X watching. Reid explained his supplier was there to 'make sure nothing went wrong'.

Each man agreed to test the quality of the other's drugs to see if they could do business. Mr Brown was confident his tests would be accurate. The undercover policeman took his ounce of heroin back to the forensic science laboratory. It tested 54 per cent pure. Not bad for the first buy.

Reid liked being a drug dealer but, like many traffickers, he thought he was too smart to be caught. He once had an argument with a uniformed policeman over a parking spot and, enraged, stormed into his real estate office, ranting that he 'would get that copper'. He immediately rang the police ethical standards department to lodge a complaint. While he was on hold, police listening devices recorded him snorting drugs on his desk.

Soothed by his chemical crutch, he lost interest and hung up.

LIKE many complex drug investigations, *Operation Carron* had begun with a seemingly unrelated case. Almost two years earlier, police had arrested a man considered the most prolific amphetamines manufacturer in Victoria. He was known to have set up or controlled seven 'speed labs' and was connected with many big drug syndicates.

Drug squad detectives spend years trying to cultivate informers. They need insiders to help set up stings to trap syndicate heads.

Experienced drug importers and distributors insulate themselves by dealing with only people they know. Undercover police – no matter how believable – cannot just knock on the door and expect to be accepted. The key to the door is an introduction from a trusted contact.

The amphetamine manufacturer was trusted – but could police make him turn? Detective Senior Sergeant Wayne Strawhorn, of the drug squad, spent more than a year trying to persuade the man to become an informer. In the end, it was a call from the other side that pushed him over.

Peter Reid, the crooked estate agent, wanted the speed manufacturer to buy heroin on a weekly basis. What Reid didn't know was that while his prospective buyer saw amphetamines as a commercial product, he saw heroin as inherently evil because his wife's sister had died from a heroin overdose. It was enough for him to agree to work with Strawhorn. He was given a code name to protect his identity. He became informer 4/65.

Operation Carron started on June 12, 1997. For a complex investigation, it ended quickly. It involved Victoria Police, the National Crime Authority, Customs and the South Australian drug squad.

Despite all the planning, undercover operations rarely go

smoothly. They run on improvisation and there can be no script. Police try to plan for all possibilities, but their targets are dangerous and unpredictable.

The undercover detective must have extensive back-up – a controller, surveillance cover, technical support and a team of investigators. Despite all that, the undercover must be able to sense danger and know when to walk away.

In *Operation Carron*, police were to extend their undercover capacity to its limits as the operation took on a life of its own and expanded into Romanian and Asian organised crime groups.

Police were to use five teams of detectives on the case at one time and run three connected investigations into a drug structure with links in South America, South-East Asia, Pakistan, Germany and Russia.

Police used seven undercover operatives, masquerading as major marijuana growers, heroin buyers, corrupt custom officers and gunmen. They were also able to infiltrate the syndicate, using their own men as drug couriers.

The investigation was to spill out of Victoria into Queensland, New South Wales and South Australia. It underlined how state and national borders do not restrict big drug syndicates, whereas law enforcement can be hampered by geographic restrictions.

Police were to identify criminals involved in selling heroin, cocaine, amphetamines, hashish and marijuana. Ultimately, the Queensland arm of the syndicate avoided exposure because of the lack of uniform national drug laws. Victorian drug squad detectives wanted to conduct sting operations on the Gold Coast but Queensland laws prohibited the plan. Six years later, police believed the Queensland cartel was still operating.

In *Operation Carron*, police ran twenty separate undercover drug buys and deliveries in five months. Locations included a real estate agency, the Airport Hilton in Sydney, the Keg Restaurant in Chadstone, two luxury Melbourne hotels, the Fitzroy Gardens, the Adelaide Hilton and Little Bourke Street.

Police used eight surveillance teams and had to write off $100,000 in one undercover buy just to establish credibility with syndicate heads. Some of the heroin bought and tested by police was 83 per cent pure and still in the original wrapper, direct from the importer.

After the five-month investigation, police used 150 officers to make 18 raids on one day. One of the main targets never got to court. He was shot dead while on bail.

Police seized almost 3000 grams of high-grade heroin, the equivalent of more than 10,000 street-heroin 'hits'. They also seized cocaine, a hydroponic cannabis crop, eight cars, firearms and stolen property.

All because Peter Reid couldn't walk away from one more deal.

REID was introduced to the undercover policeman we will call Joe Black on October 8, 1997. Black masqueraded as a Mildura cannabis producer looking to move into the lucrative heroin field.

Reid was eager to find a regular marijuana connection, so he took the bait. He told Black he had three regular heroin buyers but was keen to 'create another channel'.

Reid was quick to give Black advice on the drug trade. He told his new connection never to keep cash and drugs in the same place.

As the rental manager in his real estate agency, Reid was adept at judging the types who would make good tenants and not default on rent. He used that experience in drug dealing. He told Black that he should only sell drugs to people who had jobs because they would not have to commit crime to pay.

The only drawback was that if they were arrested, they were likely to try to do deals with police, he said. Reid was nostalgic for the 'good old days' of drug trafficking. Back in the mid-1980s, he declared, drug dealers were 'more honourable'.

Next day, Black went to the real estate office and paid Reid $3500 for about half an ounce of heroin. Within two weeks, Reid asked him if he could supply shipments of cannabis every three months, a kilo of cocaine every ten days and regular supplies of hashish. No harm in thinking big. Reid said his syndicate bought directly from Asian heroin importers in Sydney, who would buy up to $300,000 worth at a time. Reid contacted Mr X, a former panel beater turned heroin wholesaler. He said he could supply unlimited heroin.

Reid complained that the glut of heroin on the market was cutting into his profits. He didn't want to drop his standards – if he couldn't make at least $4000 a deal it wasn't worth the effort, he said.

He also complained that an associate had ripped him off – stealing $50,000 by shaving twenty per cent off two blocks of heroin. He said it was just greed. The man was making $7000 a week and didn't need to steal.

He declared the man would have to sign over the deed to his house to pay back the debt.

Black said he had made around $300,000 from his last cannabis crop and Reid, ever helpful, said he could launder the money through a real-estate deal.

Reid was not only addicted to making deals, he was addicted to the product he sold. He regularly smoked heroin in his office. When police finally raided his office they found a scorched piece of silver-foil and his rolled-up business card.

ONE of the great organised crime myths is that syndicates are divided strictly on ethnic lines. *Operation Carron* proved that in modern multicultural Australia cash crosses all boundaries and greed speaks all languages.

Reid, the Anglo-Australian estate agent, relied on Mr X, a powerful member of the Melbourne Romanian crime cell, who in turn had direct access to Sydney's Asian heroin syndicates. They were good for each other – Reid found customers who wanted bulk drugs and Mr X had access to heaps of heroin. Mr X was part of a loose group of Romanians who had direct links to Chinese heroin importers in Sydney. He had developed contacts around Australia to sell the heroin he bought in the original 12.5-ounce blocks.

Financial figures quoted about drug syndicates are often as meaningless as Monopoly money. But in this case, police identified that the main Chinese leader in Sydney gambled around $35million in Australian casinos and is believed to have moved $40million off shore in the 1990s.

Mr X had access to his own safe house in Hoppers Crossing where he would cut each block of heroin with four ounces of sugar, then recompress and rewrap the slabs for sale.

From the outside, it looked like a typical suburban home. There was a car in the drive, the lawns were mown and the lights would turn on. But no-one lived there.

Inside, police found electric scales, steel presses, blenders, sugar, plastic bags and hydraulic jacks to recompress the powder. 'It was one of the best safe houses we have seen,' a drug squad insider said.

The safe house was set up by well-known drug dealer – Dan 'The Man' Mosut. He was a man who, despite having no apparent legitimate income, owned a mansion, complete with a satellite dish to give him access to international communications. In the Romanian underworld, he was known as the King of the Gypsies.

Mr X met Mr Brown, the undercover policeman, in the lounge of the Melbourne Hyatt around 2.30pm on August 6, 1997. The drug dealer was distracted. He was worried his heroin supply network was unravelling and he needed alternatives.

Mr X moved $300,000 of heroin a week and he knew that if the quality began to drop he would lose clients all over Australia. He might have been a drug dealer but he was keen on quality control.

Mr X told Mr Brown he had been having trouble with his heroin supply since Asian gangsters kidnapped the wife of one of his big suppliers in Sydney. The career drug dealer said he needed a change. He was looking for new markets and a better standard of client. Mr X was worried about proposed legal heroin trials and thought his market could be swallowed if addicts could find a legal source of drugs. Cocaine was the future, he thought.

He told Brown he had a new business plan. He would import cocaine every four to eight weeks, depending on the demand. His plan was to begin with one-kilo lots and expand to ten-kilo importations. He said he already had access to a 50-kilo stockpile.

Mr X said he knew the market. He had rich people 'begging for' cocaine but couldn't provide it in the pure form. He planned to bring the drugs into Melbourne through his contacts in Eastern Europe. He already had connections with the 'factory' in South America to get pure cocaine at $5000 a kilo.

He knew it would not be easy. He had already lost two women couriers and two kilos of pure cocaine in Russia. The women were in Rio de Janeiro and had some trouble getting their air tickets. During the delay, one of the girls began an affair with a man whom Mr X believed was an undercover policeman. When they finally got their flight, police were waiting for them at the Moscow airport. He said they were bashed and injected with truth serum before being sentenced to four years' jail.

He also claimed he had five kilos in Europe ready to import but, as he didn't have a secure route into Melbourne, he was prepared to sell it overseas.

Mr X told Brown he had been in the business ten years and had been caught only once – when he dealt with the wrong people. He bragged that he had learnt his lesson. He was wrong.

At 3.15pm, Mr X said he needed to go to the toilet and asked informer 4/65 to go with him. When they walked in, Mr X turned and frisked him, looking for a wire. He found nothing because there was nothing to find. Earlier, at the table, he had patted down Brown and found nothing. The undercover policeman had wedged himself against the railing next to the table and Mr X just failed to reach the recording device hidden on the left side of his body.

Mr X complained that the then new commissioner in NSW (Peter Ryan) had restructured his police force and this had resulted in him losing his inside contacts. He needed bent officials to get the green light for his white powders.

He could get heroin from Pakistan and cocaine from South America but he needed protection. What he wanted from Brown was a corrupt customs officer who could ensure his couriers got through Melbourne Airport.

On September 10, Mr X met Brown in the luxurious Sofitel Hotel in Melbourne. The drug dealer said he had spent a week building his heroin business in Cairns and Darwin, where he could get $14,500 an ounce.

But he was concerned with his overheads, complaining it was costing him $10,000 a week to run shipments to Perth using a female courier accompanied by a supervisor.

But the purpose of the chat was to push for a meeting with the corrupt customs officer so they could set up the cocaine importation business. The next day Mr X met another undercover, 'Chris', who played the role of the bent customs officer the syndicate needed. They discussed their plans in room 910 of Melbourne's Hilton Hotel. Mr X was guarded. He wanted to know how his cocaine would arrive safely, as he had been burned before. 'We lost one million in the same arrangement,' he said.

'We have the stuff now ... everything is prepared.'

Chris explained they needed a suitcase that was identifiable so that when it arrived with the couriers at Melbourne Airport he could grab it before it was subjected to routine customs checks. Mr X loved the idea and paid $300 for Chris to buy the suitcase.

Mr X said he had a seemingly respectable German married couple, aged in their 50s, ready to courier his cocaine to Melbourne. He assured Chris he would have a supervisor on the same flight to make sure all went smoothly.

OPERATION Carron gave an insight into the drug world. Scheming entrepreneurs look for the best deal they can find. They fall out, only to collaborate again when they see a potential profit. It is a non-exclusive club and no-one admits to being a member.

Mr X was prepared to sell his heroin around Australia and his next plan was to take over the heroin market in Adelaide. What he needed was a trusted courier to supply his South Australian connection.

Brown introduced him to another undercover detective, who used the name Broadbent. Mr X gave Broadbent five small packages containing a total of four ounces of heroin. He also gave his new courier $800 for expenses.

Next day Broadbent met the buyer in the Adelaide Hilton bar. The South Australian connection was former light middleweight boxing champion Bora Altintas – known in the ring as the 'Adelaide Assassin'.

Altintas was a gangster – and a bad one. In 1989, he was sentenced to eleven years and four months' jail for heroin trafficking, armed robbery and assault. He served five years before he was released.

Only a year before his meeting with Broadbent, he almost died when shot repeatedly at close range with a shotgun as he sat in his car. His boxer's reflexes made him curl under the dash when he was attacked. It wasn't great protection, but it was enough. At first surgeons thought they would have to amputate his right arm but they managed to save the limb, although they could not remove more than 120 pellets in his body.

Altintas took an ounce of heroin and paid $7000 in instalments. After a phone call from Mr X, Broadbent handed over the remaining three ounces on credit.

The undercover policeman met Mr X at the Keg Restaurant in Chadstone in Melbourne at 4.15pm on November 5. He handed the drug dealer the $7000 and Mr X peeled off $800 in notes as payment. Altintas was later arrested in the final sweep – but the Adelaide Assassin was to have greater problems than the Victorian drug squad.

While on bail, in September 1998, the boxer was again blasted with a shotgun in an Adelaide street. This time he didn't survive. As the great Joe Louis once said of an opponent: 'He can run but he can't hide'.

THERE is no loyalty in the drug business and middlemen are constantly trying to find a better source. Darren Michael Jackson, a former insulation fitter from Taylors Lakes, had been buying almost 170 grams of heroin from the Reid-Mr X syndicate every week. But he was beginning to tire of the unreliability and wanted a supplier who could provide top-quality heroin on demand.

He knew the man he needed was a well-known dealer from Melbourne's west – Dragon Arnautovic. Police and gangsters rarely called him by his real name. Everyone knew him as Machinegun Charlie.

He was given the name not because of a love for guns but because of his skill as a champion kickboxer. In the ring he was known for quick combination kicks – like a machine gun. Charlie was tough and dangerous. In his last match he fought several rounds with a broken arm. Police had been chasing Arnautovic for years and he was the key target of a drug squad investigation code-named *Hamada*.

Arnautovic was a big heroin seller who had been caught several times. But each time he was caught he learnt from his mistakes and he had become a most cunning operator. He trusted few people, tried to work alone and kept a savage dog for security.

He would take his well-trained and blood-loyal guard dog, Gus, in his van when he went to deal drugs. While he talked to a buyer or supplier, the dog would bark savagely inside the van. The message was clear. You were dangerously close to a crazed, slobbering monster – who had a dog that was just as dangerous.

The Dragon had a secret compartment in the van where he would hide his heroin. Detectives said he would buy about 500 grams of high-grade heroin and then cut the drugs into one-ounce lots. He would hide his stash around the western suburbs of Melbourne in parks and public buildings. His logic was simple and effective. He did not want to be caught with large amounts of heroin and, by distributing the drugs widely, he was less likely to be ripped off and lose his stockpile.

One of his hiding spots was in a dead-end street in Sunshine. Police saw him retrieve drugs there fifteen times. They also saw him go to the Altona North Baseball Centre at least eight times. They later found about 25 ounces hidden in Berocca containers stuffed in gaps in the corrugated iron walls at the centre.

When Arnautovic was in jail, fellow inmates tried to find out where he had hidden his remaining heroin stash. He let it slip that his supply was buried at a Footscray soccer ground. On a dark and stormy night soon after, two criminal groups went to the soccer ground and began digging. They found nothing but left the pitch looking like a wombat sanctuary.

Arnautovic was good, but Jackson showed police the door and they were able to kick it down. Jackson had been supplying heroin to an undercover policeman he knew as Jack Jones. He sold Jones 28 grams of high-grade heroin for $7500 while they sat on a garden seat next to Captain Cook's cottage in the Fitzroy Gardens.

Jackson bent down and grabbed a paper bag containing the 80 per cent pure heroin from a garden bed as lunchtime tourists explored the cottage just a few metres away.

In the next deal, Jackson drove Jones to an isolated area at Laverton. They parked near a yellow van; police identified the van's driver as Arnautovic. Jackson walked to a tree stump and grabbed a package containing 56 grams of heroin.

On November 18, Jones and Jackson met at the Tarmac Hotel in Altona North. The drug dealer was to supply 250 grams of heroin for $67,500. The two met Arnautovic at the Altona North Baseball Complex and he handed over heroin in plastic bags.

As the Special Operations Group moved in, Machinegun Charlie judged the odds and dropped, face down, in surrender. But Gus the guard dog jumped on his master's back and refused to give up. He was determined to protect Charlie, come what may. It was a bad move. The SOG shot the big dog dead. A saddened Arnautovic was arrested without a yelp.

When Jackson was arrested, his automatic Beretta pistol fell from his back holster. There was a bullet in the spout and another eight in the magazine. Jackson later told police there were rabbits at the baseball stadium and he wanted to shoot them.

Police found a further 560 grams of heroin hidden at the centre by Arnautovic.

DRUG dealers can be lazy, unreliable, paranoid and often don't turn up to meetings. For police trying to organise co-ordinated raids around Australia, the odds of total success are long. It is bad enough trying to grab one group of dealers but, in *Operation Carron*, it required 150 police pouncing on several major figures at the same time so that none could be pre-warned.

They had to organise three big sting operations at the same time. Undercover police were given huge amounts of cash for the 'buy-bust' climax of the investigation. They were authorised to handle three lots of cash for the final arrest phase: $56,000, $67,000 and $348,000.

Police moved in on November 18, 1997, to run eighteen co-ordinated raids. One key target was Mr X. Police watched him drop his child off at school before going off for his day of drug dealing.

He went to The Glen Shopping Centre, bought some crockery at David Jones and then had a short black coffee outside the up-market department store while making calls on his mobile phone. He was wearing blue jeans, a blue shirt and a black vest and was carrying a black satchel.

He went to the Keg Restaurant for a meeting with Altintas and another man at 12.05pm.

He drove to several shops in the eastern suburbs and, after a short conversation with two Asian men, returned to his car with a brown paper bag. At 1.41pm he drove into Springvale Crematorium. Police believe he had heroin hidden in the cemetery gardens.

He was followed to the Hilton Hotel and arrested in room 705, seconds after he sold an undercover policeman almost 400 grams of heroin. Armed police burst in at 3pm and screamed for him to put his hands above his head. He did what he was told.

The King of the Gypsies, Dan Mosut, was arrested next day. After a long stint on remand he was bailed but within three weeks he was arrested again. This time he threw a kilo of heroin out of the window of his car while being chased. The heroin was worth $1million.

Operation Carron was one of the most complex drug squad investigations ever run. It involved more than twenty undercover drug deals ranging from 0.1 grams of heroin to 350 grams valued at $100,000.

During the operation police seized heroin valued at more than $7million, cocaine, a hydroponic cannabis crop, eight cars, cash, guns, stolen electrical goods, heroin-packaging equipment and a drugs safe house. Heroin seized on the last day alone would have made 5328 street deals.

It took five months from the start until the final arrests, but it was to take the legal system years to deal with the suspects.

In June 1999, Reid was sentenced to a maximum of 32 months' jail after pleading guilty to three charges, including two of heroin trafficking. But twenty months of the sentence was suspended, leaving him to serve a year.

County Court Judge David Jones said: 'Your role as a middle man was important and you were not an insignificant player in the (heroin) trade.'

Judge Jones said Reid had been 'ready, willing and able' to provide high-quality heroin to buyers at short notice. He said his colleagues in the real-estate business would have been unaware of his drug dealing.

In October 1998, Jackson was sentenced to a minimum of two years and eight months for heroin trafficking.

Mosut was sentenced to three years and nine months with a minimum of 21 months for heroin trafficking as part of *Operation Carron*. He was also sentenced to five years, later pushed up to eight years on appeal, over the heroin thrown from his car while on bail. His release date was set for December 21, 2005.

Mr X cannot be identified more than six years after his arrest, as he is yet to appear in court. He has indicated he will plead guilty, but police have not been in a rush to finalise proceedings. As a result of *Operation Carron* police were later to seize 50,000 ecstasy tablets at Crown Casino in Melbourne and a further 30,000 tablets in Sydney. Further information gathered in the investigation led police to seize large stores of heroin in Sydney and Melbourne.

In October 1999, Machinegun Charlie Arnautovic was sentenced to twelve years with a minimum of nine for trafficking heroin worth $1million.

County Court Judge Graeme Crossley said: 'Simply for greed and self-enrichment you set about selling and distributing heroin widely and in significant quantities available to many unfortunate addicts and victims.

'You must have understood the probable consequences on those potential victims.'

Although restricted by incarceration he still managed to maintain an eclectic friendship network. When an extreme fighter, bouncer, part-time actor and lollipop salesman, Willie Thompson, was gunned down in Chadstone in July 2003, Arnautovic found the time and inspiration to write a death notice.

He wrote of the 'many great times in our early days ... even though we drifted apart, and went our separate ways – those memories will stay with me forever'.

In prison Machinegun Charlie still managed to keep up to speed with matters underworld, partially through his own contacts, but also by reading each edition of the *Underbelly* true crime series.

Years later he remained aggrieved, not so much at his arrest but at the sudden death of his dog, Gus, at the hands of the police. 'I have lost a great, if not the best friend a person could have in this world. Yes I am talking about my dog, Gus. The reason I say that my dog was my best friend is because he never set people up, he never told on people, and, most of all, he was well aware that one day he may die saving my life and he was trained and prepared if that situation ever occurred.'

CHAPTER 17

NEVER TO BE RELEASED

*If Percy had been found guilty it might
have been him, not Ronald Ryan, to be
the last man hanged in Australia.*

HE was Victoria's longest-serving prisoner, yet in the eyes of
the law he remained an innocent man. He was declared
mentally ill, yet was repeatedly denied treatment in a psychiatric institution.

In August 1998 the forgotten man of the prison system, Derek
Ernest Percy, was put under public scrutiny for the first time in
29 years when his unique case was reviewed in the Supreme
Court. It was the first time since 1969 that he'd been given the
chance to argue why he should start his journey to freedom and
why society should no longer fear him.

Hundreds of more notorious criminals had passed through
Australian jails in the previous three decades, and few people
remembered Percy. The police who arrested him have long
since retired; his defence lawyer has moved on to be a respected

Supreme Court judge, and many of the jails that had held him had since been closed. He was a model prisoner, seemingly content to play carpet bowls, collect stamps and browse though the cricket statistics he kept on his personal computer.

A seemingly insignificant man who police suspect might be Australia's worst serial killer.

Many in the criminal justice system feared the day this seemingly harmless man would be given a legal opportunity to push for his release. On Derek Percy's first day in a cell Neil Armstrong walked on the moon, John Gorton was Prime Minister, Australian troops were fighting in Vietnam and a bottle of milk, home delivered by the local milkie, cost nineteen cents. Derek Percy was then just 21.

Percy has been in prison since he was arrested for the murder of Yvonne Elizabeth Tuohy, a twelve-year-old girl he abducted, tortured, sexually assaulted and killed on a Westernport beach, near Melbourne, on July 20, 1969.

On the fifth day of his Supreme Court trial in March 1970 he was found not guilty on the grounds of insanity and sentenced to an indefinite term at the Governor's Pleasure.

Three psychiatrists gave evidence of his 'acute psycho-sexual disorder'. A jury found it impossible to believe that a sane man could have hunted, killed and butchered a young girl like Yvonne Tuohy.

It was in the days when only the defence could raise the issue of the accused's sanity and it was also in the days when capital punishment was still on the statute books.

Percy would have been a candidate for the noose if he had been found both sane and guilty.

The defence of insanity was usually only raised as the last throw of the dice in murder cases where the evidence against the suspect was overwhelming.

But it was no real escape hatch. Those found not guilty on the grounds of insanity were sent away under the Governor's Pleasure for an indefinite sentence. Those found guilty of murder were usually released after serving less than twenty years.

Grieving relatives of Yvonne Tuohy were assured on the steps of the court that Percy was so twisted he would never be released.

In the 1960s and 1970s the difference between being found not guilty on the grounds of insanity by a criminal court, and being found guilty was more a case of semantics than of treatment. The terms 'patient' and 'criminal' amounted to much the same thing. No matter what the court found, the sane and insane were taken by prison van and dumped in Pentridge.

But in the 1980s treatment improved and inmates who, in the eyes of the law, were insane, were moved to psychiatric institutions. All, that is, except Percy.

Many were given long-term leave and were no longer seen as dangerous. In 1998 all 47 Governor's Pleasure 'clients', were told their cases would be reviewed in the Supreme Court to decide if they should be freed. One, James Henry Patrick Belsey, who had lived without incident in a Melbourne northern suburb, died only weeks before his case was to be heard. He had been diagnosed with inoperable throat cancer several months earlier.

Belsey stabbed and killed Senior Constable Charles Norman Curson on the steps of Flinders Street station on January 8, 1974, but years later he became balanced enough to live quietly, spending his days helping the aged and infirm with their mundane chores.

The changes to the law were seen by politicians, judges, police and psychiatrists as humane, progressive and just. The

Mental Impairment and Unfitness to be Tried Act took decisions on Governor's Pleasure cases away from politicians and into the hands of judges.

By the mid-1990s about half the Governor's Pleasure clients lived in the community on extended leave and were no longer seen as a danger to anyone. The rest remained under the supervision of government psychiatrists with varying levels of security. But, through it all, Percy was the exception. He stayed in jail and seventeen internal reviews all said he remained as dangerous as the day he was arrested.

GROWING up, Derek Percy was hardly in one area long enough to make friends, but he had always been so self-absorbed the moves did not seem to worry him at least outwardly.

He was the oldest of four boys, one of whom died from diphtheria as an infant when Derek was ten. His father was an electrical mechanic and the family moved from Sydney to Victoria when Derek was eight.

Percy senior was employed by the State Electricity Commission and was often moved from post to post around Victoria. In ten years, the family lived in Melbourne, Warrnambool, and in Victoria's high country. Derek went to seven schools, was brighter than average, and wanted to be an architect.

He seemed a little cold and aloof, but that was put down to the shyness that came from living on the move. No teachers or schoolmates became close enough to him to consider him as anything but ordinary.

As a child he gravitated to solitary activities. He enjoyed stamps, building up a collection of more than 10,000, and he inherited his father's love of yachting, although he preferred to sail on his own. When he was arrested he owned a Moth-class yacht. He loved to read and, like many teenagers, he took to keeping a diary to record his innermost thoughts.

For Percy, the diary was probably more important than for most kids because with his family's constant moving he didn't have a close friend to confide in.

When he was seventeen, his parents stumbled on his diary and began to read. What they saw left them horrified. Their quiet, intelligent oldest son was having bizarre sexual fantasies. Worse, many of the fantasies involved children.

His parents took him to the local, overworked doctor. According to a prison report written years later they were told not to worry, that the writings were 'just a stage of growing up'.

'No other action was taken,' the report said. But it was not just a phase but the beginning of a descent into depravity from which he would never return.

After Derek finished year eleven his father bought a service station near Newcastle, and the family moved again. The boy enrolled in his final year at Gosford High, but he gave up, tired of starting at another new school.

His new plan was to get a job in a drafting office, but he soon found he was under-qualified, and worked with his father in the service station for five months.

At nineteen, he decided to join the navy and was accepted within a week of lodging his application. For the next eighteen months he was stationed at three bases in Victoria and NSW. With an IQ of 122, he was considered a bright prospect and was offered the chance to train as an officer. He was an obvious candidate as he took orders well, was bright and loved the sea.

No-one knew that he was still keeping his diary, and far from 'growing out' of his sadistic sexual fantasies. They were getting worse.

YVONNE Tuohy was quite grown up and independent for a twelve-year-old. During the week she would play with kids from her school, but at weekends she would see the Melbourne families that came to Warneet to relax on the Westernport beaches.

Her parents owned the local shop and ran the boat hiring business, so they knew all the locals and regular holidaymakers by name.

Yvonne liked to explore with a young Melbourne boy, Shane Spiller, who came to Warneet with his parents most weekends. *Apollo 11* was circling the moon when the pair asked their parents if they could go for a hike along a peaceful strip of a Westernport beach on a winter's Sunday afternoon. It was July 20, 1969, in an era when parents were not concerned when their children were out of sight. Most kids still walked to school, played in the local streets and parks until after dark and made their own way to local sport. It wasn't until decades later that parents became paranoid about safety and turned themselves into virtual taxi drivers for their children despite the fact that childhood obesity was a greater danger than random abductions.

Frank Spiller was up a ladder painting the side of the family's weatherboard weekender when his son suggested a walk with Yvonne. It was a fine day with enough sun around to encourage the children to get some fresh air and make their own fun.

The Spillers liked to leave Melbourne at the weekends to spend their time at Warneet, less than an hour from their eastern suburbs home. It was such a nice spot that years later Frank and his wife, Daphne, were to retire there.

Daphne Spiller cut sandwiches for the kids, and Shane grabbed his little tomahawk to cut wood for a billy tea on the beach.

The country girl and the city boy walked down a vehicle track, past a small car park to Ski Beach. Shane noticed a Datsun station wagon with a man sitting behind the wheel. 'I had a feeling that day he was bad news,' Shane Spiller was able to recall almost 30 years later.

In the car was Derek Percy, who had weekend leave from Cerberus Navy Base. He had gone to the Frankston drive-in the previous night, slept in his car and driven to Cowes. On his way back he pulled into Warneet. For years, he was to admit later, he had been having dark thoughts about sexually molesting and killing children, but he was to claim he didn't believe he would ever act on these impulses.

When the kids reached the beach they remained undecided for a few seconds whether to head to a friend's farmhouse or to the nearby township. Confused, they walked in opposite directions for a few moments, and then turned to walk back to each other. They were only metres apart when Percy appeared and grabbed Yvonne. The sailor produced a red-handled dagger and menaced the girl and ordered Shane to come to him, but the young boy pulled his hatchet from his belt and waved it above his head to keep him away.

'We were there for a long time while he was trying to entice me to him. I don't know if it was minutes or seconds,' he was to say of a scene that is burned into his memory.

Percy held the knife to Yvonne's throat, forcing the young girl to try to beg her friend to give up. 'Come back or he'll cut my throat,' she is alleged to have said.

Instead, Shane ran off through 200 metres of scrub to get help. As he neared the road he saw the attacker drive off with Yvonne in the car. He screamed, but a family having a picnic nearby ignored him, later telling police they thought the kids were just playing. One of the parents was later to approach young Shane to apologise. Three decades later, he still could not forgive them.

According to police, Shane Spiller's actions saved his life and ultimately helped catch the killer. They say if he had not gone for help Percy would have killed him as well as Yvonne Tuohy. With no living witness, he may never have been apprehended and certainly would have killed again.

Police said the youngster was an excellent witness who remembered details that led them to Percy. He described the killer's car and sketched a sticker he had seen on the back window. It was the navy insignia.

BIG Jack Ford, then head of the homicide squad, and his team raced to nearby Cerberus Navy Base and found Percy washing blood from his clothes. The first police at the scene were blocked from grabbing the suspect by a navy officer who said they had no rights on the base. One policeman, more practical than diplomatic, threatened to walk through the officer if he didn't move. The officer of the day wisely moved aside and let the police past.

Detectives searched the suspect's locker and found his diary. After reading the chilling details of what he intended to do with children they were in no doubt they had their killer.

According to police this may have been a random attack but there was nothing random about Percy's planning – he had been drawing the blueprint for years.

Again and again he would fantasise about abducting children and he would write in detail of how he planned to kill them. As the hours passed, Yvonne's parents still hoped the crime would be an abduction even a rape but not a murder. But when Ford returned to Warneet it was to bring the worst possible news. He walked up the path to the Spillers' house where the Tuohys were huddled together, waiting. Frank Spiller was outside and asked if there was any hope. Ford shook his head and silently ran a finger across his own throat to indicate the child was dead.

Shane Spiller was a model witness. He gave the police the lead, then on the same night he walked through the navy base car park until he identified the killer's station wagon. Later, at a police line-up, he had to walk up and touch the man who had planned to kill him.

Nothing was too much trouble for the young boy. He posed with his tomahawk for press photographers and didn't miss a court date, giving evidence bravely and honestly, even when he believed a relative of Percy continued to stare and intimidate him inside the court, trying to bully him into a mistake.

At the end of the ordeal grateful police had their sketch artist draw a picture of the boy and gave him a show bag of gifts as a thankyou. Then they then just moved on to the next case.

But Shane Spiller couldn't move on. The bright, observant little boy didn't recover. He was afraid of the dark. He was concerned that Percy would break out and come looking for him.

Family and friends believed that time would heal the wound. They were told to ignore the trauma and to adopt the 'big boys don't cry' approach. Today Spiller would have undergone counselling. Back then he was left alone. Time did not heal the wound but turned it into an angry, festering sore.

He began drinking at fourteen, sought psychiatric help at eighteen. In an era before victim counselling Shane Spiller became increasingly bitter that no-one seemed to understand his pain, fear and loneliness.

Half a lifetime later his friends say, 'He's in a pretty bad way'.

In 1998 police found Spiller, who had tried to lose himself in country NSW, and told him that despite what had been promised, Derek Percy's case was to be reviewed. The man who had stolen Shane Spiller's chance of a normal life was going to be given the opportunity to salvage his.

'It's really knocked me around, mate. I still get nightmares. I spin out. I'm going through a rough trot now,' Spiller was to say afterwards.

The news brought to the surface fears that were never truly hidden. But it also gave him the chance to talk about the ugly things that had festered inside him. Police finally put him in touch with counsellors. He was told that he was not weak, not strange, just a victim who, understandably, couldn't cope.

'I think about it every day of my life, mate. I've searched for help. I think I'm starting to get it now.'

He said he'd been good friends with Yvonne. 'We couldn't have been closer. She meant so much to me. I've never had a decent relationship since then.' Shane Spiller lives on a disability pension, has been unable to hold down full-time work, and keeps a pick-handle next to his bed.

He admits to long-term battles with alcohol and drugs.

'What happened stuffed me. I think I could have had quite a successful life if it wasn't for that.'

He said for years he was frightened Percy would come after him. 'In the line up at Russell Street (police station) I had to pick him. I had to walk up and point right at his nose. The look he gave me. I can still remember it.'

Prison psychiatrist Dr Allen Bartholomew interviewed Percy five days after the killing. 'Bart', as he was known in prison and police circles, had known most of Victoria's maddest and baddest and he had seen the worst and the most bizarre the human condition could provide.

He was as close as you could get to being unshockable.

Percy told Dr Bartholomew he had been watching the two

children when he was 'overcome by a feeling almost a compulsion to do things to kids'. He said that over the previous four years he had weekly fantasies of sexually molesting and killing children. 'These thoughts worried him but he did nothing as he never thought he would be game enough to do it,' the psychiatrist later wrote.

Dr Bartholomew had learnt through dealing with 1500 criminal cases that time was on his side. His experience was that if you sat back you could develop a relationship with even the worst offenders and, with patience, learn their inner secrets.

But not with Percy. His few comments five days after the crime were to be his most animated. No-one could have known the window into his dark psyche was already closing.

AFTER a year in jail Percy described himself as 'a loner, not lonely', but Dr Bartholomew still hoped that over time he would be able to learn more about the distant killer.

'He demonstrates no behavioural evidence of any psychosis and his talk is rational – demonstrating reality-based thinking. He is rather retiring, having little to do with other prisoners, and only superficial relationships with the staff.

'I am quite unable, at this stage, to offer any prognosis regarding the prisoner, but clearly he is a potential danger to the youthful community. At present one can only wait and observe, and later attempt to further investigate the prisoner. I hope that he may be allowed to remain in G Division for the next few years – he is a rare and interesting case.'

An experienced parole officer observed him in the early days and stated: 'He is intelligent and his conversation follows a detailed, but matter-of-fact, cold format. He evidences no emotion and he describes his activities as if he was carving up a Sunday joint of meat.'

Most people who enter the jail system as adults without having been through the youth training system find it terrifying, but Percy adapted quickly, which was not surprising considering his lifelong capacity to withdraw into himself. 'Prison is all right if you go along with it and do what you are told and it's all right – like the navy,' he was to say during a review.

He had reasons to remember the navy fondly. After he was charged he received $1270 in back pay and a fortnightly pension cheque while in jail – making him one of the most affluent prisoners in the system.

Much later he was able to invest his pension fund in gold, build a bank account of almost $30,000, and buy a personal computer.

His interests included playing the guitar, making model boats he put in bottles, reading science fiction and maritime novels, and playing tennis. He was quiet and described by the chief of the division as 'a model prisoner (who) consistently receives excellent reports for conduct and industry'.

It might have appeared that Percy was changing, but he wasn't. A routine search of his cell on September 28, 1971, showed that he was still writing down bizarre and sadistic thoughts.

Prison officers found detailed plans of what he wanted to do with children.

They found pictures of children hidden in the cell. The brutal and graphic writings belied his passive exterior.

'Thus at about September 1971 the prisoner was behaving in a manner very similar to the year or more prior to the killing with which he was charged: apparently normal behaviour to the ordinary onlooker but a grossly disturbed sexual fantasy life,' Dr Bartholomew recorded.

As the years passed Dr Bartholomew and other psychiatrists

started to doubt if they would ever break through the walls around Percy's mind. In April 1975, he wrote: 'He is efficient, undemonstrative, quiet and never forms a relationship with anybody. Because of this withdrawal from interpersonal contact, it is impossible to have any worthwhile knowledge of his feelings and his mental state. His answers are stereotypes and safe – non-informative.

'I have to say that I can think of no valuable indices for release, and tend to wonder whether any really exist other than old age and or gross physical disability.'

The following year Dr Bartholomew described Percy as a 'colourless and somewhat withdrawn individual. His behaviour is above reproach but what thoughts go on in his mind I have no idea. Any endeavour to become to some extent involved with him is repulsed. He must be seen as a danger to children.'

He would talk to Dr Bartholomew about matters such as Test cricket, but refused to open up about his personality.

'I suspect, but cannot prove, that this prisoner has a rich (and morbid) fantasy sexual life but that he has learnt that it is to his own advantage that he covers it up. The prognosis is not good and I cannot see him being released for a long time yet,' he wrote in 1977.

Professor Richard Ball, who gave evidence at the first trial, re-interviewed Percy in January 1977. 'He volunteered nothing and extracting information was like pulling teeth …

I doubt that he is entirely without sadist fantasies.'

In 1979 he revived his teenage hobby of stamp collecting and the following year he started tertiary computer studies. He had earlier started group therapy for sex offenders, but after nine months he drifted back into his own world.

He did not want to leave a protection division in Pentridge because he had been in jail long enough to know what happened to child killers in mainstream jail. Computer nerds who cut up kids were easy prey for real crooks.

By 1980 he could be seen wandering around his division with a screwdriver, trusted to do electrical work in the jail. In his eleventh year in jail his supervisor wrote: 'One can't help but feeling that there is, in fact, much under the surface that he chooses not to reveal.'

He was then moved to J Division in February 1981 and for the first time Dr Bartholomew was prepared to write what many had suspected for years, that Percy had beaten the system. He was not mad and had never been so: 'He is not formally psychiatrically ill, and is not in need of treatment at this time'.

Another psychiatrist, Pentridge Coordinator of Forensic Psychiatry Services, Doctor Stephens, wrote: 'Percy is sexually grossly disturbed and should never be released from prison'.

In 1984 Percy told his mind minders he did not dwell on the killing of Yvonne Tuohy. 'His memories of what occurred are now faded, but that he used to feel some concern for his victim's parents, but hardly thinks of them any more.'

In the same year Dr Stephens said Percy needed to be able to offer an insight into himself if he was ever to be understood. 'I doubt whether he ever will and expect that he will remain in jail until he is made safe by advanced old age or physical disease.'

According to a parole report Dr Stephens thought Percy was 'a highly dangerous, sadistic paedophile who should never be released from safe custody. He is not certifiable neither is he psychiatrically treatable and he is totally unsuited to a mental institution. If Percy is ever so transferred he will in all probability earn some degree of freedom as the result of reasonable and conforming behaviour. The consequences of such freedom could well prove tragic.

'At this stage it remains the combined opinions of Dr

Stephens and the writer (of the parole report) that Percy be contained in a maximum security environment for the rest of his life.'

By 1985 he had not seen his family for two years. He appeared not to care. The only time he showed emotion was when it was suggested that he would be transferred to a country prison. 'Percy, whose face was inscrutable, the eyes cold and mesmeric, suddenly displayed emotion. His lips trembled convulsively as he emotionally stated that he did not want to move from J Division because he had "his computers there".'

He started to write computer programs to help intellectually disabled children learn to read and was visited once a month by a volunteer social worker. Bob Hawke was Prime Minister, Alan Bond still a national hero and Christopher Skase had a solid reputation and sound lungs when Percy had served fifteen years in jail. A prison report in 1985 said 'It has been mentioned that he is suspected of committing other child murders and if ever taken off the Governor's Pleasure list may be charged by the police with other murders'.

One of the original homicide detectives, Dick Knight, who was to go on to become a respected assistant commissioner, remained convinced that Percy had killed before he attacked Yvonne Tuohy. He argued that no-one could have committed the Westernport murder 'cold' and that it was likely he was responsible for earlier crimes.

Files from around Australia were reviewed and unsolved child killings examined. Percy was considered a suspect in the abduction murders of Christine Sharrock and Marianne Schmidt on Sydney's Wanda Beach in January 1965, the three Beaumont children in Adelaide in 1966, Alan Redston, a six-year-old murdered in Canberra in September 1966, Simon Brook, a young boy killed in Sydney in 1968 and Linda

Stillwell, seven, abducted from St Kilda in August 1968. Thirty years later the questions remained unanswered.

Dr Stephens said Percy was a dangerously abnormal personality, but not mentally sick in the accepted sense.

He was moved against his will to Beechworth prison in July 1986. At first he was unhappy because he did not have access to his computer and did not like the cold weather. He said 'he wasn't holding his breath' waiting for a release date. The penny had finally dropped.

Six psychiatrists interviewed Percy and none found signs of treatable mental disease.

Dr Richard Ball, by then professor of psychiatry at Melbourne University, saw him again in February 1988. He reported that Percy refused to talk to others and spent most of his time reading, listening to the radio or resting, staring into space.

'In a formal sense I suppose he could be regarded as without psychiatric illness,' Dr Ball wrote.

Professor Ball said he didn't believe Percy's statements that he couldn't remember what happened over the killing. He said he offered Percy the chance to take a truth drug, purely to judge his reaction. He refused the offer. 'I think this man has always been very secretive about his fantasies and his actions. It is very clear of course that for many years prior to his apprehension he had successfully hidden these from public scrutiny, even when living in a communal setting such as the navy.

'I have the feeling that this man is dissimulating and is just not prepared to admit his feelings and impulses.'

As a test Professor Ball decided to put Percy under pressure, bringing up horrible details of the torture and murder he had committed. 'He did not appear distressed in any way. There was no evidence of sweating, raised pulse rate, his respiratory rate remained unchanged, his colour was no different, his eye contact remained exactly the same. I might simply have been talking about the kinds of cheese that one eats.

'I think he must be regarded as having an abnormal personality with major sexual deviation and I cannot assure myself that this has changed for the better.'

Professor Ball added that the problem might get worse, not better. 'I suppose one needs to consider the possibility that sometimes age withers control rather than decreasing drive.'

By 1988 Percy's parents had retired to live in a caravan park and his younger brother operated the family's car air-conditioning business in Queensland. The parents went on an extended holiday, travelling around Australia.

Percy told prison officer he no longer had fantasies about children and wanted to be released. He said talk of him being involved in other child murders was a fixation of the media.

He still received an invalid pension from the navy and had saved $9000. Visits from his family became less frequent and he had not seen his brothers for five years. The mail chess games with his closest brother had stopped years earlier.

He smoked, did not take illegal drugs and was considered fit. His transfer to Beechworth failed due to some 'hassles with blokes over a number of things'. He returned to Pentridge seven months later. In September 1987, he was moved to Castlemaine jail.

His favourite television program was *A Country Practice*.

He began to age, lose his hair and develop the defeatist attitude of a man who has realised he may never be freed. 'That's what jail does to you,' he said.

His one outside friend, volunteer social worker, George McNaughton, retired and lost contact. In September 1988, another prisoner at Castlemaine, who falsely believed Percy had killed the inmate's niece, stabbed him in the chest. Percy escaped serious injury.

He had a vague interest in following Fitzroy in the football and kept an interest in Test cricket.

In 1990 Dr John Grigor from Mont Park Hospital suggested Percy be moved from prison and treated with drugs to suppress his sadistic sexuality. It was the first hope for Percy in years, but it failed to eventuate.

In 1991 he was described as an 'oddball, but no trouble whatsoever'. Prison officers said he mixed only with fellow sex offenders who, like him, refused to take responsibility for their crimes.

In his sixteenth review his interviewer tried a different approach to get through the 'cold and remote' veneer. For years Percy would answer all questions with a detached, rehearsed response. This time he was caught off-guard. 'Why do you think society takes such a dim view of people murdering children?' he was asked.

Then Percy did something he had rarely done in twenty years – he laughed.

'Why, there would be nobody left, would there?' he spluttered.

Wrong answer.

The interviewer wrote in his conclusion, 'Percy presents as an unacceptable risk and as such should be confined in the safe and, above all, secure custody of a correctional facility indefinitely'.

In 1992 psychiatrist Dr Neville Parker reviewed the case. He said Percy was not insane and the Supreme Court jury had got it wrong. 'There was nothing at the time to suggest that he was psychotic when he committed the crime, nor that he had ever had a mental illness.'

He said he didn't believe there was any treatment that 'could hold out any hope of changing this man's very perverted sexual drives'.

By 1992 he had effectively given up hope of ever being released, believing psychiatrists had preconceived ideas about him.

In 1993, when asked about his crime, he said he didn't think about it and said his victim could have been 'hit by a bus a week later and died'. He refused to join any therapeutic programs. The interviewer said Percy's only apparent regret was the crime had 'stuffed up' his life.

Professor Paul Mullen wrote in 1993 that Percy was sane. 'The wisdom or otherwise of the court's finding in Mr Percy's case may be open to question but it is not open to modification.'

He said it was unsatisfactory that Percy was still in a jail but there was no secure facility suitable for him outside of the prison system.

By 1994 he had more than $25,000 in bank accounts and investments in gold. His navy pension was forwarded to the family business.

He played cricket once a week at Ararat and worked with his computer.

In 1995 Attorney-General Jan Wade said she wanted to know if there were any moves to transfer Percy to a hospital because of the 'need for the strictest security at all times'.

In 1997 he was developing a computer program to retrieve cricket statistics and remained an avid newspaper reader. According to his prison review: 'Currently the objective with Mr Percy can only be for reasonably humane, long-term detention'.

After spending five years in Ararat he was involved in carpet bowls and organised intra-prison competitions, but only at a superficial level. He was still, in 1998, marooned on an emotional island the way he'd always been.

He'd had what was described as a 'remarkably uneventful prison history'. He had no friends and had made no efforts to deal with his problems.

He outlasted his investigators and most of captors. He outlasted three of the jails where he was an inmate: Beechworth, Pentridge and Castlemaine have all been closed.

His prison record showed he was one of the best-behaved inmates in Australia. In November 1995, he was fined $60 for having too many educational tapes in his cell.

A little earlier he had been transported from Ararat to Pentridge for an assessment. He was taken in a private prison van that had windows. He was, noted an observer, 'clearly elated by this experience as it is perhaps the first time Percy has viewed the open country side in almost 25 years'.

IN his final judgment, delivered on September 30, 1998, Justice Eames stated: 'The notes seized from Mr Percy's car after the killing of the young girl disclosed that her abduction and death were not spontaneous events, but occurred very much as the notes anticipated that such events might occur.

'In 1971, in his cell, it was discovered that Mr Percy had comprehensive notes describing even more horrific fantasies concerning abduction, imprisonment, torture, rape and killing of children. Also located was a collage of newspaper photographs of children, with obscene additional artwork in Mr Percy's hand.

'The notes are of the most horrifying nature, which, again, I consider it unnecessary to describe in detail.

'Mr Percy had written a complex chart, with first names given to proposed victims, in which he traced a pattern of conduct, which would take place over many years involving the rape, torture and killing of named children.

'Among the first names of the children referred to in these 1971 notes were some names which coincided with those of children of a family known to him, which family he remains so, because the underlying sadistic condition was then, and remains now, deeply entrenched. He has received no treatment of any kind, which might have changed that situation. He has shown no real interest in having such treatment. He has demonstrated no significant remorse or anxiety, at least none which I find credible, as to the circumstances, which caused him to kill.

'Because I am satisfied that Mr Percy holds those fantasies, then, in my opinion, the conclusion is irresistible that he remains as dangerous now as he was in 1969 and 1971.

Prior to, and during the course of, my hearings several articles appeared in the newspapers, which speculated that Mr Percy may have committed more killings than that of Elizabeth Tuohy. There is no evidence before me to support that assertion.

'Amongst the materials placed before me was a statement by Detective Senior Constable K. S. Robertson of the Victoria Police, dated May 5, 1970. In that report Robertson referred to an interview conducted with Mr Percy about the deaths and disappearances of other children, both in NSW and Canberra. I did not hear any evidence from Mr Robertson. At its highest the statement of Mr Robertson records Mr Percy's agreement that on other occasions prior to the death of Elizabeth Tuohy, whilst on beaches in New South Wales, he had sordid thoughts towards children and his agreement that he might have committed other offences had not the children been in the company of their parents.

The note records that police had no evidence to connect Mr Percy to any other killings. Only one item of "evidence" was advanced. When questioned about one killing in Sydney he is recorded as having said: "I could have done it but I can't remember".'

Shane Spiller was never to gain control of his life. Obsessed by Percy and the past, he would talk endlessly about the events that haunted him.

If anyone ever needed him all they needed to do was wait at the Robbie Burns Hotel in Wyndham in rural New South Wales. Shane would turn up there sooner or later. He lived in a neat house at the back of the pub.

More than 30 years after Percy attacked Yvonne Tuohy on the beach at Warneet, authorities finally, and at first begrudgingly, acknowledged the damage that had been done to Spiller.

In 2000 Spiller applied for crimes compensation and was initially awarded $5000 but on appeal to the Victorian Civil and Administrative Tribunal he received the maximum payout of $50,000.

It should have given Spiller a new start but some believed it could have destroyed him.

Late in August 2002 Spiller disappeared. One Victorian police source said he feared he had been killed for his compensation payout.

More than two years later, his four-wheel-drive vehicle was still parked at the front, squatters had moved into the house and his carefully kept garden was over-run.

One local who knew him well said, 'He was always saying someone was after him. No-one knows what happened to him'.

Local publican, Bernadette Godfrey said, 'He was really scared. He told me that one day he might just take off'.

Shortly before he disappeared Spiller began associating with a group of criminals, one who would be convicted over a local murder.

Spiller was scared of them – one wrecked a car he owned – but was unable to free himself from their influence.

In 2005 police from Victoria, NSW, South Australia and the Australian Federal Police interviewed Percy over the murders of Christine Sharrock and Marianne Schmidt on Sydney's Wanda Beach in January 1965; the disappearance of the three Beaumont children, Jane, Arnna and Grant, in Adelaide in 1966; Alan Redston, a six-year-old murdered in Canberra in September 1966; Simon Brook, a young boy killed in Sydney in 1968; and Linda Stillwell, seven, abducted from St Kilda in August 1968.

The move came after police were granted a magistrate's order to interview Percy, who was moved from Ararat Prison and taken to the homicide offices in St Kilda Road on February 2. He was interviewed for several hours before being driven back to the city watch-house. Percy was non-committal in some of his answers over the unsolved murders, mostly responding that he could not remember.

It had always been the same – when interviewed by police, parole officers, psychiatrists and prison officers over the decades, he has always been evasive.

Police have been able to establish that Percy was near the scene where the children were abducted, either while on holidays or while stationed at military bases while serving as a naval rating.

No-one doubts that Percy committed violent crimes – and probably murder – before he was grabbed over the Tuohy killing.

No-one doubts that Percy is not mad but evil. Over decades doctors and psychiatrists have refused to transfer him to a secure mental institution because they have been unable to find any signs of treatable mental disease.

So why was he found not guilty on the grounds of insanity

when no-one really believed he was mad? In 1969 the death penalty was still on the books and Victoria's pro-hanging premier Henry Bolte was very much in charge.

If Percy had been found guilty it may have been him, not Ronald Ryan, who was the last man hanged in Australia.

Some who remember the case say the insanity line was run to protect the jury from the grisly details of the murder.

Others say it was done under gentlemen's rules to ensure he was never released.

If he had been found guilty of murder and not hanged, he would have been back on the streets within 20 years – still young, fit and extremely dangerous.

By bending the rules of insanity to include Percy he was found not guilty – but was effectively sentenced to remain in jail until death or old age made him no longer a threat to anyone.

The last question on Percy may never be answered. Did he commit any or all of the eight unsolved murders speculation has linked to him?

Police say logically the chance of several serial killers operating in Australia at the same time was unlikely. They point out that once Percy was jailed the attacks stopped.

They can't say for certain how many murders he might have committed but he remains the red-hot suspect for the Sydney killings and the murder of Linda Stillwell in Melbourne.

Only one person knows. And he is unable – or unwilling – to tell the truth.

CHAPTER 18

DEEP UNDERCOVER

Dead men tell no tales.

IT was the spot a film director might pick for the opening scene of a bikie movie. Bleak, damp Ballarat, with the first morning of winter only hours away. Two angry, suspicious men and two detectives from the organised crime squad, collars turned up against the biting cold, meet near an isolated hamburger stand in a desolate car park.

Out of sight, armed police watch, ready to move if things turn ugly. The stakes are high. Melbourne police called the meeting to stop what was destined to be a full-scale bikie war. Trouble had been fermenting for just over a year and the organised crime squad knew that if nothing was done to prevent the slide towards armed confrontation, killings would follow.

The police wanted to get together representatives of two warring bikie groups: the Vikings, who for years had been the tough gang that controlled Ballarat, and the Bandidos, predators with a world-wide reputation for violence and drugs. The outlaw motorcycle world is always filled with tensions between groups, but usually there is a balance between the bravado of drug-enhanced macho aggression and the basic instinct of self-preservation that ensures an uneasy peace.

But it doesn't take much to upset that fine balance and turn a stand-off into a running war. The balance was destroyed in Victoria when the two heaviest bikie groups agreed to divide the state like a ripe peach, leaving the remaining gangs danger-ously exposed.

According to police intelligence, the Hells Angels, long the bikie power in South-East Australia, agreed to allow the Bandidos to expand into regional Victoria on the condition the Angels' power remained unchallenged in Melbourne. The two gangs still had their skirmishes, including the occasional drunken bashing, but in general the pact held.

The Bandidos were expansionists from way back. They moved into country centres and used their national numbers to take over local bikie groups. Join us or get beaten to a pulp was the general message. This resulted in country clubhouses being signed over, an increase in membership and new drug distribu-tion opportunities.

The Bandidos were not the only gang in the takeover business. In 1993 a man was shot dead and several others tortured when the Rebels took over the Warlocks in Geelong. In the bikie world, the strong devour the weak. Rather like the stock market, but with guns and real blood.

In April 1995, the Bandidos took over the Broke Brothers in Kyabram. Only three Broke Brothers joined, the rest were 'retired'. The next month the Bandidos absorbed the Ballarat gang the Loners. The Loners and the Vikings had been the local gangs for years and although they hated each other they managed to co-exist in an uneasy peace. The Bandidos also opened a Geelong chapter in July.

In May the Bandidos decided to take over the Vikings, but the local gang refused the 'offer'. This led to a series of increasingly violent incidents over the following year that convinced police a gang war was almost inevitable.

In April 1995, the Vikings' Ballarat clubhouse was sprayed with gunfire. In response, several Melbourne outlaw motorcycle gangs vowed to support the Vikings. In May, a bike shop owned by a Bandidos member was fire-bombed. In November, a Bandido was the victim of a hit-run. The car that struck him was driven by a Hells Angel. In February 1996, a car containing Vikings members was shot nearly twenty times in a drive-by shooting.

A man was systematically beaten with a baseball bat, another was bashed, and teams of armed bikies were seen driving through Sebastopol, near Ballarat, with shotgun barrels stuck out the car windows. Police searched the house of one bikie and found 21 sticks of gelignite and three shotguns; members of one gang were surrounded in a hotel and one bikie was beaten up at a Ballarat intersection in front of members of the public. One bikie group began to compile dossiers on rivals, including photographs, home and business addresses, and known movements.

When facing a violent feud, police often try to broker a peace deal behind the scenes. There are no sensational headlines and no spectacular arrests, but many underworld figures owe their lives to quiet police intervention before guns do the talking.

But on that Friday night, May 31, 1996, only the Vikings wanted to talk to Detective Senior Sergeant Graham Larchin and Detective Sergeant Rob Sodomaco from the organised crime squad. In the darkened car park the two Vikings office bearers told the detectives their club wanted to exist in its own right and their members would respond with violence only if attacked.

The Bandidos didn't even bother to turn up. Police telephoned them the following day, still trying to negotiate peace. The Bandidos responded with their own demands: they wanted guarantees that police would not attend, or even monitor national bike runs or fundraising concerts. They had their own plans and a peace deal with the Vikings was not part of them. The detectives concluded the bikies believed they were a law unto themselves.

Detectives reported back to senior officers that the Bandidos effectively wanted to be able to deal drugs without any police resistance. At that point the police decided conciliation and community policing had failed. It was time for old-fashioned detective work.

The target committee of the state crime squads met and declared the Bandidos a major organised crime target and a priority investigation.

Over the previous 30 years target policing had usually failed against bike gangs. Police success against bikies has involved opportunistic investigations into individual crimes, not long-term exposure of the organisations themselves.

The trouble has been that outlaw motorcycle gangs around the world have proven almost impossible to infiltrate. In one case in the US, the undercover policeman was accepted into the bike group, but he turned and ultimately became worse than the criminals he was sent to pursue.

Despite concerns over the long-term chances of success, police set up *Operation Barkly*, the secret investigation into the Bandidos. In mid-1996 the covert investigation unit briefed two of its best undercover men. Their mission: to do the impossible. That is, get inside the gang, be accepted as brothers and provide evidence that would stand up in court against a Queens Counsel's cross-examination.

Wes and Alby were born. They were two unemployed men in their late twenties on the fringes of the criminal world. Wes was to have a criminal record involving drugs. They were then set up in a rented house in Ballarat. Both were keen to make money and were happy to go outside the law to do it.

To what length the police department went to provide false identities for the men must remain secret, as these methods will be used again. Suffice to say Wes and Alby were to go deeper undercover than any police in Australia had ever been before.

THE carefully sculptured image of the Bandidos as a group of renegades who dropped out of society to share an interest in bikes, booze and broads is anything but true. The bikie world actually mimics mainstream society where money and power open doors and those who do not obey the rules are eventually shunned.

At a struggling chapter like Ballarat the fee for members was $105 per month plus $1000 to join, putting it in a league just behind an exclusive club such as Royal Melbourne Golf Club.

According to police the fees for members at the Prospect chapter in Sydney were $600 a month – seemingly steep dues given that most of the members were supposed to be unemployed battlers on the dole. Most of each month's dues were divided between the national defence fund, local legal fees, the central chapter and clubhouse rent. Members leaving the club were also expected to 'donate' their Harley Davidsons to the Bandidos. This was no glee club.

One young member without a job said he had just bought a

top-of-the-range Landcruiser for $60,000 and a Harley for $30,000. 'Paid cash,' he bragged. The gang had set up chapters in Geelong, Ballarat, Perth, Brisbane's hinterland, Griffith, Hunter Valley, Sydney, inner Sydney, Prospect, NSW north coast, inner Brisbane and Cairns.

With almost 300 members in Australia and connections with the overseas organisation, they had the power to intimidate, and apparently had access to ample weaponry to back up any threats.

Police say the Bandidos used a shoulder-fired anti-tank rocket-launcher to kill two and injure seventeen at a Copenhagen Hells Angels' party in 1996. According to police, one of the suspects later travelled to Australia for a national bike run and complained that he couldn't hear for two weeks after he fired the rocket. It is unlikely such an industrial-type injury would come under Workcover.

The Bandido Motorcycle gang was formed in Texas in 1966 by Donald Eugene Chambers, who was later convicted of killing two men after they allegedly ripped off the gang in a drug deal.

According to the FBI, the first Australian chapter was established in Sydney in 1983. The FBI found it was opened to give the gang access to Australian chemicals, banned in the US, to be used in the production of amphetamines.

For fifteen years police have regarded the Bandidos as the most violent bikie gang in Australia. In 1984 the Bandidos and the Commancheros opened fire on each other in what became known as the Milperra Father's Day massacre that left six bikies and a fifteen-year-old girl dead. The gangs gave the impression it was a romantic battle over 'turf'. It wasn't. It was over drugs.

According to US authorities the Bandidos is one of 'The Big Four' international bikie organised crime groups. It has one of the best counterintelligence systems and is considered the hardest to crack.

It was not the only international bikie group to establish strong links in Australia. Lax rules in relation to chemicals used for speed, such as P2P, meant this country was regarded as ripe for colonisation. The US Hells Angels were provided with huge quantities of P2P from their Australian connections, smuggled into America in pineapple tins. An American hit man was intercepted at Melbourne airport after police received information he had taken a contract to kill a local detective.

The federal government tried to ban international bikie leaders from entering Australia, but many still managed to arrive – some legally, and others under false names. Police around Australia were alerted in 1998 to look for an international outlaw bikie boss, wanted for questioning in the US over a series of murders and bombings linked with organised crime.

The FBI contacted the Australian Bureau of Criminal Intelligence and asked for assistance after receiving information that the international president of the Outlaws Motorcycle Club, Harry Joseph Bowman, might be hiding in Australia.

Bowman, one of the FBI's top ten most wanted criminals, was reported to be 'armed and extremely dangerous'.

According to the FBI: 'Bowman heads the Outlaws operations in more than 30 cities in the United States and twenty chapters in at least four other countries (including Australia). Bowman may be guarded by members of the Outlaws.

'Harry Joseph Bowman, international president of the Outlaws Motorcycle Club, is wanted for his alleged involvement in violent racketeering acts (that) include murders, bombings, drug trafficking, extortion, firearms violations, and other acts of violence.

'Bowman was allegedly involved in the murders of two Outlaws members and may have participated in the murder of a rival motorcycle club member. The indictment alleges that he ordered the bombings of rival motorcycle clubhouses.'

The FBI has offered a $50,000 reward for information leading to his arrest.

The Outlaws were formed in Chicago in the 1950s and Bowman, known as 'Taco', took over as national president in 1984. US authorities say the gang has been heavily involved in distributing cocaine in Florida, and has developed strong drug connections in Colombia and Cuba.

US police claim the Outlaws were responsible for at least 115 murders over thirteen years, and another 29 murders in Canada. 'The Outlaws have also utilised explosives and bombing devices in carrying out acts against perceived "enemies",' an FBI investigation found.

'The Outlaws engage in extensive witness intimidation and jury tampering efforts which closely parallel other outlaw motorcycle gang tactics.'

When Victorian police decided to try to infiltrate one of the Big Four, they knew the tactic had failed around the world. Any chance of success rested with the ability of the two undercover police selected for the job.

Alby and Wes moved to Ballarat determined to keep a low profile. Being too keen would have ruined their chances. They had to develop trust with a gang of men who seemed determined to trust nobody.

The Bandidos say they are no longer part of society. 'This is why we look repulsive. We're saying we don't want to be like you or look like you,' according to their code. Their motto is 'God forgives, Bandidos don't'.

But bike gangs can't live in isolation. They need cannon

fodder: men who want to be near the tough guys and bask in dubious reflected glory. These are the people seen to be disposable. They are used to guard buildings and run errands. In return they attend parties and can buy drugs at a cheaper rate.

When Wes and Alby drifted into town they were treated with suspicion at first. But over months they ran into the Bandidos at pubs and drinking holes in the area and the relationships slowly warmed.

To the bikies, the two seemed ideal – men who were prepared to look the other way at the right time and weren't too concerned about the subtleties of the criminal code. In November 1996, Wes and Alby were invited to the clubhouse at 4 Greenbank Court, Delacombe, for a party.

If it was a test, they passed. It was the first step in a thirteen-month journey that would lead the two undercover police to give up their professional and personal lives to become beer-swilling, foul-mouthed bikies.

They stayed on the periphery before finally being invited to become 'hangarounds'. This put them in a position where they were welcome at any Bandidos' chapter in Australia.

They were in.

Alby arrived as a would-be bikie. He had a Harley Davidson borrowed by the force for the job. Wes bought his from the president of the Ballarat chapter, Peter Skrokov, with $17,000 provided by the police department. 'We got ripped off,' a police bean counter observed later.

It might sound glamorous, to leave the mundane routine of a workaday job to ride motorbikes and live on the edge, but the edge was doubly dangerous for the undercover operators – one slip could mean exposure and death. They had to remember every lie and stick strictly to the script.

The simplest everyday occurrences could take on new and

sometimes frightening significance. Everybody has had the experience of running into an old friend or acquaintance in the strangest place. For most people it is merely an unexpected surprise. For an undercover police officer it could be fatal. During the operation one of the police, wearing his Bandido leathers, was filling his Harley Davidson with petrol at a service station. He looked up to see his next-door neighbour from his 'other life' filling the tank of the family sedan at the next bowser. To his relief he passed unrecognised.

Wes and Alby were to report, word for word, what they had learnt, including the Bandidos' greeting – right handshake, left arm embrace and kiss on the lips. Ironically, the police agents may have done the bikies they were tracking a huge favour in the long term. Senior police believe the undercovers not only gathered evidence to use in prosecutions, but saved lives with several early warnings of planned attacks on opposition bikie groups. More than once they slipped away to warn of planned ambushes and police were able to set up blitzes, roadblocks and other operations to stop the violence. Each time it was made to look as though it was just bad luck that thwarted the Bandidos' attacks.

Detective Superintendent Ian Thomas, the head of the organised crime and task force division, said: 'There is no doubt the two undercover police were at grave risk. Their work helped us move in and stop incidents with the potential to turn violent.'

But it was not one-way traffic. The club rule enforcer, the Ballarat Sergeant-at-Arms, Andrew Michlin, approached Wes and Alby and asked would they grow hydroponic marijuana in their home? It was an offer too good to refuse.

Their rented home in Lydiard Street, Ballarat, was filled with state-of-the-art recording equipment. Michlin set up one of the bedrooms as an indoor nursery, complete with lights, watering systems and tubs. It was all recorded.

Wes and Alby were promoted to 'prospects' in August 1997, and on October 21 they were promoted to full members on twelve months probation. This was personally ratified by the national president of the Bandidos, Michael Kulakowski.

The power and charisma of Kulakowski was undisputed. He was internationally respected in the bikie world, so much so that he flew to the US in July 1996 to be part of peace negotiations to stop a war between the Hells Angels and the Bandidos in Europe that had claimed eleven lives.

A former soldier and rodeo rider, 'Mick K' or 'Chaos' as he was known to his bikie mates, opted out of mainstream society at 40, but he still enjoyed the trappings of success. He drove a Mercedes, owned a luxurious home and a top of the range Harley Davidson.

The Bandidos already had a strong grip on the amphetamines market and a lucrative sideline in marijuana. But under Kulakowski the gang was moving into the club drugs of ecstasy and LSD.

According to police the Bandidos needed distribution points to move into the new wave of drugs and began to set up 'techno discos' where they could begin to cultivate thousands of new clients.

Senior Victorian Bandidos were observed in Sydney discussing plans to open techno discos in Ballarat and Geelong as fronts to sell ecstasy and LSD as part of the national expansion.

Wes and Alby were able to buy LSD from the Ballarat Bandidos for $5 a tab. Later they were able to buy it for $3.50 from the Sydney chapter as brothers were prepared to undercut brothers. They transferred money to a Bandido-controlled bank account in NSW and the drugs were moved by express post to a designated post box.

The profits were massive, with each tab selling for $7 retail. Each sheet contained 200 tabs and the Bandidos bragged that their courier was walking in through Sydney airport carrying a bundle of LSD sheets 25 centimetres thick on every smuggling run.

Bandidos were selling LSD stamped with the Sydney Olympic logo, a smiley design, love hearts, and Beavis and Butthead. According to the Melbourne undercovers, the Victorian Bandidos planned to move into the party drug scene. Police were later to say that Alby and Wes were involved in more than 30 deals buying marijuana, amphetamines, LSD and ecstasy from Bandidos in three states during their thirteen months living undercover. They were so trusted that Alby became the secretary-elect for the Ballarat chapter, giving him access to the club's financial records.

The Bandidos continued their plans to expand through regional Victoria. The next target was Wangaratta and that meant an attack on the local club, the Tramps. In February 1996, the president of the Tramps received a letter in the post. It said the Tramps, their friends and children, would be in danger if the gang did not disband and leave town.

In May 1997, the Broke Brothers tried to reform for a run. About 30 Bandidos from Ballarat and Geelong rode to Kyabram for a show of strength.

But Wes and Alby were able to report the planned attack in enough time so that police gathered at Kyabram in such force they were able to keep the hostile groups apart.

Despite the ongoing violence the bikies continued to refuse to co-operate with police. The Sergeant-at-Arms, Andrew Michlin, made the mistake of allowing police to conduct a search without a warrant. He was busted back to the level of 'prospect' as a punishment.

The power of the group over the individual is complete. A member of the Griffith chapter, Dean Francis Corboy, declared that a member of the Tramps looked the wrong way at him at Wangaratta on October 3, 1997. He summoned 60 members from Geelong, Ballarat and Griffith for a confrontation at Wangaratta.

According to the Bandidos' code, members were expected to just walk out of their jobs and drive. When a brother needed help, whether he was right or wrong, you must support him. But one of the undercovers managed to get the message to police and when the Bandido strike force turned up, there 'just happened' to be a major police blitz on in Wangaratta. Wherever the bikies went they were pulled over. Also unexplained was why no members of the Tramps were anywhere to be seen that night.

Just to show their strength the Bandidos started their 1997 National Run in Wangaratta on October 23, with more than 250 bikies from Australia and around the world present in full colours. To make matters worse for a country town with limited police resources it was the break-up day for VCE students. The town would be filled with drunken bikies and drunken teenage girls. It was every parent's nightmare. Police had a meeting with Kulakowski and explained the situation. He agreed to keep control and 'Chaos' sent out the message to his troops – stay cool. The night passed without incident. 'That was his power,' a senior policeman said. The power to make peace, or war, at whim.

The 250 bikies moved on to Geelong and, according to police, went to a popular local nightclub. The owner set up a special room for them but they wanted the run of the nightclub and the manager baulked. Kulakowski gave the nod and they trashed the place and bashed the bouncers. No official complaint was ever lodged.

On October 24, 1997, some of the gang, including a few international Bandidos, went out to test fire their illegal firearms. One of the overseas visitors had to be dissuaded from opening fire on a passing Geelong-Melbourne train.

The National Run was to prove the highlight of Kulakowski's reign. He had charisma and power, but that won't stop a bullet. On November 9 Kulakowski, Sergeant-at-Arms Bruce Harrison and fellow member Rick De Stoop, were shot dead in the basement of a Sydney dance club. Another Bandido was shot in the head, but survived.

Bandidos from around Australia, including the two undercover police, drove to Sydney for the funeral. In a ritual fit for royalty more than 200 bikies filed past for a brief moment with their dead leader.

It is alleged one of the undercover officers bent over to embrace the deceased leader and whispered into the casket, 'I'm a copper, you know'.

Dead men tell no tales.

But while the bikies were grieving, business was still business and life went on. Wes and Alby were able to buy a thousand LSD tabs from one of the Sydney leaders of the Bandidos straight after the funeral.

With the danger of revenge killings after the death of the three Bandidos, police had to move quickly.

Wes and Alby were called back in so they wouldn't be at risk. On December 11 more than a hundred police in four states made co-ordinated raids. Nineteen people were arrested and drugs with a street value of more than $1million were seized. They also found chemicals suitable for making amphetamines worth $6million, and seized firearms, including an AK-47 rifle and pen pistols. The head of *Operation Barkly*, Detective Inspector Andrew Allen, said: 'Some outlaw motorcycle gangs seem to think that the law does not relate to them. I think we have shown that no-one is beyond policing.

'These gangs must learn that if you traffick drugs and engage in unlawful activities, sooner or later you will be locked up.

'While *Operation Barkly* has made inroads into the Bandidos, history has shown that these gangs must be continually monitored. Some outlaw bikie groups make a public show of supporting charities to clean up their images when the truth is many are heavily involved in major criminal activities.'

Wes and Alby had gathered so much evidence that most of the bikies charged decided to plead guilty. But the main players, such as Peter Skrokov and Andrew Michlin, were destined to spend only about six months in jail, less than half the time the two police risked their lives infiltrating the group.

In 1998, the last of the arrested bikies, Dean Corboy, pleaded guilty in the Wangaratta Magistrate's Court to trafficking amphetamines. He was sentenced to eight months, with six months suspended – an effective jail term of two months.

But justice sometimes moves in mysterious ways. Another court has also passed judgment on the main players. According to police intelligence, the national chapter of the Bandidos has sentenced the bikies who embraced Wes and Alby to be flogged when they are released from jail. There will be no appeal.

Police say Wes and Alby have received professional counselling so they can re-enter mainstream policing.

Intelligence reports indicate there are still contracts out on their lives.

CHAPTER 19

A CONCRETE CASE

'No, you just chop into four pieces
... with a chainsaw.'

'FRANK' was a devoted family man and volunteer firefighter who worked in the Melbourne wholesale fruit and vegetable market

The market is a small city filled with hard-working men who rise before dawn to buy and sell the produce of the land to be consumed by city people who neither know nor care about the journey from soil to plate.

But there has always been another side to the market. For decades the cash economy of the industry has made it a fertile spot for organised crime to flourish.

From the 1963-64 market murders until the present day, bad men have made a living in an industry where most work is still conducted under the cover of darkness.

Many became rich selling not only fruit and vegetables but

also another easily grown crop – marijuana. So when Frank was asked to deliver a package, no questions asked, the father of three did as he was told, although he knew the package contained cannabis. He was given $1000 cash for his trouble.

For Frank, it was the start of a decade in which he went from being a low level courier, carrying drugs and cash, to become the confidante of the bosses of five drug syndicates.

Frank was also to become one of Victoria's most important police witnesses. Known by a codename, he gave detectives the key to drug syndicates that had proved virtually impenetrable.

Confidential police documents say that he provided enough evidence and information to short-circuit the crime rings that provided most of the drugs in Melbourne's western suburbs.

A secret police review concluded, 'It is accepted by many that it would have taken up to eight years by conventional policing methods to achieve what this operation has in eleven months.'

According to Detective Sergeant Stephen Cody, Frank had always been known in drug circles as a man of his word. The major dealers loved using him. He wasn't an unreliable junkie, he didn't try to rip them off and he kept his mouth shut.

He acted as a human buffer for the syndicate heads. He handled the money and the drugs so that if there were any arrests, the heads remained a step removed. He took the risks, but he was always assured that if things went wrong his family would be looked after.

Eventually he was arrested and sent to jail. As a man of his word he did not implicate any of his superiors and, as expected, took the rap. But, his family members were left to fend for themselves, even after his daughter was hit by a car and suffered brain damage.

The so-called men of honour refused to repay his loyalty. He was seen as expendable. It was to be a major lapse of judgment.

On his release Frank returned to work for the same men but this time he knew he would have to look after himself.

Late in 1990 police raided Frank's house and he was arrested again. His wife was furious. She saw the family being dragged into the underworld. A few months later, aged in her late 30s, she suffered a stroke and became paralysed on one side of her body.

Normally police have to pressure low-level criminals into giving evidence against members of a drug syndicate, but this case was unique. Frank approached police and offered to become an informer. 'He wanted to make sure he didn't go back to it. He wanted to burn all his bridges so that he would be forced to make a new start,' Detective Sergeant Cody said.

And so Frank became Informer 108. As a unique go-between, '108' introduced police to five separate drug syndicates. The resulting investigation began as *Operation Pipeline* in 1991 but expanded into *Operations Advance, Exceed, Extra, Overflow* and *Bluestreak*. Even though the investigation itself ran for eleven months and resulted in 68 arrests it was not completed until late 1995 when the final court hearings were completed.

It involved more than 30 police from the drug squad and the Altona district support group and more than 80 police were called in when the final arrests were made.

Police seized or purchased cocaine, heroin, amphetamines, cannabis and hashish to the value of $6million and observed drug deals totalling $7.5million. It resulted in the arrest and conviction of two drug millionaires, solved a previously unknown murder and led to the discovery of an Uzi machine-gun.

Police seized assets, including a farm at Laverton valued at $350,000, nine cars, including a Porsche and a new $47,000 four-wheel drive, two motorbikes, including a Harley-Davidson 'Fatboy', and $500,000 cash.

Pipeline provided a snapshot of the real drug world in any big Australian city: a fluid, turbulent mix of individuals and syndicates always on the make. It wasn't a neat pyramid structure with one Mr Big or a series of criminals running well-defined organised crime groups.

Rather, it showed how different gangs did business with each other when it suited. It also showed how a generation of minor criminals, who in another time would have just been bottom dwellers in the underworld food chain, were able to make millions from drugs.

The five syndicates were basically broken into ethnic groups – Chinese, Italian, Lebanese, Greek and Anglo-Saxon – but while they were independent, they were all prepared to co-operate on major deals.

'They were into everything and anything. Greed was the only common interest they had,' was the pithy judgment of the head of the operation, Detective Inspector David Reid.

An example of the wealth that can be made from drugs was the rapid rise of John Falzon.

In the mid-1980s Falzon lived in a housing commission flat in Sunshine. In 1984-85 he put in his only known tax return and declared an income of $10,000. Although he did not work or claim social welfare he was able to acquire assets worth more than $1million, including houses, cars and two farms.

Police watched him dig up $230,000 in cash, hidden in a plastic drum under a sleeper in the backyard of a friend's parents' house in Sunshine. Days earlier he had loudly criticised his wife for spending $20 too much at the supermarket. 'She used to have to provide receipts to him after she'd done the shopping,' one investigator said.

'He was a miserable, self-centred, selfish, secretive individual,' he said. 'Falzon spoke in code when discussing drug transactions within his network and refused to deal with anyone he didn't know,' according to a confidential police report. He would only deal with Informer 108. It was to be his downfall.

Informer 108 introduced undercover policeman David Barlow to the syndicates. The second time Barlow met a millionaire amphetamines distributor called Atilla Erdei, the drug dealer stuck a gun in his ribs. 'He nearly broke them,' Barlow was to recall. 'He was a violent man with no regard for anyone else.'

Before *Operation Pipeline* police were unaware that Erdei, a clothing manufacturer and millionaire property owner, was a heavyweight drug distributor. During the investigation they found he had already killed one man and was planning to murder a second.

Erdei was eventually arrested and convicted of murdering Anh Mal Nguyen on Good Friday 1992, by strangling him with his bare hands and then dumping the body in a concrete-filled 200-litre drum in Pyke's Creek Reservoir, near Ballarat.

After the arrests police were told that a $100,000 contract had been taken out on David Barlow's life. He married during the undercover operation and spent his first anniversary in the witness protection scheme. He was eventually forced to sell his heavily fortified eastern suburbs home at a loss of $24,000.

Some members of the syndicates were not content with making threats. They also offered inducements. Drug squad detectives were offered $100,000 in cash for the undercover operative's original secret tapes. They were promised the money in two $50,000 lots, one before and the other after the committal.

It was no idle promise. When Senior Detective David Harley from the drug squad parked his car near the corner of Park and Nicholson Streets, North Fitzroy, to meet syndicate member

Frank Dimos, he was ready to gather evidence for the bribery sting.

He didn't have to wait long. Dimos walked along the road clutching his stomach but it was not a case of bad indigestion. When he hopped into the car his shirt was unbuttoned and $40,000 cash was spilling from around his belly. He said that he was ten pairs of 'socks' short and would pay the rest the next day. He threw the bundles of cash into the driver's side foot well.

The group also wanted police to raid selected drug dealers, keep a small percentage for evidence and then return the rest to be resold. Police were to be paid a retainer and a share of the profits.

Two of the men were arrested in a Melbourne motel room viewing 40 kilos of cannabis valued at $72,000, which they thought they were buying from corrupt drug squad detectives.

Three men involved in the syndicate were later charged with attempted bribery and conspiracy to pervert the course of justice. Two received no effective jail terms as the sentences were made concurrent with drug terms and the third, Dimos, received an effective sentence of only four months.

Police privately say the courts should be tougher on criminals who offer bribes. 'The crims have nothing to lose. If someone cops a bribe they can get away with it, but if they are arrested for it they don't do any real jail time anyway,' comments one investigator.

After appearing in court, a process that took five years, Informer 108 moved interstate with his family under a new name. According to Detective Sergeant Cody: 'He is doing well. He is one of the success stories of the system. He has a full-time job, is looking to buy a house and is supporting his family.'

But while confidential police documents described *Operation*

Pipeline as 'one of the most significant drug operations undertaken in modern Victoria Police history' detectives remain convinced they were not backed up by the courts. They believed that light jail sentences and flawed asset seizure laws made it impossible to make serious inroads into the drug racket.

Detectives, who arrested the 68 people in *Operation Pipeline*, claimed some of the major dealers were back selling drugs even before the five-year operation was completed.

Police in *Pipeline* said that though they arrested the main dealers in heroin, amphetamines, cocaine, hashish and cannabis, the operation had no long-term effect on the drug industry.

'As soon as we arrest a major player there is someone else who is prepared to walk in and fill their shoes,' complained the then acting head of the drug squad, Detective Inspector Reid.

Police in the western suburbs reported that there was a slight increase in the price of drugs, and minor supply problems for about four months after the arrests, but then the industry returned to normal.

'The profits are so great. People can amass more money in a few short years than they could ever acquire in a lifetime of legitimate work,' Detective Inspector Reid said.

Some of the major drug dealers arrested through *Operation Pipeline* were fined or given jail terms of two years or less. The longest sentence was for one of the main targets, John Falzon, who was sentenced to seven years with a minimum of five.

'I think everyone agrees there is a need for the major dealers in the drug industry to be subjected to severe jail terms but it doesn't seem to regularly happen,' Reid says. 'I know we are fair-dinkum about doing something. I just wonder if others are.'

The maximum sentence for drug trafficking is 25 years jail and a fine of $250,000.

'In *Operation Pipeline* more than 80 police were involved. It involved time, resources and effort and personal risk for a number of people. An undercover officer, an informer and their families were placed at great risk and the maximum sentence for any of the offenders was seven years with a minimum of five,' Reid said.

'I think the only way to make inroads is when people selling drugs at the highest level go to jail for long periods and come out broke.'

Police in *Operation Pipeline* and associated investigations tapped into a group of drug cartels with links in China, Thailand, Western Australian and South Australia. One gang ran a separate drug syndicate inside Loddon prison.

The operations identified hundreds of drug deals worth more than $13million and resulted in the seizing of assets of more the $1.1million, although further assets of more than $1million allegedly acquired with drug money could not be touched.

Police believe at least three Melbourne legal identities help organise removal of assets so they could not be traced to drug purchases.

In *Pipeline*, a new four-wheel-drive vehicle bought with $47,000 cash of drug money and with 40 kilometres on the clock was kept in a police compound for nearly three years before it was sold at a heavily discounted price.

For most police, it is possible to move on after a major arrest. The brief of evidence has to be completed and there may be several court appearances to come, but largely the hard work is over. In some ways the detectives are like film directors. They plan and control the whole production, but they are not the stars. It is the witnesses and the hard evidence that ultimately matter. Confessions are recorded, tapes produced and witnesses swear statements.

But when an undercover policeman is used, the stakes become higher. Undercover work is specialised. Recruits have to be gregarious, likeable and able to think on their feet. They can't make a mistake or freeze under pressure. A slip can be fatal.

Undercovers have to be carefully controlled. In New Zealand and the US some have gone 'wild' and crossed the line. They often see a different world, well away from the humdrum life of a wage earner. No mortgage problems, no saving for a holiday or a second-hand car. It is cash city. If you want something, then buy it. The restaurants, the bars, the girls, and the partying all seem to be on tap.

Often, when the sting operation is completed the criminals caught in the net are doubly outraged. It is a personal insult that someone they trusted and liked turns out to be a policeman who betrays them. The added concern is that the undercover is the key player in any successful prosecutions. It takes the police-criminal relationship to a different – and dangerous – plane.

In one big Victorian police operation into a Griffith-connected Honoured Society group, the cartel took out a million-dollar contract on the undercover operative, who eventually left the job.

In *Operation Pipeline* the undercover, David Barlow, actually had to slip out of his role to get married. At the time he looked more like Frank Zappa than a clean-cut police sergeant.

Barlow was introduced to the syndicate as a major drug dealer and was soon accepted by the main players. In a restaurant in Carlton in May 1992, he was on the mobile phone to a drug dealer in Hong Kong when Attila Erdei walked in. 'I said I was talking to my Chinese connection and he said he had a Chinese problem, but it was gone,' Barlow said.

What Erdei had referred to was the cold-blooded murder of an

Asian victim. 'I always knew he had the capacity to do it. At one meeting at a service station near Westgate bridge he pulled out an Uzi machine gun and started waving it about.'

He said that when he realised Erdei was talking of a recent murder he tried to get him to provide details without appearing to be too pushy: 'I went into evidence gathering mode.'

'I put my finger up to indicate pistol. He put his hand up to indicate he had strangled him. He said his thumbs were sore for three days.'

'He said it took about ten minutes and the victim kept screaming and fighting. He called him a dirty little monkey.'

Barlow said Erdei told him he put the body in a drum and filled it with concrete. The next morning the concrete had dried and shrunk and the head was visible. 'He said he gave it a pat on the head and filled up the rest of the drum with concrete.'

Erdei told the policeman that when he rolled the drum into the dam it had bounced on rocks before disappearing. Police divers were able to estimate the point of entry and recover the drum with the body.

After the arrest, Barlow's wife started to get strange telephone calls. The family started to receive letters about pre-paid funerals.

Police installed two security systems, bulletproof glass and a video surveillance system. Armed police moved into their house. His wife was followed by police. Barlow was armed 24 hours a day. Every time he arrived home he would check outside and inside looking for gunmen. 'It was like living in a fishbowl. Every time I went home I was waiting for someone to jump out of the bushes.'

The couple's first anniversary was spent in witness protection with armed police. Eventually things began to settle down. They were at a formal ball enjoying themselves when a work call came through for Barlow.

The Coburg police had received a tip. 'You've got an undercover named Dave who lives in Ringwood. There's a $100,000 contract out on him.'

For the Barlows it was the end. They decided to sell their suburban home with the security systems more in keeping with a city bank than a family house. They sold the house for a loss of $24,000. They were glad to get rid of it.

Meanwhile, the wheel of crime and detection keep turning. By the time the Barlows had regained a semblance of normal life, some of the men convicted of dealing drugs had been released from prison and were back in business.

Time: 12.22pm, May 1, 1992.

Place: Genevieve Cafe, Faraday Street, Carlton.

Present: Informer 108, police undercover operator David Barlow and target Attila Erdei.

Edited transcript of Erdei bragging of killing Anh Mal Nguyen on Good Friday 1992, by strangling him with his bare hands, then dumping the body in a concrete-filled drum.

The three men are sitting at a table and have ordered lunch of soup and chicken parmigiana.

ERDEI: 'My problem, my problem, gone my little problem.'

BARLOW: 'Is he? What is he?'

ERDEI: 'Holiday.'

BARLOW: 'Where?'

ERDEI: 'Long tour.'

BARLOW: 'Did you, did you knock him?'

ERDEI: 'Good Friday. Yeah.'

He then indicated he strangled the victim.

BARLOW: 'Yeah.'

ERDEI (a body builder): 'My hands ... hurt for three ... days.'

BARLOW: 'Do you know what? You're … mad.'

ERDEI: 'He … owe me 60 grand.'

ERDEI: 'I start squeezing his throat like hell you know. And he going "Err" like that and fifteen minutes I got him down on the ground.'

Informer 108: 'That's life, murder.'

ERDEI: 'Yeah, so what.'

108: 'I'd hate to see if you got upset with me, mate.'

BARLOW: 'You'd have to get a bigger drum.'

108: 'Bigger drum all right.'

ERDEI: 'No, you just chop into four pieces … with a chainsaw.'

ERDEI: 'Five years ago we go to hunting. And I shoot one horse, not me, one friend of mine. White horse, I like horses and the … shoot him. And I go to him (the horse) and you know, he not die, so I put five or six bullets in the head. And believe it or not, I never go hunting after because I so sorry for the horse. And after three weeks, four weeks, believe it or not, I start sleeping, always come that horse in my mind. I can't sleep.'

Then Erdei talks about the difference in killing the horse to murdering Nguyen. 'I feel nothing, man … Believe me, I feel nothing.'

ERDEI: 'Now it's two weeks ago tomorrow morning, exactly, tomorrow morning. And once not he comes into my dreams or something. I got good sleep and everything because he is a piece of shit, not a human being.'

Police recovered the body on the basis of details from the taped conversation, sixteen days after the murder.

Erdei was convicted of murder and sentenced to 22 years with a minimum of seventeen.

CHAPTER 20

DEAD MAN TALKING

The job sounded perfect ...
almost too good to be true.

FOR Ron Williams, it was the beginning of a new beginning. Warmed by summer's setting sun and a rare inner glow of satisfaction, he stood on an isolated beach in Western Australia, indulging his passion for surf fishing. He was – if not a world – then at least a continent away from decades of disappointment.

For the first time in years the battler from Melbourne could see a future that gave him hope for a better life.

No longer would he struggle in low-paid jobs, a potential casualty in every economic downturn. He felt he was going to crack the big time and become, finally, master of his destiny.

Standing next to Williams on the deserted beach near Albany, was his new boss and confidant, a man who called himself Paul Jacobs, a successful company director and the driving force behind a national geological firm.

Although the two were the same age and physically similar, Ron Williams looked up to the man he'd known only a few weeks for having the qualities he lacked – drive, ambition and a sense of purpose.

Until they met, Williams had been convinced he was going nowhere. He had worked hard in Melbourne in a variety of dead-end jobs, but had nothing to show for it but a hard-won reputation for dedication. Pats on the back don't pay the mortgage.

In his last job, he'd worked six days a week for a second-hand car parts firm in a southern bayside suburb. Yet he still lived with his elderly mother, lacking the money for a deposit on his own unit. His redundancy payment from Dulux, an earlier job, had long gone. Like many a lonely bachelor, he liked a drink, and found it hard to save money.

Now, aged 45, it seemed he finally had a break. In his kit was a signed, legally-binding, two-year contract to work in the mining industry at $60,000 a year, more than twice his wreckers' yard wage back in Melbourne.

Even weeks afterwards, he must have marvelled at the good luck that had changed his life, when he'd spotted a classified advertisement in the *Herald Sun* newspaper on 26 January, 1996.

It read: 'GENERAL HAND GEO. SURVEY. Duties include camp maint. D/L essential. Suit single person 35-45 able to handle long periods in remote areas. Wage neg. Contract basis. Call 9423-8006 between 6-9 pm.'

He rang the number and found himself speaking to a Mr Jacobs, the man who would be handling the interviews. The nervous applicant slurred his words slightly but the prospective employer didn't seem to notice – or didn't care that the man on the end of the phone sounded a little drunk.

The prospective employer could afford to be selective. After all, fifty people had responded to the advertisement, but he was looking for a particular type, someone with special qualities. Ron Williams sounded most promising.

The first interview was held in modest surroundings – a small unit in the north-eastern Melbourne suburb of Greensborough, rather than a flash city office. That was easy to explain, and Jacobs explained it: he invested in WA exploration, not useless business status symbols.

For Williams the job sounded perfect – adventure, coupled with two years security and the chance to have another go at life, three thousand kilometres from past failures. Much better money, the possibility of being a key player in a small team, and the chance to work with an understanding boss who acted like an old mate. It sounded almost too good to be true.

Jacobs had sifted through the job applications looking for a man who was around his own age, had few ties and would not be missed if he disappeared. He short-listed fifteen names. Not a bad return from an ad that cost him $103.60 to run over three days.

Over the next few weeks Williams returned to the unit for follow-up interviews, each one bringing him closer to the job of a lifetime.

Slowly the form of the interviews changed and the questions became more personal. Williams found himself confiding in the man who could be his boss, telling him of his broken marriage, of childhood difficulties and of changing his name by deed poll fifteen years earlier.

This was new ground for Williams, who tended to be a loner and who tended not to speak freely of his personal life, even to workmates he had known for years.

But Jacobs was a good listener, and a sympathetic one, so the story of Ron Williams's life came out, piece by piece. Finally, Jacobs told him he had passed muster. He had the job.

It was to cost him his life.

THE problem with Paul Jacobs was that he wasn't. His real name was Alexander Robert MacDonald, a Vietnam veteran, bomber, prolific armed robber and escapee. He had escaped from the Borallon Correctional Centre, near Ipswich in Queensland, in September 1995. He had been serving twenty-three years for armed robbery and escape.

In the next two years MacDonald robbed seven banks in three states and got away with a total of $320,800. He was possibly Australia's last bushranger. He robbed country banks, taking hostages to try to prevent bank staff from activating security alarms, and then he used his bush skills to camp out until police road blocks were removed days later.

MacDonald would hike hundreds of kilometres and drive thousands to rob banks in NSW, Queensland and Western Australia. While most modern bandits used high-powered stolen cars to get away from crime scenes, MacDonald used push bikes, small motorbikes or his hiking boots. He'd been out of jail only two months when he first developed a plan to take on a new identity. But, as the plan grew more sophisticated – and cold-blooded – he decided he needed a patsy. Someone whose life he could take over.

Which is how Ron Williams came by the worst lucky break of his life. MacDonald was only three months older than Williams and they had uncannily similar faces and builds, although the escaper was slightly taller.

Williams provided documentation such as driver's licence, deed poll papers and birth certificate for his prospective boss.

MacDonald used them to set up two accounts, one in a bank and the second in a credit union, so he could channel his armed robbery funds. He went to the Registry of Births, Deaths and Marriages to get a copy of the birth certificate he would later claim was his. He was to end up with a passport, driver's licence, five credit cards, a Myer card, ambulance subscription and private health insurance under Ron Williams's name.

But the trouble with taking someone's identity is that there is a living, breathing witness who can expose the fraud at any time.

MacDonald believed he had that base covered. His credo was as old as crime: Dead men tell no tales.

It was brutally simple – and breathtakingly callous. So much so that Senior Detective Allan Birch, an armed robbery squad investigator, later had trouble grasping the ruthlessness of the quiet middle-aged man he was interviewing.

Puzzled about the identity swap, the detective said to MacDonald during an interview on 26 July, 1997: 'Can you explain to me how you would assume the identity of a person who responds to an advert for employment?'

MacDonald responded quietly: 'You kill them.'

Birch: 'Did you kill Mr Williams?'

MacDonald: 'I did.'

THE VICTIM

RON Williams was a loner who spent most of his spare time fishing in Port Phillip Bay. He had married in July, 1981, and fathered a daughter but the marriage failed quickly. He legally changed his name from Runa Chomszczak to Ron Williams the same year he was married. He was a handyman who could make a fist of most trades.

He had plenty of workmates but few, if any, who ranked as true mates. He dreamed of adventure, but couldn't see a way out of the rut his life had become.

He lived with his mother and spent as much time as he could at work, not because he was well paid or loved his job, but because it gave him company.

His former boss, the owner of Comeback Auto Wreckers, Kevin Brett, was to say of him: 'He was a great little bloke. He was an all rounder. You name it, he could do it. He was a human dynamo.'

Brett said Williams was a gardener, handyman, storeman, painter and delivery man. He was a statewide reliever for Brett's three car spare parts businesses.

'He would have worked seven days a week if you let him. He lived for his work.'

He was later to die for it.

While Williams didn't speak freely about his private life, his former employer sensed a sadness in his eager worker. 'He was a little timid and easily let down. He'd had some knocks in his life.'

His only outside interest appeared to be fishing and restoring his car. Workmates said he would often head straight to the bay after knocking off work. He worked until the week before he was to go to Western Australia, but also kept a promise to paint the ceiling of a sandwich shop near his old job. That's the sort of bloke he was.

Brett was happy to see his trusted handyman kick on to a new job, but he couldn't help having a twinge of doubt – particularly when he found Williams had to sign a contract with secrecy provisions, and was being paid a retainer for weeks before he was to take up the new position.

His generous new benefactor was paying Williams around $500 a week not to work, which was more than he had been paid to work in Melbourne. It didn't make sense to Kevin Brett, but he kept his doubts to himself, not wanting to dampen the enthusiasm of a man who, he felt, deserved a break.

Brett was to recall: 'He was very secretive about his new job. I asked him about it and he said I had paid him peanuts and we had a laugh. He said the main reason he got the job was that he had no ties.

'He said he took on the job because he wanted to get enough money to buy a unit. I told him there would always be a job here for him.'

His former boss said Williams would never have suspected he was being set up. 'He just wanted to believe in people.'

THE MURDER

THE new hand asked surprisingly few questions about the work he would be expected to do in the outback. 'Mr Jacobs' told him the business was 'a family concern doing geological survey on order from mining companies in Western Australia'.

He asked Williams to sign an employment contract saying he would not seek, or take any other type of work before they travelled west.

When Senior Detective Birch asked him later, 'Why did you do that?' MacDonald was to answer: 'That was purely and simply because the guy was a little unstable and really didn't seem fully committed to the new employment, and I wanted to have him locked in to the program.'

They left for Western Australia in MacDonald's Toyota Land Cruiser utility in late February, a month after the job was advertised. Williams packed light. The boss already had any provisions they would need. Like any seasoned camper, he had a shovel in the back.

They drove across the country for four days, staying at motels, and drinking and eating together. Both men were excited. Both were looking forward to starting a new life.

Williams wrote postcards to his old workmates, relatives and his few friends. His new boss and mate was his usual helpful self and said not to worry about mailing them. He promised he would do that later.

But one postcard was sent straight after it was written, when the two men arrived in Albany, about four hundred kilometres from Perth. Williams couldn't resist a little good-natured gloating to his former workmates at the car wreckers in Melbourne. He sat down and wrote a card in a pub. It read: 'Hello boss. I'm sitting with the new boss eating oysters kilpatrick. Got to go, new boss is bringing the beer over.'

The condemned man ate a hearty meal. His last.

Soon after they left Albany, MacDonald turned the dusty four-wheel-drive on to a dirt track to Cheyne Beach. He suggested they go fishing, knowing Williams was certain to be keen.

He had selected the beach by looking at a map because it was isolated. He remembered the district from his last visit, twenty years earlier. They walked down to the beach from the utility, Williams carrying his fishing rod, MacDonald a khaki knapsack he'd bought in an army disposal store in Melbourne.

Williams fished and the two men chatted for about an hour. Both were waiting for sunset. Williams because he hoped it would make the fish easier to catch. MacDonald because he wanted to catch his prey unawares in the twilight.

As they chatted, MacDonald bent over slowly, undid the knapsack and slipped his hand in. Inside was the ten-shot, sawn-off, semi-automatic .22 that he had tested months earlier by firing into the Mary River, near Gympie in Queensland. He lifted the gun out and, as he was to describe it later, brought it to his shoulder in one smooth motion and fired. He was about a metre away. The last thing Ron Williams saw was the flash leaping from the barrel as the bullet hit him between the eyes.

'He was just standing there … I shot him once in the forehead and again in the back of the head when he fell to the ground,'

MacDonald was to tell police, as dispassionately as if he was talking about slaughtering a sheep.

Senior Detective Birch asked him: 'With what intention, if any, did you take Mr Williams to that location?'

MacDonald: 'Of killing him … I stopped the motor vehicle, we took some fishing tackle from the rear of the vehicle, proceeded along the beach, fished for perhaps an hour and then I shot him.'

MacDonald said he checked Williams' pulse to make sure he was dead, carried him thirty metres up a sand dune and buried him. 'I dug a hole, placed the body in it, covered it with sand, smoothed out the area (and) put branches and shrubbery over it.'

Senior Detective Michael Grainger: 'You say your intention was to kill him – were you apprehensive or were you just – you – you had a job at hand and you were doing that job?'

MacDonald: 'It was a job at hand.'

He said that as he prepared to shoot he 'just switched off, I guess'.

Birch: 'What do you mean by that?'

MacDonald: 'When you cut off your emotions … I guess it's part of military training that sometimes you need to switch off your emotions … To be able to perform anything that needs to be done.'

It took him two hours to murder his travelling mate, bury his body and clean the area of clues. He left at 10pm.

Grainger: 'Why – why did you kill him – what's your reason for murdering Mr Williams?'

MacDonald: 'To assume his identity.'

He was asked by police if he had any mental illnesses and he said he had been diagnosed with a personality disorder.

MacDonald: 'Perhaps I don't share the same emotions that other people do.'

Grainger: 'Do you know that killing someone's wrong?'

MacDonald: 'I know that many people consider it to be, yes.'

Grainger: 'Did you consider the killing of Ron Williams wrong?'

MacDonald: 'No.'

Grainger: 'Why?'

MacDonald: 'To me, it seemed appropriate.'

Birch: 'Have you found yourself in other circumstances where you've found it necessary to kill someone?'

MacDonald: 'Yes.'

Birch: 'When?'

MacDonald: 'In Vietnam.'

But that interview came later. What he did when he left Cheyne Beach was dump his car, throw the number plates into a river, hitchhike back to Melbourne. He'd also discarded two identities, Paul Jacobs and Alexander MacDonald. But he kept the postcards Williams had trusted him to post. And post them he did, gradually, over several months. No-one who got the postcards could know that the return address scrawled on the back didn't exist, any more than the man who'd written them. But his name did. The Vietnam veteran, bank robber and killer had become Ron Williams.

THE CROOK

ALEXANDER Robert MacDonald was a Queenslander. The first time he saw the inside of a police cell was when he appeared at the Brisbane Magistrates' Court on 1 December, 1967, charged with theft. He was fined $100 and given a two-year suspended sentence.

Perhaps it was suggested that military discipline might help him from returning before the courts because a month later he joined the army, entering the Recruit Training Battalion. In April, 1968, he transferred to the Artillery School in Manly, NSW, to train as a gunner. He had two tours of duty in Vietnam, the second at his own request.

Much later, he was described as having been a commando in the Special Air Services. This was untrue. But police believe he may have learnt about explosives in Vietnam when he was involved in jungle clearances, and he would have become familiar with firearms.

In 1972 he was charged with 'unlawfully killing cattle', fined $50 and ordered to pay $80 restitution at the Caboolture Magistrates' Court in Queensland.

In October that year he literally walked away from the army, going absent without leave from his base. He never returned, and was discharged a year later under a rule for long-term absentees.

Ten years later he would write to the army and ask for his service medals for his two tours of duty. He was told he was not entitled to the medals as he had gone absent without leave.

In March, 1978, the licensee of the Crown Hotel in Collie, Western Australia, found a plastic lunch box at the rear of the hotel with a note addressed to him. It said the box contained a gelignite bomb that had not been primed. It was a warning.

MacDonald demanded $5000 from each hotelier in the district and threatened to bomb their pubs if they didn't pay. He kept his word. Three months later a bomb exploded at the Crown, badly damaging the hotel, and it was only luck that stopped MacDonald being a cop killer. A local policeman handled and examined the gelignite package only two minutes before it exploded.

MacDonald was arrested after he made an extortion demand for $60,000 from the hotels. He had built a bomb with four sticks of gelignite and had another sixteen sticks hidden in the bush. Police had no doubt he would have continued blowing up pubs until he was paid his extortion money.

He was sentenced to seven years over the bombings and extortion but served far less. He was released in September, 1981, and headed to Queensland.

Thirteen months later MacDonald was again a wanted man. Police said that between November 1982 and March 1983 he robbed several banks and service stations in central and northern Queensland.

It was during this time that MacDonald began to take hostages during robberies. In three bank robberies he took a staff member with him to ensure the police were not immediately called.

On 11 February, 1983, he robbed the National Australia Bank at Mossman of almost $10,000. He took a staff member to the edge of cane fields almost five hundred metres from the bank and then vanished into the cane on foot.

Police believe he used a CB radio to contact his partner to pick him up.

In July, 1983, MacDonald was arrested in the Northern Territory as he was about to return to Perth. Again, the former soldier showed his extraordinary single mindness. On 28 July he escaped from the Berrimah Jail while awaiting extradition. In the escape he broke his ankle but still managed to travel four painful kilometres. He was forced to surrender after twelve hours on the hop.

He was sentenced to seventeen years jail. In 1984 he was given another six months for attempting to escape from Townsville's Stuart Prison. Not to be deterred he tried to escape again, this time bashing a prison officer and trying to take a female nurse hostage.

He was given another five years for his efforts.

He had served twelve of his twenty-three year sentence for eight armed robberies, two charges of conspiracy to commit armed robbery, four counts of unlawful imprisonment and the attempted escapes, when he decided he'd been in jail long enough. This time his escape was successful.

Despite the fact he was serving a long sentence for crimes of violence and had tried to escape repeatedly he was given a position of trust. At the Borallon Correctional Centre, near Ipswich, he was allowed outside on gardening duty. On 12 September, 1995, he simply walked off. 'I guess I couldn't see the end of it,' he later told police. He had three years to serve until he would have been eligible for parole.

He said he walked away and 'skirted the general Brisbane area'.

Birch: 'So how far would you have walked on foot?'

MacDonald: 'Over a period of a week, a couple of hundred k's I guess.'

He said he camped in the bush near Gympie for about three weeks after the escape.

On 20 October, 1995, he robbed the Westpac Bank in the Queensland town of Cooroy, near Noosa Heads. Then he escaped on a pushbike.

He went into the bank carrying his ten-shot .22 semi-automatic rifle. He said he selected the bank because it was near scrub where he could disappear.

He rang the manager earlier that day to make an appointment. Six staff members were in the bank. He was politely ushered into the manager's office, where he produced the gun and demanded money. He was given $15,000, stuffed it into a travel bag and walked out. 'I got on the pushbike and rode off along some back roads into the scrub.'

He camped out for two nights to beat the police road blocks.

He used the money to set himself up with camping gear that he planned to use for more robberies.

He then robbed the Westpac bank at Airlie Beach on 15 December, 1995. 'While I was in prison in Stuart Creek, a chap there had told me how he robbed the bank in Airlie Beach.'

He got there by walking and hitchhiking and then camped in the scrub. He needed only to glance at the bank the day before to know his prison mate had been right. It was an easy target.

Next day he went into the bank and said he had a complaint about an account. Then he produced the gun and demanded money. He walked out with $83,000 and a female teller as hostage. After they'd walked about 80 metres he let the frightened woman go, then walked into the bush.

After murdering Ron Williams he was to use the same method to commit five more bank robberies in Yepoon, in Queensland, Airlie Beach (again), Laurieton and Coonbarabran in NSW and Busselton in Western Australia.

Unlike most bandits he made little effort to hide his identity. He didn't use the usual armed robber's disguise of a balaclava or rubber mask. He wore a white Panama hat, almost as an identifiable trademark, until he lost it during one robbery when he was chased into the bush.

He was a disciplined, cool, loner who went to great pains to cover his tracks. He lived quietly in Victoria as Ron Williams and would never pull a robbery there, instead travelling big distances interstate to pull bank jobs. He wanted police to believe that one of Australia's most wanted men was half-hermit, living in a tropical rain forest, coming out only to rob banks. No-one, he believed, would look near Melbourne for the Queensland bushranger.

He even had a fresh tattoo, a parrot with the name Megan, put on his left arm, covering an older tattoo that was recorded on his police record. He was asked by Senior Detective Allan Birch why he travelled out of Victoria to rob banks. 'You could drive to Tocumwal or to Geelong. Why is it that you went north?' the policeman said.

MacDonald answered matter-of-factly: 'Well, to hopefully convince the police in Queensland that I was still in that area.'

Bizarrely, MacDonald was to come within metres of creating a huge international incident during an attempt to rob a bank at a tropical beach resort.

He took four days to drive from Melbourne to Cairns in his four-wheel-drive, and then took a bus along the winding coast road, past crocodile farms, caravan parks and five-star resorts to Port Douglas, later to become a popular holiday destination for American presidents, publishers and journalists. He took with him a second-hand black mountain bike he'd bought for $100 at the Cairns Cash Converters, and his dismantled double-barrel shotgun in his knapsack.

For a week he camped near the beach and walked around town. Like any other tourist, he wandered down the main street, past pubs, cafes and the prestigious Nautilus open air restaurant favoured by Bill and Hillary Clinton in happier times. But, unlike most tourists, he kept his eye on the Commonwealth Bank branch in the centre of the town.

He noted staff movements and saw that one man always arrived at the same time and parked his white Falcon in an underground car park, before walking a few metres to the bank.

He decided to abduct the staff member and demand that cash be delivered to him.

On Friday, 30 May, as the young staff member walked out of the carpark, MacDonald strolled over and grabbed him. He walked quietly with the man to the bank and then slipped a note to a female teller. It demanded that all the money in the bank be delivered to a spot on the banks of a river, eight kilometres from Port Douglas, in exchange for the staff member's life. The gunman and the hostage drove to the river to wait near a disused bridge next to the highway. It was a popular fishing spot but MacDonald knew it was low tide and the area should be empty. But a fisherman, who obviously could not read a tide chart, went up to the robber and his nervous hostage as they waited.

'A chap who had been fishing in the river came along and I had to take him in tow, so to speak,' MacDonald was to tell police.

The three waited about near the road. MacDonald knew there was only a few police at Port Douglas and he could slip into the cane fields or rainforest if they began a search.

But his plan unravelled when he spotted a huge contingent of police on the main road. When he saw four marked police cars, motor bikes and unmarked units he believed he was in big trouble. 'It didn't pan out the way I figured it would.'

What he didn't know until much later was that it was Murphy's Law at work. MacDonald had done his homework on the bank – but he hadn't read the local papers. The Chinese Vice Premier, Zhu Rongji, was in town after a tour around Australia.

Mr Zhu was heading for the Cairns airport with his massive police escort when he passed over the bridge near where MacDonald was hiding.

No-one knew that a killer with a loaded gun got within metres of one of the leaders of the biggest country in the world. But the killer didn't know either. He thought that half the Queensland police force was about to descend on him, so he let the two men go and pedalled his second-hand bike about three kilometres, in one of the slowest getaways on record, then disappeared into the bush once more. He then walked more than forty kilometres back to Cairns, collected his car and drove to Airlie beach to rob the Westpac branch a second time.

On 2 June, 1996, he turned up at a Somerville boat yard, Yaringa Boat Sales, saying he wanted to buy an old timber cabin cruiser that had been advertised in a boat magazine for $23,000. He didn't seem too worried about the price. He would have been churlish to quibble. Three weeks earlier, on 10 May, he'd robbed the Yepoon Commonwealth Bank of $107,000.

He produced a $500 deposit to settle the deal on the cabin cruiser. He returned ten days later with a briefcase. He opened it and took out $10,000 in cash. Three days later he was back with the same briefcase and another $12,500.

He was going through a messy divorce, he explained, and didn't want his ex-wife to know about the money. So he carried it in the briefcase. It seemed reasonable to the salesmen.

He was to spend $80,000 on the boat, Sea Venture, fitting satellite navigation gear and reconditioned motors.

He paid $1200 cash to moor the boat at Yaringa and began to live on board. He told locals he was a builder and renovator who dabbled in prospecting. He began to drink at the Somerville Hotel and developed a group of mates. At least six times he disappeared for up to eight weeks at a time. He told his new friends he was prospecting in Queensland. Which, in a way, he was. But not with a pick and shovel.

Just before Christmas, 1996, he threw a huge party for his friends, supplying all the food and liquor to celebrate completing the main work on the boat. During the refit a worker opened a waterproof case in the boat. Inside he found a sawn-off shotgun. He decided, perhaps wisely, not to ask questions.

In June, 1997, MacDonald told his friends he was short of cash and needed $10,000 before he could finish the boat and sail to the Solomon Islands where, he said, he was going to hook up with a friend.

He said he would head north on 27 June. Police believe he

was going back to Queensland for one more armed robbery before sailing out of Australia to freedom.

He loaded up his Toyota with camping gear and provisions, then drove to the Hume Motor Inn in Fawkner and booked in to room eight.

While he was preparing to head north the television program, *Australia's Most Wanted,* screened a segment on the escapee-bandit. Police received a call to look for a Toyota four-wheel-drive in Melbourne's north. Within hours they found the car, registered to Ron Williams. A police check confirmed that a Mr Ron Williams was a reported missing person.

A detective walked into the restaurant where MacDonald was sitting and immediately knew he was the wanted man. He was arrested by members of the Melbourne armed robbery squad outside the motel at 5.15pm on Thursday, 26 June, with his brother. He was extradited to Perth, pleaded guilty to murder and sentenced to life in prison.

When police went through his papers they found documents from the Christian Children's Fund. Here was an armed robber who could kill a harmless stranger and steal his identity without a moment's guilt, and yet sponsor a poverty-stricken child in South America.

THE INTERVIEW

RECORD of interview between Senior Detective Allan Birch and Ronald Joseph Williams, of Ford Road, Shepparton, conducted in the offices of the armed robbery squad on Thursday, 26 June, 1997. There is a long discussion where the suspect refuses to agree to be fingerprinted until it is explained that the prints can be taken by force.

BIRCH: 'I suspect you of armed robbery and escape. In

simple terms, Mr Williams – I believe you are actually Alexander MacDonald. I have information that Alexander MacDonald is responsible for the commission of a number of armed robberies and has escaped a prison in the state of Queensland.'

Birch then informs the suspect that police have the legal authority to take fingerprints forcibly.

BIRCH: 'If you don't comply or you don't want to comply with that request, then I'll seek authorisation from my superior to take them forcefully from you. All right?'

MacDONALD: 'And who would that superior be? The man who assaulted me earlier?'

BIRCH: 'Well, I don't know what you are talking about.'

MacDONALD: 'The gentleman who was here earlier on with you.'

SENIOR DETECTIVE MICHAEL GRAINGER: 'What I suggest we do at this stage, Mr Williams, is that we suspend the interview.'

(After long discussions, MacDonald agrees to be finger-printed.)

MacDONALD: 'Well, it would seem that I have no option.'

(After the fingerprints are taken MacDonald knows it is useless to continue the charade of pretending to be Ronald Williams.)

BIRCH: 'Can you please state to me your full name and address?'

MacDONALD: 'Alexander Robert MacDonald, no fixed place of abode.'

BIRCH: 'Right. Mr MacDonald, how did you come to be here in the office of the armed robbery squad?

MacDONALD: 'I was apprehended, shall we say, on Sydney Road at Fawkner.'

BIRCH: 'Where have you been residing for the last, say – six months?'

MacDONALD: 'I live on and off in the Millewa State Forest.'

BIRCH: 'And whereabouts is that situated?'

MacDONALD: 'It's near Tocumwal in New South Wales.'

BIRCH: 'Right, and you live in the forest?'

MacDONALD: 'I use tents and tarpaulins.'

Police asked MacDonald how he came to be known as Williams.

MacDONALD: 'Well, it's an identity I've assumed since being an escapee.'

BIRCH: 'Right. Now how did you assume that identity?'

MacDONALD: 'By taking identity from the actual person.'

BIRCH: 'Right. Who is Ron Williams?'

MacDONALD: 'He's a guy from Melbourne.'

BIRCH: 'Right, do you know Ron Williams?'

MacDONALD: 'Yes.'

BIRCH: 'How do you know Ron Williams?'

MacDONALD: 'I met him on the pretext of employing him.'

BIRCH: 'Under what circumstances did you meet him?'

MacDONALD: 'I needed an identity. I ran an advertisement in a newspaper … the *Herald Sun* … For someone to take up a position with a geological survey.'

BIRCH: 'And what was the intention of placing the advert?'

MacDONALD: 'My intention was to find a person of suitable age, background. No – no close relatives, and assume his identity.'

BIRCH: 'Right. How many persons responded to that advert?'

MacDONALD: 'Fifty, I guess.'

BIRCH: 'Over what period of time did those fifty people respond?'

MacDONALD: 'Within the space of – yes – a week.'

BIRCH: 'Can you explain to me how you would assume the identity of a person who responds to an advert for employment?'

MacDONALD: 'You kill them.'

BIRCH: 'Did you kill Mr Williams?'

MacDONALD: 'I did.'

BIRCH: 'Can you approximate for me when that occurred?'

MacDONALD: 'Early March, 1996.'

BIRCH: 'Right, and how did you kill Mr Williams?'

MacDONALD: 'I shot him.'

BIRCH: 'And what were the circumstances … ?'

MacDONALD: 'I required his identity. I transported him to Western Australia. Took him to a beach, and shot him there.'

MacDonald then explained how he put an advertisement in the paper, under the name Paul Jacobs, for a field hand for 'geological survey work,' and how he had formed a short list of men 'with no dependents, no close relatives.'

MacDONALD: 'He (Williams) was quite drunk at the time (when he rang) which was one of the factors that decided me to interview him further. A few days later Mr Williams turned up at the flat for the interview and looked even more promising.'

MacDONALD: '(He was) a guy of my build, roughly – maybe a little shorter. Obviously of the same age group.'

The prospective employee and employer had chatted for about an hour in the flat.

BIRCH: 'When did you form the opinion that he was a person of whom you wanted to assume his identity.'

MacDONALD: 'At that time I was about eighty per cent certain that he was suitable, so I asked him back for a second interview … at which he could supply more personal details … educational background, family background, employment.'

BIRCH: 'Was that – in what way was that necessary to you?'

MacDONALD: 'To give me the background story of the person.'

About six other men had telephoned for interviews but MacDonald put them off. At his second interview Williams said he had been brought up in orphanages, had no close family ties and had changed his name from Chomszczak. MacDonald had diligently written down all these personal details.

MacDONALD: 'Yes, he was married to Margaret Joy Manning in 1981, July 1981.'

BIRCH: 'And where is Mrs Manning now?'

MacDONALD: 'He didn't know … they divorced in 1982.'

BIRCH: 'At the times you were writing down (the personal details) what was your intention with Mr Williams?'

MacDONALD: 'To kill him.' MacDonald then described how he had congratulated Williams, telling him he was the successful candidate, that he would be employed in WA for two years, and would be paid $60,000 a year if he signed a contract that he would not take up alternative employment. Until then, he had promised him a retainer of $500 a week 'to lock him into the program.' He then spoke freely to police about the murder.

MacDONALD: 'It took place on Cheyne Beach in Western Australia at approximately 8pm. I shot him once in the forehead and again in the back of the head when he fell to the ground.'

BIRCH: 'With what intention, if any, did you take Mr Williams to that location?'

MacDONALD: 'Of killing him … I stopped the motor vehicle, we took some fishing tackle from the rear of the vehicle, proceeded along the beach, fished for perhaps and hour and then I shot him.'

BIRCH: 'Right, where was the firearm?'

MacDONALD: 'It was in a fishing bag that I had with me.' (a khaki knapsack from a Greensborough army surplus store).

Senior Detective GRAINGER: 'You say your intention was to kill him – were you apprehensive or were you just – you – you had a job at hand and you were doing that job?'

MacDONALD: 'I had a job at hand.'

He explained he had previously tested the gun at a bush camp on the Mary River, near Gympie in Queensland.

He said he and Williams arrived at the spot and fished several areas along the beach before he committed the murder.

BIRCH: 'What was he doing?'

MacDONALD: 'I believe he was just standing there. We were talking about something or other.'

GRAINGER: 'So how was it that you were able to distinguish him and kill him in the dark?'

MacDonald: 'I have reasonably good night vision.'

He said that he had been a gunner in the regular army, serving for five years from 1968, and trained to use machine guns, rifles and grenade launchers.

MacDONALD: 'I dug a hole, placed the body in it, covered it with sand, put branches and shrubbery over it.'

BIRCH: 'What were your duties to perform, or that you performed, in Vietnam?

MacDONALD: 'I'd rather not go into that.'

BIRCH: 'Did you cause a death of any persons in Vietnam, by way of shooting them with a rifle?'

MacDONALD: 'I'd rather not discuss that.'

GRAINGER: 'Prior to the actual killing of Mr Williams, when was it that you decided, right – this is the spot – this is where it's gonna happen?'

MacDONALD: 'When I first saw the area.'

GRAINGER: 'And how long was that before you actually killed him?'

MacDONALD: 'An hour and a half.'

He said that as he prepared to shoot Mr Williams he 'just switched off, I guess.'

BIRCH: 'What do you mean by that?'

MacDONALD: 'When you cut off your emotions … I guess it's part of military training that sometimes you need to switch off your emotions … To be able to perform anything that needs to be done.'

GRAINGER: 'Why is it that you – you're telling us all this? Do you have any reason for that?'

MacDONALD: 'Well. It's a foregone conclusion that you would've found this all out anyway.'

GRAINGER: 'Why – why did you kill him – what's your reason for murdering Mr Williams?'

MacDONALD: 'To assume his identity.' He was asked by police if he had any mental illnesses and he said he had been diagnosed with a personality disorder.

MacDONALD: 'Perhaps I don't share the same emotions that other people do.'

GRAINGER: 'Do you know that killing someone's wrong?'

MacDONALD: 'I know that many people consider it to be, yes.'

GRAINGER: 'Did you consider the killing of Ron Williams wrong?'

MacDONALD: 'No.'

GRAINGER: 'Why?'

MacDONALD: 'To me, it seemed appropriate.'

BIRCH: 'Have you found yourself in other circumstances where you've found it necessary to kill someone?'

MacDONALD: 'Yes.'

BIRCH: 'When?'

MacDONALD: 'In Vietnam.'

He then explained buying the boat to sail to the Solomon Islands.

GRAINGER: 'Would that be in an endeavour to flee Australia?'

MacDONALD: 'I don't know quite how to phrase this. A terminal effort, shall we say.'

GRAINGER: 'You intended to kill yourself in the Solomon Islands?'

MacDONALD: 'That's correct.'

GRAINGER: 'Why is that?'

MacDONALD: 'Because I didn't see any future.'

GRAINGER: 'Why would it be necessary to kill yourself in the Solomon Islands?'

MacDONALD: 'More pleasant surroundings.'